LANDLOCK

Paralysing Dispute over Minerals on Adivasi Land in India

LANDLOCK

Paralysing Dispute over Minerals on Adivasi Land in India

PATRIK OSKARSSON

PRESS

ASIA-PACIFIC ENVIRONMENT MONOGRAPH 14

Published by ANU Press
The Australian National University
Acton ACT 2601, Australia
Email: anupress@anu.edu.au

Available to download for free at press.anu.edu.au

A catalogue record for this book is available from the National Library of Australia

ISBN (print): 9781760462505
ISBN (online): 9781760462512

WorldCat (print): 1052587980
WorldCat (online): 1052587899

DOI: 10.22459/10.22459/L.09.2018

Cover design and layout by ANU Press

Cover photograph: 'Elected representatives taking part in a dharna conducted by CPI (M) in Visakhapatnam on June 25, 2007 by projecting bauxite mining in the scheduled areas as a demon which would eat tribals', by K.R. Deepak.

Contents

Tables

Figures

Abbreviations

APMDC	Andhra Pradesh Mineral Development Corporation
Balco	Bharat Aluminium Corporation
CPI	Communist Party of India
CPIND	Communist Party of India (Marxist-Leninist) New Democracy
CPM	Communist Party of India (Marxist)
EIA	environmental impact assessment
GVMC	Greater Visakhapatnam Municipal Corporation
HRF	Human Rights Forum
IBM	Indian Bureau of Mines
IT	information technology
JSW	Jindal South West
JSWHL	JSW Holding Ltd
MLA	member of (state) legislative assembly
mm&P	mines, minerals & People
MoEF	Ministry of Environment and Forests
MoU	memorandum of understanding
MP	Member of (national) Parliament
Nalco	National Aluminium Corporation
NEAA	National Environmental Appellate Authority
NGO	non-governmental organisation
PCB	Pollution Control Board

PESA	*Panchayat Extension to Scheduled Areas Act 1996*
RTI	Right to Information
TDP	Telugu Desam Party

Acknowledgments

This book was made possible through institutional support from the Azim Premji University, Bangalore, which allowed the author to spend three months on a book-writing sabbatical in 2012 at The Australian National University. In the latter stages of book production, support from the Swedish University of Agricultural Sciences contributed to the cost of copyediting. Thanks also to Patrick Wennström of the Swedish University of Agricultural Sciences for making the map reproduced as Figure 1.1.

Parts of the argument presented in Chapters 4, 5 and 6 have previously been published as articles in *South Asia* (Oskarsson 2013a), *Development Studies Research* (Oskarsson and Nielsen 2014), and *Extractive Industries and Society* (Oskarsson 2015), but have been revised and updated for the purpose of the present volume.

The author would also like to acknowledge the valuable comments of two anonymous peer reviewers, and the editorial work of Colin Filer and Philippa Mulberry, which has greatly improved the quality of the text. All remaining errors rest with the author.

1. Mining Conflicts in Liberalising India

In the late 1980s, the small social advocacy organisation Samatha ('Equality') started working with impoverished Adivasi communities[1] facing land alienation in the Eastern Ghats hill range of northeastern Andhra Pradesh. Members of the organisation had earlier experienced first-hand how outsiders, whether for private gain or through government projects, were acquiring land that was intended to be reserved for Adivasis, thus pushing people into deep poverty. Realising the lack of understanding of the formal procedures of the government on the part of the Adivasis, Samatha started helping people to secure the land documents they needed in order to make use of existing legal protection.

In the early 1990s, villagers approached Samatha when a subsidiary of the Birla Group, one of India's biggest industrial conglomerates, wanted to mine calcite in their village. As the mining plans were believed to violate the *Andhra Pradesh Scheduled Areas Land Transfer Regulation 1959*, which bans the sale or transfer of land from a tribal to a non-tribal person, what came to be known as 'the Samatha case' was taken to court in 1993 and later appealed to the Supreme Court in Delhi (Vagholikar and Moghe 2003; Krishnakumar 2004).

1 The term 'Adivasi' is widely used as an alternative to the official designation of 'Scheduled Tribes' (or 'tribals') as groups of people with special constitutional benefits who mainly live in central India's forested hill region.

A final verdict in the Samatha case was reached by the Supreme Court in 1997. Relying on a combination of the Indian Constitution's Fifth Schedule, set up to protect and support Adivasis across the country, and Andhra Pradesh state land transfer legislation,[2] the court reached the conclusion that no land, including government (or 'revenue') land, private land or forest land, could be leased out to non-tribals or to private companies for mining or industrial operations. The judgment stated that '[i]f the government was allowed to transfer or dispose of its own land in favour of non-tribals, it would completely destroy the legal and constitutional fabric made to protect the Scheduled Tribes' (India 1997). The court ordered an immediate closure of all existing private mines in Andhra Pradesh, and suggested a process for other states with Scheduled Areas[3] to review their laws in accordance with the judgment.

The Samatha judgment has been widely acclaimed for reaffirming the constitutional right to land for Adivasis. But where the similar Mabo judgment in Australia in 1993 successfully opened up a space for Aborigines to become participants in all discussions over what should happen on their traditional land, and resulted in strengthened overall environmental protection (O'Faircheallaigh 2006), the efforts of the Indian authorities have mainly been directed to limiting the impact of the Samatha judgment by confining its application to Andhra Pradesh. As the Fifth Schedule of the Indian Constitution applies to some of the country's main (existing and potential) mining areas across nine states in central eastern India, the judgment at the time created a lot of unease among policymakers across the country. If it was implemented in Andhra Pradesh, and even expanded to the other states with similar legislation, a large share of India's main reserves of iron, bauxite, chromium and coal would be off-limits to the private investment that was supposed to be the basis of future expansion since the new national mineral policy was announced in 1993.

2 The new state of Telangana was separated from the state of Andhra Pradesh on 2 June 2014, but the tribal land transfer legislation has been retained by both states.

3 The Scheduled Areas are the territories reserved for India's tribal communities in the Fifth Schedule of the Constitution. It applies to the states of Andhra Pradesh, Bihar, Chhattisgarh, Gujarat, Haryana, Jharkhand, Madhya Pradesh, Maharashtra, Odisha (formerly Orissa), Telangana, and Rajasthan. Due to migration, the tribes do not exclusively live in the Scheduled Areas nowadays. Similarly, there are parts of the Scheduled Areas where non-tribal peoples are now the majority.

The judgment continues to stand but has not been implemented outside of Andhra Pradesh. The current impasse has thus been interpreted as a ban on private mining in Andhra Pradesh despite continued mining in other states. Mining across much of central, tribal India has even been able to expand despite the many controversies repeatedly surrounding mineral projects. These have perhaps been most severe in Odisha (formerly Orissa) State, where clashes between the police and local people protesting against land alienation have resulted in violence on several occasions, with casualties suffered in specific protests against bauxite mining in Kashipur (Reddy 2006; Goodland 2007) and a proposed steel plant at Kalinganagar (Mishra 2006; Padhi and Adve 2006). Also, in the states of Chhattisgarh and Jharkhand, Adivasis have been at the receiving end of violence when finding themselves caught between Maoist Naxalite rebel groups and the government, including the allegedly state-sponsored Salwa Judum militia. This was seen by some as a conflict over access to valuable mineral resources (Sundar 2006; Lahiri-Dutt et al. 2012). It is clear that the present approach to industrialisation is one that leaves large parts of the rural population alienated, despite much protective legislation and at least some supportive court verdicts.

Reinterpreting the Samatha Judgment to Allow Mining

In Andhra Pradesh, and in the newly formed state of Telangana, private-sector mining is still unable to encroach on Adivasi lands, yet these lands are in great demand for many government projects seen as operating in the public interest, including coal mines and irrigation dams. Since 2005, new attempts have been made to exploit the bauxite ore in this region, even though the Samatha judgment is an accepted part of the legislation. The relevant project instead relies on a weakness of the Samatha judgment by using an Andhra Pradesh Government company to carry out the mining while the private investor, Jindal South West (JSW), which is financing the entire project, locates its associated refinery just outside of the Scheduled Areas, where private land ownership is allowed (see Figure 1.1). A confident state government with a strong role to play in national politics, and the support of one of India's major business families, at the time looked certain to be able to implement the project in this new form of public–private partnership, which in large part appeared to have been designed to circumvent the Samatha judgment.

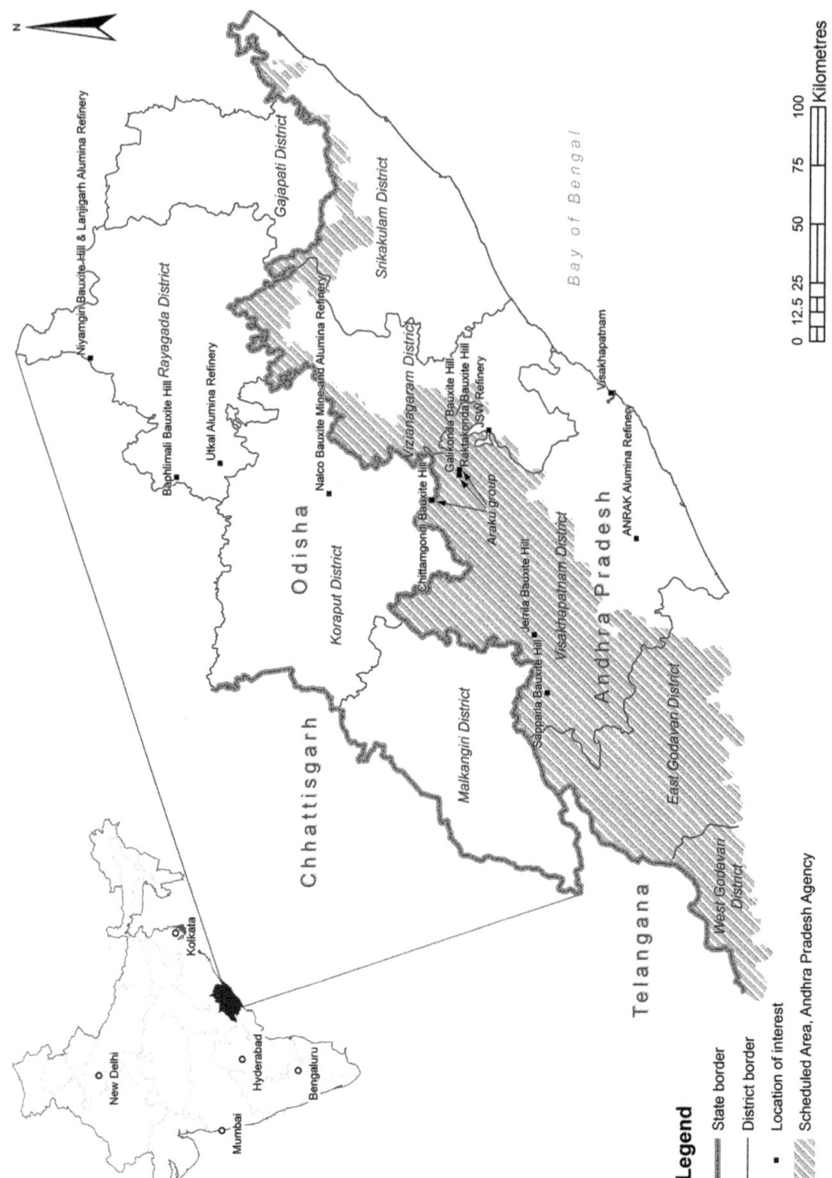

Figure 1.1 Map of northern Andhra Pradesh with proposed bauxite mining and refining locations.

Source: Cartography by Patrick Wennström, Swedish University of Agricultural Sciences.

The legal form of this public–private partnership was perceived by anti-mining activists as an overly generous interpretation of the law in favour of private-sector interests. However, given the slow pace and unpredictability of court procedures, it was still possible to launch this major investment. Along the way, significant protests were staged, not only at the sites chosen for the mine and refinery, but also in the wealth of local, state and national government and other forums that form part of India's extensive framework for democratic debate and decision-making.

Since its inception, a great amount of uncertainty has characterised the project implementation, allowing it to linger for many years in a condition similar to that of a range of other high-profile mineral projects in central eastern India's mineral tracts.[4] Government responses continued to indicate that bauxite mining and refining was still under implementation, with tangible signs on the ground when land was acquired, and some—but crucially far from all—administrative approvals provided for the refinery. In 2013, however, the company confirmed in a newspaper interview that it had cancelled its investment because of the slow pace of implementation and a lack of government support (Anon. 2013). Without an officially declared cancellation, and in any case all too experienced with radical about-turns for controversial projects, civil society actors continued to be vigilant, fuelling further media speculation about renewed mining in 2014 (Patnaik 2014). The continued vigilance after the 2014 elections appears to have been well founded, since the new state government quickly initiated discussions about restarting the controversial bauxite mining and refining projects (Anon. 2014).

This book examines the controversial attempt to start new private mining in the state of Andhra Pradesh in 2005. This was one of many conflicts over (and acts of resistance to) economic reform involving tribal land that have been happening across central eastern India.[5] It explores, on one hand, the tension between existing tribal land rights legislation and concerns over land use changes resulting from mining industry operations, and on the

4 The Posco steel plant in Odisha State was proposed in 2005 and officially cancelled in 2016. Vedanta Resources planned a bauxite mining project that has remained locked in local protests over land, but also in various legal and other disputes, since 2003 (Pingle et al. 2010; Amnesty International 2011).

5 Tribal land is here defined as any land in areas traditionally inhabited and/or used by people officially categorised as members of Scheduled Tribes, whether this land is officially designated as private, forest, revenue or any other form of land, or is located within or outside of the Fifth Schedule areas, since many tribal villages are outside of these borders.

other hand, the potential profitability of mining projects, especially for politically influential interests. A key issue at stake is the choice between alternative uses of the land for mining or for low-intensity cultivation and extraction of forest products. The choice is either to prioritise the protection of Adivasis from absolute poverty or to promote economic growth through mining, thus reflecting alternative visions of development and justice.

In this case, the many different forces and processes working to promote or frustrate industrialisation developed into a paralysing stand-off. This book explains how this unexpected outcome was the result of permanent distortions in the way that different groups understood one another and dealt with their differences about how Adivasi land and natural resources should best be used. The core concern over how land should be used resulted in a deadlock—here described as a 'landlock'—in which the extension of local cultivation and forest use was just as impossible as the extraction of mineral ores. This outcome was to no one's benefit, since the minerals are not being used yet stronger tenure rights for local people cannot be translated into improved livelihoods. It is argued that the sort of long-running conflict detailed here, while perhaps not paradigmatic, offers insights into the deeply ingrained inability to resolve the differences expressed in countless conflicts over Adivasi land and resources in recent decades.

Mineral Extraction, Land and Indigenous People

In many parts of the world, the conflict between mining projects and indigenous people has become an increasingly significant issue. In these conflicts, not only are different uses of land and resources under contestation; often it is two entirely different views about what is of value and how society should progress (Godoy 1985; Ballard and Banks 2003; Bebbington 2011; Gilberthorpe and Hilson 2012). As mining imposes radical transformations on indigenous territories, with potentially permanent changes to local environments and societies, long-running conflict has been the result.

Among the most difficult conflicts to reconcile have been the conflicts on indigenous lands. India's Adivasis, like indigenous populations in Australia, Melanesia or South America, continue to suffer disproportionately when their lands and cultures are disrupted as a result of mining. However, a history of exploitation, combined with modern-day dispossession, has also generated wider support for the 'indigenous' cause, even to the point where the term 'has come to be embedded in discourse surrounding resource extraction' (Gilberthorpe and Hilson 2012: 4–5).

Even so, the struggles of Adivasis in India cannot be fully and easily reconciled with indigenous struggles elsewhere. The basic point that most Indians are indigenous, given that they have lived within the country's present borders for many centuries, is hard to ignore. Even more so, the internal variations and divisions among those designated as Adivasis make a unitary struggle harder to envision (Baviskar 1995; Guha 2007).

At the same time, while global mineral investment offers opportunities, it provides new challenges for accountability. As Hilson argues:

> circumstances are severest in developing countries, where governmental intervention is minimal, regulatory frameworks are commonly incomplete, and fewer effective support schemes are in place for community and industrial groups. Compounding the problem is the fact that a number of these countries' governments, which have heavily promoted foreign investment in their minerals sectors in recent years, almost exclusively side with mining companies on key land use issues (Hilson 2002: 65).

The difficulties of relying on a mineral-dependent development strategy have been the subject of frequent discussion in the literature. Developmental failures resulting from a heavy reliance on minerals have led to a broad acceptance of the 'resource curse' theory (Ross 1999; Auty 2002) amongst policymakers. However, the extraction and sale of minerals remains a tempting pathway out of poverty, especially in times of high mineral commodity prices, and this has driven the combination of continued mining with attempts to improve policy measures to avoid the resource curse.

Some of the efforts to improve social and economic outcomes nationally, as well as in mineral-producing regions, have focused on getting international companies to implement best practices in all their project locations around the world through corporate social responsibility programs, often following the recommendations of the Extractive Industries Transparency Initiative. These efforts have nevertheless tended to work on terms set by the companies themselves rather than by the affected communities (Gilberthorpe and Banks 2012). In some countries, attempts have been made to provide local people with a share of mineral benefits, and sometimes the right to participate in decision-making, but even when there are mandatory negotiations between indigenous communities and mining companies, as in Australia, uneven power relations tend to be significant and local outcomes are highly variable (O'Faircheallaigh and Corbett 2005).

Despite India's long history of mining, the industry did not attract much interest from social scientists before it started to expand, and therefore become more visible, as the result of the liberalisation of the mining legislation in the early 1990s. There has since been a growth in the number of civil society publications (e.g. Reddy 2006; Kalshian 2007; Bhushan and Zeya Hazra 2008; Amnesty International 2010) and in more academic works (e.g. Herbert and Lahiri-Dutt 2004; Padel and Das 2010; Bedi 2013; Kumar 2014; Lahiri-Dutt et al. 2012; Oskarsson 2013a, 2015; Lahiri-Dutt 2014, 2016). Research on mining in India has been particularly concerned with the negative consequences of displacement, especially for the Adivasis, and the effects of deforestation. Coverage of current conflicts is part of a larger body of literature on land and natural resources in tribal India, and on the social movements that have worked towards securing land rights in the face of threats from non-tribal farmers and moneylenders, from forest departments and commercial forestry operations, or from the building of large dams (e.g. Baviskar 1995; Balagopal 2007a; Guha 2007; Springate-Baginski and Blaikie 2007; Kumar and Kerr 2012). When violence became more common in central India, Arundhati Roy (2009) referred to this as a struggle between the Maoists and the 'MoUists' because of the large number of mining deals—known as memoranda of understanding—that had been signed.

India, however, represents something of a special case within the international literature, given its surprising degree of insulation from international mining industry practices and actors. While the country has nominally opened up its economy, and now has a policy framework designed to attract foreign investment, the investors in mining remain overwhelmingly domestic, and it is mainly the technology that is sourced from abroad. Some of the raw materials and end products, especially alumina and aluminium,[6] are exported, but the domestic market is more

6 Aluminium production is a three-stage process of bauxite mining, alumina refining and aluminium smelting. Alumina is aluminium oxide, an intermediary product usually manufactured close to the mine site.

significant. International financial institutions like the World Bank, while active in the country in many other ways, are not involved in mining projects (Herbert and Lahiri-Dutt 2004), and indications are that most of the future expansion is going to be funded either by domestic banks or by the mining companies themselves.

The virtual absence of international companies or financial institutions in the mining sector has resulted in an avoidance of the international discourse on best practices in the sector, including the discussion of corporate social responsibility and community relations programs. Indian legislation on mining, while certainly extensive, has not been significantly influenced by international policies or standards. The result is an industry characterised by insularity in both policy and practice, with only very modest improvements in community relations in recent decades. While this might represent a seemingly difficult scenario, there is a possible upside, given that the industry is more locally accountable and less dependent on decisions made by foreign companies with headquarters far away, as has often been the case, for example, in Africa or Melanesia (e.g. Ferguson 2006; Bainton 2010).

This is why it might make more sense to situate the conflict over mining on Adivasi land in India within the broader literature on land rights. Land continues to be the most important productive asset for rural communities in India, and ownership of land is linked to a reduced incidence of poverty (Mearns 1999). The Samatha judgment has strengthened tribal rights to this crucial asset by preventing the development of several proposed mining projects. Yet the contested nature of its implementation, as well as continued attempts to mine the mountains, make it doubtful whether local people have been able to utilise these stronger rights for economic improvement. This is especially the case since private landholdings are still frequently denied to tribal farmers in forests controlled by the government.

> Because tribals have no security of tenure and live under the constant threat of eviction, they cannot invest in improving their land. Their poverty prevents them from planting tree crops that have long gestation periods, and the illegality of their position precludes their receiving loans from the government to make their agriculture more productive (Baviskar 1994: 2500).

Although alienation of the best agricultural land has been a serious issue in many Adivasi areas, access to land has often been a somewhat less important issue, with the average landholding size being larger than the Indian national average. Instead, infertile soils, a lack of agricultural inputs and poor infrastructure, including a lack of irrigation facilities, have been among the main reasons for low productivity (IFAD 1991; Purushothaman 2005). When settled agriculture has not been sufficient, the commons—especially forest lands—have been an important additional resource (Mearns 1999), but even in the case of forests, there continue to be significant challenges to local access and management.

India has been characterised as having experienced 'thousands of small wars against land acquisitions' (Levien 2011: 66) in recent decades, when farmers, forest-dwellers, herders and many other groups dependent on land for their survival have fought with the state and private companies over increasingly scarce pockets of land. Land is a very sensitive subject anywhere in India, with a close relationship to the livelihoods of the poor, but also to social identities, the food security of the nation, and the desire for industrialisation and progress. In tribal, central India this connection is even starker due to the intense poverty of the region, people's inability to move into alternative employment once land has been lost to mining or other industries, and a lack of other possibilities for economic improvement. Adding to this already bleak picture, there have been violent clashes between Maoist groups and counter-insurgency forces, partly related to the process of industrial expansion on tribal land (Sundar 2006).

When Adivasis across India have been unable to participate directly in political debate (Guha 2007), demands for protection of their rights have instead been organised through social movements, mainly engaging directly with the bureaucracy or the judiciary (Katzenstein et al. 2001). This approach to strengthening tribal claims to resources seemed to be successful in parts of central India as mass movements for the protection of *jal, jungle* and *jameen* (water, forest and land) became increasingly common in recent decades. But the failure to achieve significant change, as in the case of opposition to the Sardar Sarovar dam on the Narmada River, seems to have provided the opportunity for counter-claims. One example of this is the way that right-wing Hindu organisations have made significant inroads into tribal India in recent years (Chatterji 2004; Baviskar 2005). This ongoing fight for the right to interpret tribal identity remains uncertain and, like the many other contestations underway at any point in time in India, is cross-cut by a multitude of different issues and voices.

As a result of centuries of struggle, Adivasi land protection and a wealth of other Adivasi rights continue to exist in different forms with widely variable implementation across central India. Adding to this complexity is a significant expansion in rights for disadvantaged groups that has been secured in recent years, coupled with other legislation that has been added or altered in favour of mineral-led industrialisation. And while the overall thrust of national economic policy is in favour of private investment, the public sector continues to be a major participant in all forms of mining, as well as in refining and thermal power generation. What emerges is a mixed picture, not only of mineral governance and land rights, but also strategic approaches somewhat at odds with the official rhetoric of economic liberalisation, as various forces within and outside of the political establishment struggle to influence the way that various resources are best utilised and by whom.

The landscape of rights is constantly changing across India, with local adjustments as well as laws targeted to certain socio-economic groups. The result is a confused mix of laws that, though significant on paper, take on a much less clear meaning on the ground. Frequently, the intended beneficiaries need to mobilise in order to demand their implementation. In worst-case scenarios, rights passed into legislation become little more than empty rhetoric when politicians seek re-election. The resultant governance framework contains a multiplicity of institutions, following regulations that often overlap, are at odds with one another, or with contradictions that are unresolved. Governance often comes with great democratic ambition, but is fuelled by much uncertainty and controversy.

The strongly stated intention of the state to work for economic growth with the private sector as its partner have combined, in a somewhat ad hoc manner, with a significant expansion of social legislation meant to strengthen local people's rights. Many active participants, plenty of forums in which to debate development, and very extensive legislation thus characterise India's democracy. However, the reach of participatory democracy does not easily extend to the pursuit of industrialisation and economic growth. Here uncertainty, secrecy, complexity and overlapping authorities are some of the underlying factors that have resulted in much controversy between supporters and opponents of industrialisation on Adivasi land. While these concerns have long existed in India, recent controversies in the extractive industry sector have been exaggerated by the combination of national economic liberalisation with an international resource boom and the seeming contradiction between the pursuit of public goals and personal profits by many of the key actors.

Private-Sector Mining for Economic Growth and Political Patronage

The language of liberalisation commonly used to describe India's economic reform process (Bhagwati 1993; Krueger 2002) suggests that the country should end up with a rule-bound, transparent economy that uses the market to allocate resources. When India continues to have significant government interventions in the economy, there has been a tendency to explain this as a result of the liberalising reforms not proceeding as far as was intended. An alternative and more credible characterisation of the economy views it as one based on the preferences of a narrow public–private alliance with limited intentions to let go of earlier opportunities for control. The political system remains remarkably similar to that which existed before the onset of economic reforms, with the same drivers that invited Indian politicians to look for opportunities to control the economy for political and personal gain, and with the same business groups willing to bargain for preferential treatment. According to Kohli (2007: 113), 'the development model pursued in India since about 1980 is a pro-business model that rests on a fairly narrow ruling alliance of the political and the economic elite'. A pro-business approach favours established interests by means of active state intervention. Reasons to support existing businesses may be nationalistic or may be based on other ties—including monetary ones—that cause decision-makers to intervene.

Before the economic reforms, patronage was largely based on opportunities for bureaucrats and politicians to selectively award licences and contracts, or simply to accept kickbacks for the grant of particular administrative approvals (Kochanek 2007).

> The essential business of a state minister is not to make policy. It is to modify the application of rules and regulations on a particularistic basis, in return for money and/or loyalty. The telephone is his essential instrument, for his orders modifying the application of general rules are only rarely written (Wade 1985: 480).

The state–business developmental alliance is able to use old-style political control techniques to gain benefits in the newly 'reformed' economy. The system of regulation and control in the sphere of industrialisation remains impossibly complex for any administrator to manage effectively, despite the recent reforms intended to simplify the system. Lack of information, split responsibilities in the federal system, multiple laws with overlapping and often contradictory content, unclear implementation procedures, and frequent changes to the rules make it impossible to stay up to date with regulatory demands. This regulatory complexity is a key factor that continues to allow politicians to use their discretionary power for the benefit of select business partners in a system of legally reasonable market orientation and democratic division of power. 'At a very basic level, politicians continue to be needed as fixers' (Jenkins 1999: 116).

The best opportunities for earning additional direct incomes in the reformed economy are to be found in land transactions. Land acquisition cannot take place without state government cooperation, and within each of the states, fixers are needed from each particular area of acquisition. Direct kickbacks for enabling land transactions might not even be necessary, since opportunities will exist to divert funds from the purchase, including diverting land to relatives and friends, or simply to profit from knowing that the value of land next to any industrial project will inevitably rise (Jenkins 1999).

Whenever cases questioning the public purpose of certain land acquisitions have been made, the courts have generally said that whatever democratically elected governments decide counts as a public purpose, so long as rules are followed regarding compensation for those losing land (Iyer 2007). But the acquisition of land for private companies is politically sensitive, so there is indecision as to whether or not governments should intervene and on whose behalf they should act (Fernandes 2009). Just as in the distribution of benefits, informal possibilities exist for politicians to negotiate compensation whenever enough power can be assembled to seriously challenge development plans. The opportunities rest with individual political brokers who can use personal influence to intervene on a case-by-case basis (Jenkins 1999; Newell and Wheeler 2006).

Since the early 1980s, with a radically reduced level of national public investment, state governments have been forced to compete for private investment in a completely new way. In some sectors, like mining, state governments nevertheless have some means to strongly influence—if not control—decisions about who gets to operate where. The exploitation of especially valuable ore deposits depends on investment in plants to refine the ore, otherwise contracts will not be awarded. A complete lack of transparency in the award of these contracts ensures that consideration will only be given to politically favoured investors. Even for smaller mining leases, administrative approval procedures remain complex and hidden from the exercise of any independent authority, thereby allowing scope for manipulation. Industrial investment also creates opportunities beyond those associated with land acquisition, as in the sub-contracting of construction or other activities. These contracts can either be won by companies owned by politicians or distributed to other contractors as a form of patronage.

The chief ministers are key actors in the process of seeking out sources of private investment.

> In the 1990s drama of economic liberalisation state chief ministers play leading roles in India's emergent federal market economy. They are seen on front pages, covers of news magazines and television screens, making and breaking coalition governments, welcoming foreign statesmen and investors, dealing with natural disasters and domestic violence (Rudolph and Rudolph 2001a: 1541).

Having never been especially prominent among Indian states, either economically or politically, Andhra Pradesh shot to sudden fame in the early 1990s when Chandrababu Naidu of the Telugu Desam Party (TDP) became the first state government politician to openly embrace a package of economic reforms (Rudolph and Rudolph 2001a; Suri 2005). Whether Naidu was as reform-minded as he claimed to be remains uncertain, since many of the welfare programs instituted by previous governments continued during his period in office. Eventually, his government was damaged by the accusation of neglecting the countryside (Suri 2004), and once the Congress Party came back into power in 2004, there was a return to standard state government behaviour, with reform measures carried out by stealth, and the promulgation of well-advertised populist welfare packages for the poor (Srinivasulu 2009).

It was in this highly politicised setting that proposals for a number of large-scale bauxite mining and refining projects were made from the early 1990s onwards. India's significant bauxite ore deposits, confined to a relatively small geographical area in the Eastern Ghats hill range in the states of Odisha and Andhra Pradesh, were first identified in the 1970s. The first—and to date the only—large-scale mining operation to be established was implemented by the public company Nalco (the National Aluminium Corporation) in Odisha in the 1980s, with the French company Pechiney involved as a supplier of technology. Direct private-sector involvement only began with the economic reforms of the 1990s, but despite significant efforts, such attempts by Indian and multinational companies have so far not resulted in new mining operations. This has forced related alumina refineries, like Vedanta's Lanjigarh refinery in Odisha, to operate with a mix of bauxite ore from other parts of India or from abroad.

The world aluminium industry, like much of the metals sector, underwent rapid expansion in the 2000s, with the price of alumina reaching an all-time high in the summer of 2007.[7] An important factor behind the sustained growth since the early 1990s has been Chinese demand (World Bank 2006). China is now the world's largest aluminium producer, and Indian bauxite deposits have been among those geographically best placed to cater to this demand. China accounted for as much as 82 per cent of Indian alumina exports in 2006/07, with a value of US$339 million. The aluminium industry is the biggest metal industry in the world after iron and steel, and production of its raw material has been shifting towards the tropics over the course of the last 50 years as new deposits have been found in countries like Brazil, Guinea and Jamaica (Barham et al. 1994). At the same time, the industry has been constrained by the high energy costs and increasingly stringent environmental norms applied in the Western consumer countries, while ore-producing nations have long sought to obtain a greater share of the final value of processed aluminium (Francis 1981; Bunker 1994).

Economic and technical obstacles to the growth of this industry in India have been reduced by the availability of international technology and private-sector funds, and by greater access to the world market. But as far as Adivasis are concerned, the continued lack of benefits from this or any other changes to the modern economy might not make much difference.

> Adivasis were displaced from their lands and villages when the state occupied the commanding heights of the economy. And they continue to be displaced under the auspices of liberalisation and globalisation (Guha 2007: 3306).

The main difference in recent years may not have consisted of formal policy changes, but rather the scale of the threat of displacement as the mineral industry has looked to expand its operations by means of private-sector investment and the importation of large-scale technologies of extraction.

7 The onset of a global recession towards the end of 2008 significantly reduced prices—a trend that has since continued.

Whether the developmental alliance will be able to implement its plans is not so easily predictable when its discourse of economic growth and export-oriented industry is clashing with a strong oppositional discourse. As is clear from the public interest litigation that enabled and later defended the Samatha judgment, there is significant capacity in civil society to support continued Adivasi land and livelihood protection in Andhra Pradesh, and this is supported in turn by a well-established—even if at times unpredictable—democratic framework.

Deliberative Democracy in India

Indian democracy affords opportunities for widespread deliberations over the reasons for and against a certain choice. These deliberations take place in upper and lower houses of the national parliament, in state government assemblies, in district and local councils, as well as in many other forums, such as print media and television. They extend over geographical scales, and are increasingly conducted in local languages, allowing the inclusion of a wider group of people than at any earlier point in time (Kohli 2001). Furthermore, the issue of tribal land protection has been defined as a matter of public policy through earlier struggles. Legal protection is prescribed in the national constitution and in state land rights acts, and it is therefore open to public debate. The Supreme Court has reaffirmed in the Samatha judgment that governments cannot diminish the importance of this legislation in favour of other societal goals such as promoting broader economic growth.

As part of the dominant discourse on land use, the extraction of mineral ores from central India is justified by an ideology of modernisation and economic development through industrialisation that has been present in top policymaking circles ever since Independence (Chibber 2003; Kohli 2004). Minerals are seen as vital inputs to industrial processes or as sources of crucial export revenues, which are key for progress technically and economically, and one of the few realistic hopes for impoverished central Indian states to improve their economies. The focus is on economic growth rather than on mitigating the costs borne in the Scheduled Areas, or ensuring that a significant share of the income is returned to the mineral-producing areas. A related and influential factor is the unreformed nature of the political system, where the need for resources to fund political patronage incentivises politicians to attempt to extract rents by controlling access to land and natural resources.

Habermas treats systematically distorted communication, the failure to reach the goal of communicative action and therefore to reach mutual understanding (Edgar 2006), as unintentional, thereby indicating that a refusal to participate in deliberations is not part of a conscious strategy of domination. But Bohman (2000) argues that this is not necessarily the case, and that there are situations of purposefully distorted communication. In his view, domination is often based on the avoidance of consensus building, and that is how elites can best assure themselves of a disproportionate share of resources. Avoidance of debate over the bauxite project discussed in this book is exemplified by the way that the state government secretly signed a deal with JSW in 2005 and proceeded to make comprehensive plans without sharing the details with the public.

Indian laws, however, require certain documents to be produced as part of government procedures. At least some parts of the administration cannot remain completely silent on what is being planned: there may be attempts to prevent information from reaching the public, but legislation exists to ensure at least some degree of transparency, which can open matters up for wider debate. In addition, the media produce many stories, often based on protests or controversy, but also allowing a voice to project proponents. In these cases, the nature, its quality and timing of the information that reaches the public are likely to be crucial for the stimulation or suppression of public deliberations. Even if project promoters attempt to suppress such deliberations, it might be possible to create alternative public spheres in civil society to support communication on such matters of concern. The varying capacities and interests of the actors in the bauxite project opposition, first to access, and then to interpret and share, information in various forums, is decisive for the success of such alternatives.

The many years of delay in the development of mineral projects in central India seem to show that it is not merely the available material resources and capabilities that are important for the outcomes. If this were the case, the promoters of bauxite mining would be certain to come out on top due to their ability to influence state functions and their greater command over technical and financial resources. A starting point for the need to extend a political economy analysis is the subject of land rights that constitutes the focus of this book. The demand for tribal land rights depends on claims to identity, in addition to material livelihood needs, rather in the way that other natural resources have come to be imagined and contested in the cultural politics approach favoured by Baviskar (2008). But while the symbolic opposition to polluting extractive industries proposed in the green hills reserved for Adivasis continues to provide support for traditional land uses, this book is focused on the possibilities for affecting policy preferences and implementation across a range of different forums across the whole of India. A discursive model can here be seen as more appropriate, since it involves:

> a plurality of forms of association, roles, groups, institutions, and discourses … [where] the means of interpretation and communication are not all of a piece. They do not constitute a coherent, monolithic web but rather a heterogeneous, polyglot field of diverse possibilities and alternatives (Fraser 1989: 165).

In this cacophony of claims and counter-claims, the outcomes sought by the groups involved are not necessarily the same, and different groups may not even use the same discourse.

A core difference does exist where the developmental alliance favours a discourse based on economic growth while civil society concerns over Adivasi land rights are based on the politics of identity. Additionally, there is a significant geographical dispersion of forums across the country as a whole, despite the physical challenge of gaining access to national forums, particularly for those losing land to extractive projects in remote, central eastern parts of the country. And different forms of communication are being used, both in terms of the common language being spoken and the technical vocabulary required by those identified as experts, as for example in the domain of environmental science. The claims for redistribution and recognition (Fraser 1989, 1997), or claims about economic growth as opposed to the protection of Adivasi identity, are thus not able to speak back to one another. The analysis offered here is therefore broadened to include the ability to make claims embedded in material and cultural discursive contexts in a setting where vast differences between decision-makers and citizens call for attention to a third term that is crucial for Fraser (2009), namely representation.

Information is crucial to communication, since without it very little purposeful communication can take place. If people do not know the what, where and how of the planning made for a bauxite project, there is really very little that can be learnt, even if more inclusive deliberations take place. Informational issues are particularly relevant when significant knowledge exists, even though such knowledge is often fragmented among many different actors, and this point applies to the extension of bauxite industry operations in the country and the work of oppositional groups whose members have used the law to improve the realisation of rights in support of tribal livelihoods.

Genuine deliberations resembling the Habermasian ideal of inclusive, deliberative democracy, where all citizens can engage in open and unhindered communicative exchanges, require that 'information about state functioning be made accessible so that state activities would be subject to critical scrutiny and the force of "public opinion"' (Fraser 1997: 72). Without basic information flows in place, it becomes difficult to even start imagining new and better ways of understanding the changes brought on by large-scale extractive industries in tribal India, and how the current social and economic development dilemmas should be resolved.

Nowadays, some Indian government agencies are pursuing increased openness in policy implementation, and to some extent in policy deliberations, while other agencies seem to want to keep that space closed. Different federal ministries have vastly different approaches, as shown by comparison of the drafting and implementation of the *Special Economic Zone Act 2005* by the Ministry of Commerce with that of the *National Rural Employment Guarantee Act 2006* by the Ministry of Rural Development. Where the former has been made without any civil society influence, the latter has a *lok adalat* (people's court) as part of its mandatory monitoring mechanisms (Dreze and Khera 2009). When specific information-sharing and public accountability provisions are lacking, as in the Special Economic Zone Act, then the *Right to Information Act 2005* allows every citizen to access a wide range of information related to government action. Before this important act was passed:

> [a]ctivists had to rely on 'leaked' documents and information gleaned from government responses submitted to the courts and to donor organizations such as the World Bank which had a more liberal public disclosure policy (Baviskar 2007: 5).

Meaningful deliberations depend not only on the ability to access information, but also on the possibilities for people to convert this information into useful knowledge (Thomas and Parayil 2008). The average citizen cannot be expected to understand technical planning reports relating to the mining industry, and indigenous people around the world 'often lack the financial resources and the access to "technical" information and expertise required to ensure effective participation' (O'Faircheallaigh 1999: 64).

In India, the environmental impact assessment report, normally written by environmental engineers for decision-makers who are also environmental engineers, is the only mandatory piece of public information about a proposed industrial project that has to be translated into the local language. Due to the technical approach adopted in such documents, the critique of them depends on middle-class activists who have the formal education and other necessary resources to understand and challenge the legalities and technicalities of extractive industry plans.

Since basic information flows about a project are already guaranteed through the independence of the media and a few legal transparency clauses, complete secrecy is not likely to be a viable option for those promoting them. Instead, 'the powerful use control over the production of knowledge as a way of setting the public agenda, and for including or excluding certain voices and participants in action upon it' (Gaventa and Cornwall 2008: 175). These actions can include the framing of scientific rules that exclude certain people and/or claims in favour of decisions made by technical experts, or the denial of representation in various democratic forums. However, if the right kind of information can be accessed, it might be possible to reorganise the terms of deliberation; for example, by means of a court case. In the present case, oppositional groups and individuals with relevant skills might be able to counter their exclusion by using new information technologies and rights to information legislation in addition to the forms of opposition that have previously prevented mining on tribal land. The struggle over tribal land can thus be seen as being just as much a struggle over the right to define who is affected and who is not, and who is supposed to make decisions about the use and distribution of resources. In the contestations over tribal land, information is a resource that can be used to blunt the overt exercise of power.

This book uses an analytical framework based on Fraser's (1989) 'three moments in the politics of needs interpretation', but also draws on her more recent work (Fraser 1997, 2009). This allows a transition from an initial examination of the natural characteristics of the resource and its political economy, to the mediation of the state and the possibilities for different oppositional claims to be heard across India's many deliberative forums during project implementation, and finally to an examination of the outcomes of the contestation.

The Legitimisation or Denial of Needs

The legitimisation of the need to protect Adivasi land has both a material and cultural basis. The strength of this need ensures that the proponents of mining cannot easily and completely deny the value of tribal land protection, especially since the Samatha judgment. Instead, if industrialisation is allowed to proceed, alliance members must attempt to modify the interpretation of what is meant by these rights by emphasising other forms of material gain. Oppositional groups may point to the strong cultural image of the tribal people to show the need to continue with land protection or justify it as a means to livelihood protection. These interchanges create a tension between demands for redistribution and recognition.

The first part of the legitimisation or denial of needs, as detailed in Chapter 3, is the way in which the mining project is formally organised and what its terms of reference mean for the distribution of material benefits derived from it. The proponents rely on significant advantages in accessing state and market resources when attempting to use tribal land for industrial purposes. The ability to formalise a business agreement that sets out certain rights and obligations between those who are party to the agreement, but also conditions the way that future costs and benefits will affect third parties, involves an apparent use of power. The issues are political economy questions concerned with the creation and organisation of the bauxite project itself, and how political and economic power has directed its design towards certain outcomes.

The second important legitimacy concern is with the specific pieces of land, and their current users, located at the centre of the contestations, as detailed in Chapter 4. The importance of land rights for tribal people has been well established as a general principle, but the particular ways in which the bauxite project proposes to divert and use the land, and how these new uses compete with existing livelihoods, affects the perception of the need to protect existing land use in each specific case. This need is shaped by the compensation offered to the land users and the opportunities to build new livelihoods when old ones are no longer possible. Environmental degradation will indirectly affect local livelihoods beyond the experience of immediate displacement, and to some extent will also generate wider regional concerns over the condition of water and forests.

The Negotiation over Needs

Analysis of the negotiation over needs is still concerned with the material issue of tribal land and its many uses, but shifts to a discursive arena of government mediation and competitive bargaining processes, where the claims of different actors are voiced at different discursive sites, ranging across scales from specific project locations to the state and central capitals. The exercise of power and the complexity, not only of the planned bauxite project and its many potential 'externalities', but also of the legal and administrative processes that are meant to mediate its implementation, contribute to the contested and uncertain nature of the process.

The government is meant to mediate between different claims by application of the rule of law to ensure justice for all citizens, and additionally to ensure special affirmative rights for especially disadvantaged groups like tribal people, as detailed in Chapter 5. For example, the way that issues are framed over land acquisition, compensation policies, or forest and water use will have crucial importance for the way that these issues are discussed. In the former statist economy, the bureaucracy almost took on a life of its own with regard to promoting or preventing different programs and plans, but this autonomy is seen here as having been significantly curtailed by the action of the most influential politicians, even if other forums might be able to counteract this dominant influence. Representation is therefore a key issue in the negotiation over needs, since it determines who is allowed to voice a claim in relation to the project.

Furthermore, opportunities to mediate are offered by actors and organisations in civil society, including those immediately affected by the prospect of displacement and pollution, as detailed in Chapter 6. The many forums that exist across India's federal democratic system can be used to stake oppositional claims on issues related to the alienation of tribal land and the way that these concerns have been framed in government procedures. Issues of representation are also important for the ability of opposition groups and individuals to claim legitimacy when speaking on behalf of those who are negatively affected. Politicians in power may have an advantage on this score, despite the many problems associated with the way that elections are fought, since they can claim that they were democratically elected, as opposed to most of those who disagree with their plans.

The Satisfaction of Needs

The final stage in the analytical framework is the satisfaction of needs, or the extent to which it is possible to reach the outcomes that are being sought. The model of communication proposed by Habermas treats access to information as the basis for people to debate how they wish to have their societies organised. However, differences in access to—and use of—information across India's many public forums can limit deliberations, thus creating openings for those in power to shape future tribal land use according to their own wishes. Resourceful civil society organisations and actors may be able access the informational resources that would allow for challenges to be made to the power of the developmental alliance. Whether the alliance is able to control access to information, rather than rely on the exercise of overt power based on its superior material resources, is thus seen as a crucial factor in satisfying the need to protect tribal land rights. Chapter 8 uses informational problems experienced during my own fieldwork as a way to understand the eventual outcomes of this process.

Methodology

Due to the crucial role that information is found to play in struggles over land and mineral resources, this book frequently mentions the informational problems experienced by various actors, including myself as a researcher. This reflexive approach was chosen in order to emphasise the way that context-specific informational resources are crucial to an explanation of outcomes in a setting characterised by a great deal of uncertainty and apparent gross inequality of power, not only between the two opposing sides but also within these broad coalitions. The capacity to access and process information was found to vary enormously from one individual to the next, and I was one such individual during the course of my fieldwork.[8] The strategies that I used to uncover information are taken as further evidence of the depth and nature of these informational problems, illustrating the need to move beyond standard political ecology explanations, as shown in Chapter 7. Information is here seen not only as a vital resource, with access determined by sheer power, but also as being uncertain, complex, full of contradictions and coded in particular languages that determine who can and cannot access and make use of it.

8 Fieldwork was carried out during three visits, lasting a total of 10 months, between 2006 and 2008. Another, shorter visit was made to the proposed mine and refinery sites in June 2012.

It was far from obvious where I should start enquiring about the planned bauxite industry operations during my fieldwork. If you try to see company representatives in their local registered offices, you will find JSW located on the outskirts of Visakhapatnam, in the housing estate built for employees from their other small facility in Vizianagaram District. A few rooms seem to function as temporary offices, while others are reserved for managers staying overnight. There are no reception staff other than the local security guard; in fact, the office seems to have very few, if any, permanent employees. Similarly, AnRak Aluminium, the other proponent of an aluminium project in Andhra Pradesh, is housed in a plain family home in the upmarket suburb of Jubilee Hills in Hyderabad,[9] without any hint of it actually functioning as an office space. There is not even a company name to be seen there.

The state government offices are only marginally more approachable, since they at least have official addresses with signboards. Key in the Andhra Pradesh Government planning effort is the Mines and Geology Department and its head, who is designated as the vice-chairman and managing director. This department operates on the seventh floor of the extremely worn-down BRK Bhavan building in central Hyderabad, where the lifts rarely work, adjacent to some of the most insignificant departments of the state government. There was an air of efficiency about the managing director's dealings, and I encountered a significant number of other visitors on several of my own visits. Nevertheless, whenever one approached him with specific questions, some obstacle or another would make an appearance. In the end, these personal interactions were curtailed by the absence of a second authorisation from the state government, despite the grant of a research visa by the central government, which supposedly required the state government's approval.

My fieldwork strategy then changed from making largely unsuccessful attempts to find company representatives or meet policymakers in Hyderabad to engaging with the vocal and widespread opposition in the more directly affected city of Visakhapatnam. This is where bauxite mining had become a major issue, perhaps even disproportionately so when compared to its actual economic importance, or even to the area of land to be acquired or the amount of pollution to be caused. Many other

9 Visakhapatnam District is located in the residual state of Andhra Pradesh, while Hyderabad is now the official capital of Telangana. However, Andhra Pradesh will have Hyderabad as its capital until the construction of a new state capital has been completed.

projects were being proposed at the time, in and around Visakhapatnam city, such as the expansion of the Vizag Special Economic Zone, with its focus on information technology, and a 'coastal corridor' made up of other infrastructure and industrial projects.

The various opposition parties and activist groups that had been campaigning on the bauxite issue, as well as local journalists, would not necessarily be close to the corridors of power in Hyderabad and Delhi, where all decisions and detailed plans were being made, but they had often managed to get hold of some government document or other piece of information that could reveal something about what was being planned. Much effort had been put into the discovery of such information by a dedicated set of groups and individuals, but there was little coordination in the analysis and dissemination of their findings. Only an outside researcher could manage to stay sufficiently clear of the politics of information access amongst these oppositional groups to gather the data presented in this book.

The politics of information access worked in many ways—sometimes unexpected or even quite random. Claiming neutrality as a researcher was a good start when meeting people for the first time. Nonetheless, the topic was highly politicised, with no apparently neutral position. Not taking a stance might seem suspect and thereby limit my own access to information. Affiliation with a foreign university only worked to some extent to establish trust with respondents. Introductions were much more reliable, and these opened up opportunities for further enquiries with the project's opponents, but almost never with the government, and especially not with the company, which was unknown to just about everyone in the state. Connections established in my previous work as a volunteer in a non-governmental organisation (NGO) could open some doors, but could also be a drawback; for example, when I encountered one of the many feuds between various civil society groups and political parties.

Sheer luck was certainly also an element of my fieldwork. I came across a person who had a good friend and former 'junior'[10] who was high up in the local administration. When the senior made a request on my behalf, it was possible to get access to a wide range of government documents that would never have been made available otherwise, or at least would have taken months or even years to obtain.

10 A 'junior' is someone a year or two below you in university.

As the research moved from policy corridors to the project opposition and then to the sites of implementation, issues of access to information became less and less problematic. In the towns and villages on and next to the proposed project sites, people would even go out of their way to contact others I might be interested to meet, irrespective of their particular position on the issue.

It was known that some activists had been very active in obtaining information through the recently introduced Right to Information (RTI) Act. As it turned out, almost every respondent had some document to add to the puzzle of what was actually being planned. They rarely divulged the manner in which these had been obtained, other than by saying that RTI and other methods had been used. It is assumed that NGOs had mastered RTI procedures well enough to mainly depend on this legislation for information access, whereas journalists and other independents lacked the time, knowledge and resources for RTI requests, and therefore had to depend on other methods. Data collection was thus a combination of ethnographic work and documentary analysis aimed at understanding a very fluid situation spread out across different geographical scales. This combination has much to offer as a methodology to investigate resource contestation, especially the translation of government policy into project implementation (Randeria and Grunder 2011).

The existence of a multitude of planning documents, and the ability to access internal government communications, allowed for at least some insights into the meticulous work of reasonably high quality that was being carried out inside government departments. Although there were indications of rules being bent to favour project implementation, this was far from being a complete picture in a state with a relatively well-trained administration following a detailed set of regulations.

Outline of the Book

This book examines the paralysing stand-off on bauxite mining and Adivasi livelihoods in three parts. The first (Chapters 2–4) connects the historical and recent struggles for Adivasi land rights in Andhra Pradesh with the way that a bauxite mineral project was planned; the second (Chapters 5–6) deals with the contestation of the project during its implementation phase, both at the actual project sites and across a multitude of state and national forums; which leads to the third part (Chapters 7–8), in which an explanation is sought for the experience of paralysis.

Chapter 2 provides the historical context of longstanding struggles, at times of a violent nature when other means of protest have not been possible, to protect Adivasi land from outsiders, not only in Andhra Pradesh but across large parts of central India. Since the issues around land use and forest access for traditional inhabitants remain largely unresolved, opposition to the present wave of private sector–led investment in the bauxite industry has been heavily influenced by this historical context.

Chapters 3 and 4 examine the details of how and by whom the project was planned, and how Adivasi livelihoods would be affected at the two sites chosen for it. This sets the foundation for understanding the way that wider concerns about social justice were addressed as part of the planning process. The existing land transfer legislation and the many actors supporting it provide a foundation for the tribal people to realise their land rights. There is a very stark contrast between land transfer laws and the Samatha judgment, on one hand, and economic policy in general, specifically the new mineral policy framework, with its emphasis on economic growth through private investment, on the other hand. Yet these seemingly incompatible policies and laws continue to live side by side, their interaction shaped by ongoing contestations and the amount of pressure that various influential groups can exert in each particular case. The contest over bauxite mining in Andhra Pradesh is here seen as one instance of hundreds of similar battles currently raging across central India.

Chapters 5 and 6 examine the way that project implementation has been mediated in government processes and through civil society interventions, first at the local project sites and then across the wider institutional framework of the state. In these chapters, the mediation processes move away from the immediate struggles over access to, and control over, various natural resources, to address the unique character of the contestation that came to be defined by the question of who could access key information and then master the techno-bureaucratic language and complicated procedures required in order to access forums where challenges could be launched. State mediation processes offer opportunities to find a middle way between the two conflicting positions, because the state is in charge of ensuring that the rule of law is followed. However, the state comes with many internal contradictions, most clearly seen in this case in the role of politicians as promoters of industry and that of the judiciary as upholder of the law that bans the transfer of tribal land to non-tribal actors. Chapter 6 discusses the role of civil society in circumstances where government mediation has limited effects.

Chapter 7 returns to my concern with informational problems as seen through the eyes of the researcher, to illustrate the difficulty of generating a larger, common understanding when so many fractured understandings exist, in government agencies as well as among groups and individuals in wider civil society. Finally, Chapter 8 provides an overall conclusion, including a discussion of the larger theoretical implications of this analysis for the future relationship between land, minerals and people in central India and beyond.

2. Adivasi Land Rights and Dispossession

Land as a social justice concern for Adivasis has a long historical precedent in rebellions and struggles across central India (Arnold 1984; Pati 2011; Bates and Shah 2014). Claims for land rights make emotive demands for both the recognition of a unique identity and the material redistribution of resources. On paper, strong laws exist to give formal support to these rights, but these have never been implemented more than half-heartedly, and even then with much variation between states and even across territories within states. However, rights enshrined in laws remain as important mobilisation factors for movements working towards their actual implementation. While significant similarities exist across the Adivasi areas of central India, specific historical circumstances differ, owing, for example, to the fragmented governance of British India, with its many princely estates, or to cultural and ecological variations across regional landscapes. These factors continue to influence present-day legislation and the possibilities that exist for different groups of people to be heard and to effect change.

Movements are built on local grievances but are also influenced by outside events. Place-specific contexts are interrelated across regions, especially through the legislative centres in the state capitals and in Delhi. At times, certain actors have the ability to jump from one context to a completely different one, as was true in the Samatha case, where a national court was persuaded to protect local land rights. These openings across India's fragmented federal framework represent great sources of hope for improvement, while simultaneously creating fractures when only certain actors are able to operate across scales to bring about change.

This chapter presents a historical overview of land struggles in Adivasi India, with a specific focus on Andhra Pradesh. It shows how centuries of unrest over land relations have been crucial in shaping the present-day social movements protesting against bauxite mining. And it provides a deeper consideration of the Samatha judgment itself, which initially appeared to protect all the Adivasis of central India from dispossession.

Past and Present Adivasi Land Uses

The history of land relations in tribal Andhra Pradesh, as well as in much of the rest of tribal central India, is one of recurring struggles against the transfer of farmland in the valleys to non-tribal farmers and moneylenders, and against the government's claim to own forest land on and around the hills (Balagopal 2007a). Successive efforts have been made by state governments to strengthen tribal legal rights to agricultural land in the valleys, especially as part of attempts to restore peace after rebellions, but state governments have retained control of forest land, leaving many tribals living under insecure circumstances for generations. The *Scheduled Tribes and Other Traditional Forest Dwellers (Recognition of Forest Rights) Act 2006* (otherwise known as the Forest Rights Act) provided some hope for change in favour of forest-dwelling communities, many of which are tribal communities.[1] Yet threats of dispossession by development projects, including dams and mines, have become common in the last 50–60 years.

A special legislative area with strong land rights, still today widely known as 'the Agency', was created in the northern part of Andhra Pradesh as a result of recurrent struggles against externally driven resource exploitation (see Figure 1.1). This process had three distinct moments: the creation of the area as a separate administrative region by the British colonial government in 1839; the declaration of state ownership of all forested land in 1882; and the reservation of private agricultural land for tribal farmers in 1917.

1 According to one estimate, about 10.7 million people, or 14 per cent of the total population, in the former state of Andhra Pradesh (prior to the separation of the new state of Telangana) live in forested landscapes (Reddy et al. 2010).

Land on the plains, beyond the boundaries of the Agency, was formally titled in the early 1800s under local intermediary landlords, known as zamindars, who collected revenue on behalf of the colonial government. The zamindars, often minor chieftains who had inherited their titles, had great powers within the territories assigned to them, but could be evicted if they did not perform according to set criteria, especially if they did not pay the required taxes (Saxena 1997; Rao et al. 2006). Within the Agency itself, a distributed system of authority developed through the appointment of local hill zamindars, known as muttadars, who in turn were subordinate to the bigger zamindars on the plains.

> The muttadars were the vital links in an extended chain of authority and subordination stretching from the villagers in the hills to a raja in the plains and hence, far more hazily, to a distant suzerain in Hyderabad, Delhi or Madras (Arnold and Guha 1995: 101).

Baken describes the establishment of land tenures around the city of Vijayawada in Krishna District, south of the present Visakhapatnam District, during the 1840s as an arrangement that built on earlier patterns of ownership and use:

> [T]he land revenue arrangements prevailing in [the 1840s in] Vijayawada were a continuation of old local traditions in which specific (land owning) caste groups in each village had the exclusive right to the possession and yield of the soil, in return for paying taxes (Baken 2003: 121).

Not only were upper- and middle-caste groups able to command large areas of land; the quality of their land, including access to water sources, also tended to be better than that held by members of lower castes (Hjejle 1988).

The former (and larger) Visakhapatnam District,[2] on the very outskirts of British colonial rule, on the border between the Madras and Bengal presidencies, proved to be a difficult area to control, despite the use of zamindars as intermediaries, and there were frequent violent rebellions, especially in the hills (Arnold 1984; Atluri 1984). Without strategic importance or enough (known) resources to warrant the despatch

2 Visakhapatnam District under the Madras Presidency of British India comprised what today are the Visakhapatnam, Srikakulam and Vizianagaram districts of Andhra Pradesh, as well as parts of southern Odisha (see Figure 1.1).

of sufficient troops to control the situation, the solution adopted in 1839 was to set aside seven-eighths of the district's area from the normal rule of law through the creation of the so-called Agency.[3]

The provisions for the Agency included special courts of law and the ability to exclude or modify existing laws not deemed appropriate for the area. Significant powers came to be held by the District Collector who was the 'Agent' of the British Government—hence the continued reference to 'the Agency' in coastal Andhra Pradesh (Carmichael 1869). It was, in a sense, a practical solution for the colonial power to strengthen its local authority while removing some of the demands on hill zamindars to produce the same amounts of revenue as other zamindars in exchange for the return of peace in the hills.

Despite this, the rebellions continued, and even became worse after passage of the *Madras Forest Act 1882*, which put ownership of most Agency land in the hands of the government as 'reserved forest'. This included all land not under continuous cultivation but subject to the practice of shifting cultivation, known locally as *podu* (Saxena 1997; Rao et al. 2006). Another device was to declare land on hill slopes to be unsuitable for agriculture.[4] In the hilly Visakhapatnam Agency, this process ensured that most of the land came to be vested in the government, leaving only the flatter valley land to be recognised as private land. For these reasons, the forest dwellers, hunter-gatherers and subsistence farmers of the Agency were rarely included in any formal system of property rights, and this situation has continued to the present day (Balagopal 2007a).

Arnold (1984) argues that the nature of the rebellions showed that the grievances of the people were longstanding and served to unite the many different groups of people who inhabited the area, often including the locally influential muttadars, against the outsiders. This does not mean that the distinction between 'tribal' and 'non-tribal' identities was particularly important in such movements. Some of the best known rebel

3 This was done by means of the *Ganjam and Vizagapatam Act 1839*. Similar areas had been excluded in other parts of British-ruled India, including the Chota Nagpur area in present-day Jharkhand in 1833 (Maharatna 2005), and in the Godavari and Ganjam agencies in what is now Andhra Pradesh. The special Meriah Agency was carved out of the Visakhapatnam Agency in what is today southern Odisha in order to deal specifically with the perceived problem of human sacrifice among the Kondh people (see Padel 2009).

4 A 10 per cent slope was used as a relevant measure in parts of Odisha, which has a similar land settlement history (Kumar et al. 2005).

leaders were non-tribals, such as the Hindu Alluri Sitarama Raju, from the Kshatriya caste, who led the 1922–24 uprising against the restrictions on *podu* and on access to forests.

The result of a century or more of frequent unrest influenced the first legal protection granted to private land in the Agency. The *Agency Tracts Interest and Land Transfer Act 1917*, also emanating from the Madras Presidency, attempted to regulate land transfers, but also to limit the prevalence of usurious interest rates that indirectly led to land loss when farmers were not able to repay their loans. Specifically, no land was allowed to be transferred from a person belonging to a so-called 'hill tribe' to an outsider. It was, however, possible for the Agent to grant an exemption from this rule, so the land alienation could continue (Sastry 2006).

Subsequent legislation created further restrictions on land transfer, culminating in the passage of the *Andhra Pradesh Scheduled Areas Land Transfer Regulation 1959* (hereafter called the 'Land Transfer Regulation'). The seeming incapacity of such legislation to resolve the issues was indicated by amendments to this regulation that were made in 1970 after the outbreak of a rebellion in Srikakulam District (Reddy 1977). Again, violent protest had erupted in the hills over restrictions on forest use imposed by the government, but it was also partly due to limited implementation of the 1959 regulation and the prevalence of low wages in the region that it covered (Dasgupta 1973).

The Land Transfer Regulation, as it currently stands, completely prohibits the transfer of any type of land to anyone but an Adivasi person or a registered Adivasi cooperative society. This crucially includes forest land owned by the government. The law further presumes that all land in the state's Scheduled Areas originally belonged to a tribal person, which means that land found in the possession of a non-tribal person should be restored to the original owner. Nominal tribal landholdings in which the real beneficiary is a non-tribal person, which are known as *benami* titles, are also prohibited (Balagopal 2007a). However, the regulation does not attempt to resolve issues related to ownership of, and access to, forest land. Nor does it propose a solution for the problems of the rural but non-tribal poor, who outnumber the tribal population in some parts of the Scheduled Areas.

In comparison to the exhaustive provisions of the Land Transfer Regulation, the Fifth Schedule of the Indian Constitution, the second legal precedent cited in the Samatha judgment, makes far less distinctive provisions for the protection of land rights. Instead, it leaves specific regulations to be determined by each state government or governor through repeated use of the word 'may'. For example:

> The Governor may make regulations for the peace and good government of any area in a state which is for the time being a Scheduled Area … such regulations may … prohibit or restrict the transfer of land by or among members of the Scheduled Tribes in such area (India 2007a: 288).

So it is not surprising that interpretations of the constitutional mandate to protect Adivasi landholdings have been highly variable.

Ever since the first land transfer legislation in Andhra Pradesh, the only amendments that have been enacted have been meant to further strengthen land rights. Civil society protest and electoral pressure on politicians has so far prevented open market reform of tribal land tenure in the state (Reddy 1988; Balagopal 2007a). Across tribal India, as far as is known, not a single land transfer act has been repealed, or even weakened, despite repeated attempts, such as those made in Jharkhand (Rao 2003; Kumar et al. 2005; Vijay Murty and Saran 2016) and also in Odisha. The continued formal strength of tribal land rights is quite remarkable, given the marginalised position of tribal people and the ongoing process of economic reform.

It might be possible to see the continued existence of land transfer legislation alongside the government's intent on promoting industrialisation as the result of the wide legal and administrative loopholes that exist in its implementation (Rao et al. 2006).[5] One example of this is that, if a non-tribal farmer gained possession of land before 1959, or with the consent of the Collector prior to the 1970 amendment, this land is allowed to stay in his or her possession. The most common loophole, however, is failure to act on the many surveys and reports that over the years have identified

5 An especially high incidence of farmland held by non-tribals is reported for the new Telangana State, with more than 50 per cent land being alienated, as compared to Vizianagaram and Srikakulam Districts, with 0.2 per cent and 2.2 per cent of land respectively in non-tribal holdings. Land alienation data is not reported for Visakhapatnam District, but more than 9,000 hectares of non-tribal landholdings were detected in a 1997 survey of the district (Rao et al. 2006).

particular non-tribal landholdings across the Scheduled Areas of Andhra Pradesh. Administrative inaction and long drawn out court procedures have prevented the settlement of many land issues (Balagopal 2007a).

At the time of Independence, the Agency areas were incorporated into India's collection of Scheduled Areas.[6] But the process of settling its borders excluded many of those it was meant to protect. The Srungavarapukota (S. Kota) Mandal, a sub-division of present-day Vizianagaram District,[7] was one such area that was declared to be 'non-scheduled', despite a history of being part of the larger colonial Visakhapatnam Agency and having traditionally been a forested area inhabited by tribal groups.[8] The way the Agency border was drawn proved absolutely crucial for possible locations of the alumina refinery and for the people it would displace, since private industry has not been allowed in the Scheduled Areas after the Samatha judgment.

At the non-scheduled refinery site, several tribal villages were among those most severely affected by land acquisition in an area that had been excluded from the tribal land rights legislation (see Chapter 4). Campaigns have been running since the 1970s to include 796 tribal villages across Andhra Pradesh, with a combined population of 140,186 according to the 1981 census, within the Scheduled Areas. The number of non-scheduled tribal villages is especially large in the coastal districts, with 170 villages and 45,149 people in Vizianagaram District, and 33,939 people in neighbouring Srikakulam (Ajay Kumar n.d.). However, despite official recognition of the problem, there seems to be no scheduled status forthcoming for the land in question. Indeed, most of it is likely to have already fallen into non-tribal hands.

6 A clear definition of the extent of the Visakhapatnam Agency is difficult to find despite its importance for Scheduled Area governance. A practical definition would be the area in which the Andhra Pradesh Government's Integrated Tribal Development Agency operates, that is to say, the mandals (or sub-divisions) known as Ananthagiri, Araku Valley, Dumbriguda, Hukumpeta, Pedabayalu, Munchingiputtu, Paderu, G. Madugula, Chintapalli, G.K. Veedhi and Koyyuru. The non-tribal part of Visakhapatnam then becomes the remaining 32 mandals of the district, but given the larger size of the mandals in the Agency, this would mean that the latter makes up roughly 56 per cent of the total geographical area (Gopal 1996).

7 A mandal is also known as a 'block' or *tehsil* in other parts of India.

8 It is possible that S. Kota Mandal was already excluded from the Agency in 1863 when, according to Carmichael (1869), the Vizianagaram and Bobbili zamindars were moved into the regular area of the Madras Presidency.

Land and Adivasi Culture

The early history of the Agency thus revolved around rebellions in defence of material resources like land and forests. However, to fully understand the enduring support for special land provisions, it is not enough to merely examine the history of these material struggles. The discourse around tribal people and the impact of modernity upon them started to change in the late nineteenth and early twentieth centuries towards a view of the people as ecologically benign and therefore virtually guaranteed not to be able to cope with social and economic change. It is this representation of tribal people as having a special relationship with their natural surroundings that continues to reinforce the protection of tribal land, just as much as their direct livelihood needs as farmers or forest dwellers. The appeal of 'the tribal' has been remarkably durable despite India's changing economic priorities.

This modified view of tribal people, which came to be widely accepted from the early years of the twentieth century, was most clearly articulated by Verrier Elwin, a British missionary who arrived in the late colonial period and, after many years living in central India, became an authority on tribal issues, even to the point where he was appointed as an adviser to the Government of India (Guha 1996). In sum, Elwin argued that the tribal person was as much culturally as economically tied to his or her natural surroundings, and that tribal society was based on a special kind of unity and solidarity, with significant elements of fraternity and equality, and with a much higher status afforded to women when compared to the rest of India. Elwin's characterisation of the tribes thus positioned them against Western modernity as well as the traditionally rigid and unequal Hindu caste society. According to him, 'it was only the tribal isolated in the highlands who really lived; his religion characteristic and alive, his social organisation unimpaired, his traditions of art and dance unbroken, his mythology still vital' (Guha 1996: 2378–9). From this characterisation came the demand to protect tribals by upholding the sanctity of the separate areas created by the British, wherein they would remain free from the influence of modernisation as well as of Hindu caste society.

On closer examination, however, the division between tribal and non-tribal peoples that is maintained in national policy is not quite so clear-cut. At least in central India,[9] the 'tribal' social category comprises a wide range of peoples living across a number of different states, some of whom have their own religion, language or other customs that separate them from 'mainstream' India, while others do not, or else have adopted a religion, language or customs that resemble those of other, 'non-tribal' social groups (Xaxa 1999; Roy Burman 2003). To find a common denominator between all these groups of people is not a straightforward task, and most probably never was so in the past (Guha 1999).

The designation of Adivasi is increasingly used to build a claim for recognition as 'indigenous' people, yet it is doubtful whether the groups now officially categorised as Scheduled Tribes can claim to be more 'native' to India than other populations, such as the Dravidians of southern India (Xaxa 1999). In addition, many 'tribal' groups have migrated to their present locations from elsewhere, which makes it difficult to claim that they are the original inhabitants of the places where they now live (Guha 1996; Prasad 2003).

The supposedly egalitarian nature of Adivasi society does not seem to be supported by evidence from within the Agency that shows some striking resemblances to the caste divisions that exist on the plains. The traditional social order of the Agency has maintained the status of members of the Bagatha tribe as the main landowners, with the Valmiki tribe having a status similar to that of low-caste Hindu Dalits, with virtually no land of their own (Rajpramukh and Palkumar 2005). Similar divisions have been shown to exist between different sub-tribes (Reddy 1971). There is evidence of more freedom for women, in the form of higher female work participation rates, but this has not entailed a greater inclusion of women in decision-making forums or even in access to education, where tribal women still lag far behind men (India 2001a, 2001b).

9 The Scheduled Tribes of the Sixth Schedule states of northeastern India are not discussed in this book because of significant differences in their cultures, as well as the legal framework, when compared to central India.

Figure 2.1 Adivasi village with bauxite hill in Araku Mandal.
Source: Photo by author, June 2012.

Perhaps the most distinctive feature of the 'tribal' category is instead the high incidence of poverty, or low levels of human development, that continue to plague the people within it (Kapur Mehta and Shah 2003; Gang et al. 2008). Despite its relatively strong overall record of poverty reduction, Andhra Pradesh is still worse off in comparison to other states with large Adivasi populations.[10] Other indicators of their intense poverty are evident in the high incidence of malnutrition and disease.[11] Nationally, Adivasis continue to be significantly worse off compared to India's other disadvantaged communities, such as Dalits and Muslims (Guha 2007).

10 As recently as 1990, the tribal literacy rate was as low as 7.7 per cent in the Visakhapatnam Agency, with a female rate of only 1.8 per cent (Gopal 1996). By 2001, 37 per cent of tribals were recorded as being literate, with a female rate of 26 per cent. Only Uttar Pradesh and Bihar have lower tribal literacy rates than Andhra Pradesh. By comparison, the Dalit literacy rate in Andhra Pradesh was 60.5 per cent in the same year (India 2001a, 2001b).

11 The infant mortality rate is between 120 and 150, compared to 72 for the whole of Andhra Pradesh. There is a 30 per cent mortality rate for under-5s, but for some tribal groups (like Savara and Gadaba) it is over 50 per cent. The incidence of tuberculosis is twice as high in the tribal population, and 75 per cent of all cases of malaria in the state are recorded in tribal areas (Reddy et al. 2006); 65 per cent of children aged 1–5 suffer from malnutrition, and only about half of all households consume adequate amounts of protein and energy, according to a survey conducted in the Khammam District of the new state of Telangana (Laxmaiah et al. 2007).

The Indian Constitution has recognised close to 650 different groups as Scheduled Tribes. These are not identified as 'indigenous' groups, but rather as being historically disadvantaged and in need of state support, like the Dalits. Extensive welfare programs have thus been designed specifically for these tribal groups and, like the Dalits, they have been allocated quotas in educational facilities and government jobs and reserved seats in elections to bodies that range from local councils all the way to the national parliament. Combined with state-level support for Adivasi land rights and other forms of protection, the legislative framework is significant on paper and continues to evolve.

The enduring representation of Adivasis as 'noble savages' in much academic writing owes something to the critique of modernity in post-development theory and to the women-in-environment literature (e.g. Shiva 1988; Escobar 1995). Examples of this representation can also be found amongst those working to protect Adivasis from mining incursions (e.g. Padel and Das 2010). However, this view has been exposed to criticism for resting on a form of deterministic romanticism that presupposes the natural ability of these people to take care of the environment and live sustainably (Guha 1999; Prasad 2003). The tribal category, and the more popular term Adivasi, is here understood as one that was originally imposed on a wide range of hill peoples. Nowadays, tribal people might be seen as a collection of people who are not necessarily 'indigenous', or even originally related to one another, but have a shared experience of marginalisation and relative isolation that has shaped their identities over past centuries (Xaxa 1999).

The overwhelming majority of the 5 million Adivasis in Andhra Pradesh and Telangana live in the northern hilly parts bordering India's main central-eastern Adivasi region. The 14 officially recognised groups of the Visakhapatnam Agency live in the southern end of the Eastern Ghats hill range, at the junction between the Gondi-speaking peoples, who migrated there from the west, and Kui-speaking Kondhs to the north. In addition, there are a number of native Telugu-speaking communities like the Kondha Reddy, who possibly migrated from the Andhra Pradesh plains (Arnold 1984; Pingle and von Führer-Haimendorf 1998). With such a diversity of peoples, it is perhaps not surprising that it has been difficult to gather support for local movements with a unified Adivasi identity.

Nevertheless, based on both material and cultural values, strong support continues to exist amongst tribal peoples themselves, as well as from sections of civil society and the state, for continued protection of land rights. Ownership of agricultural land and access to forests are both seen as important elements of social justice. The *Forest Rights Act 2006* is the most recent example of the way in which the image of the tribal as a caretaker of the environment is still very much alive, including among policymakers. As expressed in the Government of India's Bhuria Committee report on local decision-making in the Scheduled Areas:

> Tribal life and economy, in the not too distant past, bore a harmonious relationship with nature and its endowment. It was an example of sustainable development. But with the influx of outside population, it suffered grievous blows (India 1995: 1).

Social Movements and Bauxite Mining in Central India

One way to understand the changes brought about by mining is to examine the forms of social movement, and other forms of resistance, that it has created. These can be divided by between those concerned with *exploitation* (mainly of labour) and those concerned with *dispossession* (of people living above or near the mineral resources) (Bebbington et al. 2008). Strong labour movements have historically been built around the first set of concerns, where the key issue has been working conditions, but in more recent years, new movements have been created around the issue of dispossession, as modern industries have tended to employ fewer people and have moved into remote geographical areas where local people may have little hope of gaining employment from industrialisation. Concerns over dispossession have come to embrace:

- *land use changes*, including the extent of the land required for mining and the compensation paid for it, but also the effects of pollution;
- *social changes* imposed on previously coherent communities; and
- *resistance to people perceived as outsiders*, who remove valuable resources from the local population instead of providing them with a greater share of royalties or other forms of income.

Protests against bauxite mining in India have tended to focus on land use changes, with the aim of protecting local peoples from dispossession, mainly by preventing their displacement and pollution of the environment. Such protests have demanded the abandonment of mining plans in areas where the ensuing changes will be too great for the local people to cope with (Ramamurthy 1995; Reddy 2006; Amnesty International 2010; Padel and Das 2010; Patra and Murthy n.d.). In some cases, a demand for environmental conservation has also played an important role in these protests (Mishra 1987; Oskarsson 2013b). Alumina refineries, on the other hand, like other industrial facilities, have tended to create resistance because of their use of agricultural land and the poor employment and compensation benefits provided to farmers, with less concern about environmental conservation. In both cases, the option of demanding better business practices, remunerative employment and a local share of the profits has been eschewed in favour of an oppositional path of resistance to dispossession.

The reasons for the strong opposition to dispossession are not hard to fathom. Though exact numbers are not available, it seems clear that mining is the biggest source of displacement in India after dams, with victims potentially numbered in millions. Very few of them have been resettled, and the problem has been especially acute for those displaced by mining. Even when a program of resettlement has been agreed, the implementation of land-for-land compensation policies has proved to be impossible. One important explanation for the lack of compensation, let alone full rehabilitation, is the strong connection of mining to forest land owned by the government. For tribal peoples, the denial of rights over forests has meant the denial of compensation when a tract of forest has been converted into a mine (Fernandes 2009). The denial of compensation for land also means a denial of other potential forms of compensation—jobs or education—that could help people to rebuild their livelihoods. The development of industrial facilities tends to take place on flatter stretches of land with more formally recognised ownership rights. However, this has not prevented controversy over the acquisition of this type of land, which is often seen to involve a choice between livelihoods and food security, on one hand, and industrialisation, with manufacturing jobs, on the other (Fernandes 2007).

Concern over the social changes brought about by mining has occasionally been voiced in India, but has so far found little high-level policy support, despite the fact that many mining operations taking place in the

Scheduled Areas. Acts of resistance to the appropriation of the benefits by outsiders, which have been a common theme in the international representation of resource struggles involving indigenous peoples, have received remarkably little attention in India. Even when state governments have presented arguments to the national government for higher levels of compensation from mining, local tribal movements have seemingly refrained from making claims to mineral resources as a collective right. The greater threat of dispossession has apparently precluded attempts to secure greater local benefits from mining, despite the opening made for tribal cooperative mining in the Samatha judgment.

Large-scale aluminium production started under British rule in 1943, when Indal, a subsidiary of the Canadian firm Alcan, started operating in Kerala, with access to both bauxite ore and hydropower for smelting. A number of joint ventures followed, on a relatively small scale, but the discovery of larger bauxite deposits in other parts of the world made the Indian operations uncompetitive. Efforts to expand the industry came much later, in the form of a joint venture between the Hungarian and Indian governments, known as Balco (Bharat Aluminium Corporation), in the present-day state of Chhattisgarh in 1965. However, technological problems prevented Balco from operating properly for many years, and when these problems were finally overcome, the ore reserves turned out to be insufficient.

The Indian aluminium industry would probably have remained in this semi-dormant state had it not been for the discovery of the east coast bauxite reserves in the mid-1970s. Despite the conduct of surveys by British and Indian geologists for well over a century, these deposits, in parts of the Scheduled Areas of southern and western Odisha and northern Andhra Pradesh, had not previously been detected (Rao and Ramam 1979). The Nalco (National Aluminium Corporation) bauxite mine and alumina refinery complex was opened in southern Odisha, in cooperation with the French firm Pechiney, and with financial support from the French Government, in 1987. A few years later, an aluminium smelter was constructed in Angul, in northern Odisha, close to the coal mines that would provide its source of power. Nalco remains the by far largest bauxite miner in India, and the only one that is currently exploiting the vast bauxite deposits of the Eastern Ghats.

The Indian bauxite industry's first encounter with protest movements occurred in the late 1980s, when Balco's search for additional ore reserves brought it to Mt Gandhamardhan in western Odisha (Mishra 1987). This mountain is known for its biodiversity but also as a destination for Hindu pilgrims. A significant opposition movement was established when local and national activists objected to the company's statement that 'Gandhamardhan will truly come of age with old holy temples of Nrusinghanath and Harishanker and modern industrial temples co-existing and enriching each other' (Concerned Scholars n.d.: 2). In the end, it was mainly the mobilisation of local livelihood concerns that forced the company to abandon its plans, at a time when protests against displacement, especially by dam construction, were growing across India. The difference between the widespread protests against dams and those against bauxite mining at Gandhamardhan and other locations is that the latter have been less concerned with direct displacement, with a greater focus on the indirect loss of livelihoods from the disturbance of water and forest resources. In addition, the proposed bauxite mining areas have often had environmental values that justify conservation. These concerns, which have been voiced with growing strength since the late 1980s, have largely been ignored by the promoters of mining projects.

Aside from the Gandhamardhan protest, the late 1980s and early 1990s were relatively quiet years, in which there was little government support or private capacity for further expansion of the mining industry. The lack of interest or capacity is evident in the Andhra Pradesh five-year plan for 1992–97, which merely suggested a start to 'preliminary studies for exploitation of the Araku group of bauxite deposits for which no other government agency has expressed interest' (Andhra Pradesh 1991: 39). The bigger deposits of the northwestern part of the current Visakhapatnam District were not even mentioned as a topic worthy of study, presumably due to security issues in areas that were virtually under the control of the Naxalite 'Peoples' War' group.

The interest in developing the east coast bauxite deposits increased dramatically in the 1990s after the Indian economy was opened to private investment in export industries. These changes coincided with the start of a period of higher mineral commodity prices in world markets and the loosening of control over refining and smelting technologies by a handful of Western companies, which allowed these technologies to be purchased on the open market. Among the first attempts to exploit these new opportunities was the Utkal Alumina project at Kashipur in Odisha in the early 1990s (see Figure 1.1). However, the experience of the nearby Nalco mine and refinery fostered strong resistance that evolved into possibly the longest running protest movement against any form of industrial development in the state of Odisha, which culminated in the police shooting of three protesters in 2000. These and other human rights violations have been extensively documented but are still largely unresolved (PUDP 2005; Reddy 2006; Goodland 2007; Padel and Das 2007). While the ongoing protests caused the withdrawal of international investors Hydro (from Norway) and Alcan (from Canada), and even the Indian Tata Group, the project has continued, and is now wholly owned by Hindalco (part of the Birla Group), which is proposing to expand the operation.

Bauxite projects in Andhra Pradesh have remained secondary to those in Odisha, partly because the former has smaller deposits and more difficult terrain, but also because of the failure of attempts to establish a local industry with Soviet support in the early 1980s (Srinivasan et al. 1981).[12] It was not until 1999 that the Government of Andhra Pradesh, together with an unnamed Dubai partner, made another attempt to exploit its bauxite deposits, but these plans made little progress before they were dropped in 2003 as a result of civil society pressure based on the Samatha judgment's ruling against private mining on tribal land (Prasad 2000; Ganjivarapu 2007).

Privatisation and restructuring has concentrated the Indian aluminium industry in the hands of three companies: Nalco, Hindalco and Vedanta. Vedanta Resources, registered in the United Kingdom but with its main operations in India, is a relatively late entrant to the aluminium industry. It quickly grew to become a major player through the purchase of two former state-owned companies, Balco in Chhattisgarh and Madras Aluminium Company in Tamil Nadu, while also attempting to establish some new projects of its own, especially in Odisha.

Vedanta's Balco compound in Chhattisgarh was large enough to accommodate an entirely new aluminium smelter with a dedicated coal-based power plant, so the old Hungarian and the new Chinese-built smelter continue to operate on the same site. For its part, Nalco is doing very well financially, but as its various attempts to create new facilities in India have failed at the planning stage, apparently for political rather than technical or economic reasons, it has been forced to look abroad.

12 These attempts were finally abandoned with the subsequent demise of the Soviet Union.

Hindalco appears to have started mining on a small scale in Kashipur, in close collaboration with the state-owned Odisha Mining Corporation, to supply raw material for its Utkal refinery.

The key test case for this new wave of expansion has been Vedanta's plan to follow a similar course of action to supply its Lanjigarh refinery in the same part of Odisha (see Figure 1.1). In 2003, three activists filed a case in the Supreme Court of India alleging that the company was making illegal use of forest land. After long deliberations, the mine was controversially allowed to proceed in August 2008 (India 2008a), but local protests continued, supported by national and international campaigns (India, 2007b; Norway 2007; Amnesty International 2010, 2011). In 2010, the mine failed to secure an operating licence from the Ministry of Environment and Forests (MoEF), but this merely led to a new round of litigation and appeals to the MoEF's 'expert committee'. With no resolution in sight, Vedanta seems to have undertaken a six-fold expansion of its refining capacity, despite not having the required regulatory approvals (Orissa 2011) and without a local supply of raw material.

This case has received so much publicity, both nationally and internationally, that it is not easy to envision any form of resolution to the conflict. The expansion of social media networks in recent years has ensured that the issue is kept alive, including by means of 'annual global days of action' against Vedanta that coincide with the company's annual general meetings in London (Foil Vedanta 2015). Any attempts at resolution on the part of state actors thus risk being seen either as disincentives for the investors who count as key figures in the 'new economy' or as attacks on the human rights of marginalised groups.

Unfortunately, Indian governments were unable to learn from mistakes already made during the long-running controversy over bauxite mining when they allowed AnRak Aluminium to build a refinery in Andhra Pradesh without having first secured their ore supplies, thus replicating the establishment of Vedanta's refinery without a mine in Odisha. It was therefore predictable that Adivasi rights activists would protest against mining in the hills while investors had predicated construction of a refinery on access to ore that cannot easily be sourced from elsewhere (Oskarsson 2012). The AnRak Aluminium investment, just like the Jindal South West (JSW) project that is the focus of this book, had to contend with the Samatha judgment's ban on private ownership or lease of land for mining in the Adivasi areas. While this has led companies to rely on state governments to provide them with access to mineral resources, it has also created a susceptibility for future legal challenges in any case where resources from Adivasi areas look as if they are being used for private rather than public benefit.

The Samatha Case

The Samatha Supreme Court case in 1997, crucial to the controversies examined in this book, is perhaps best seen as one of the final cases of success during India's phase of public interest litigation that started in the mid-1980s. Only a few years after the Samatha judgment, a claim for rehabilitation of people affected by the Sardar Sarovar dam was decided in favour of the industrialists, and the trend has not been reversed to date. There have been a few positive court verdicts for activist plaintiffs since then, but certainly fewer than in the past. While legal activism remains a popular option for social movements, it is not the main tactic that it once was (Epp 1998; Gustavsson et al. 2013).

Shortly before Samatha brought its case to the courts, an organisation called Sakti ('Power'), with similar goals, had been litigating against mining companies in the same hills, close to Visakhapatnam, based on similar breaches in the protection of Adivasi land rights. Sakti won this case because the companies were deemed by the court to be 'non-tribal' and therefore ineligible to own or lease the land. The judges in Samatha's initial High Court case were somehow not aware of the earlier judgment, so when Samatha lost this case in 1995 there was no other option but to appeal to the Supreme Court through public interest litigation involving the Government of Andhra Pradesh as well as the companies. This was a crucial difference because the government was supposed to operate in the public interest, including the interests of tribal people, as well as to contribute to national economic development.

The court was well aware of the conflicting issues at stake.

> The object of [the] Fifth and Sixth schedules to the Constitution … is not only to prevent acquisition, holding or disposal of the land in Scheduled Areas by the non-tribals from the tribals or alienation of such land among non-tribals inter se but also to ensure that the tribals remain in possession and enjoyment of the lands in Scheduled Areas for their economic empowerment, social status and [the] dignity of their person. Equally exploitation of mineral resources [for] national wealth undoubtedly, is for the development of the nation. The competing rights of tribals and the state are required to be adjusted without defeating [the] rights of either (India 1997).

According to Vagholikar and Moghe (2003: 69), the Samatha judgment itself can be summarised in three key points that apply specifically to the state of Andhra Pradesh:

1. State, forest and tribal private lands in the Scheduled Areas cannot be sold or leased out to non-tribal persons, including private industries, since this would contradict the Fifth Schedule of the Constitution and the Andhra Pradesh Scheduled Area Land Transfer Regulation.
2. Mining activities in the Scheduled Areas can only be undertaken by the Andhra Pradesh State Mineral Development Corporation or a tribal cooperative acting in compliance with the *Forest (Conservation) Act 1980* and the *Environment (Protection) Act 1986*.
3. At least 20 per cent of the net profits from such activities, aside from any mandatory environmental protection costs stipulated by other laws, are to be set aside in a permanent fund for the improvement of local education, health or other social services.

While the judgment provided improved protection from development-induced displacement in Andhra Pradesh, it came with some difficulties. Adivasis, unable to obtain employment in mining projects because of their lack of qualifications, are likely to face overwhelming obstacles to the exploitation of minerals through cooperatives in a manner that promotes an equitable distribution of the benefits. On the other hand, the decision to allow the government to do the mining was motivated in a fairly simplistic manner by the assumption that public corporations act in the public interest. The court thus took the view that the mineral resources had to be used for the benefit of the nation, despite the risk that the government would cause much the same problems for tribal people as would private companies. Indeed, the court did not even prescribe any particular measures to ensure that state-owned mines would actually produce any public benefits.

The status of the 20 per cent of net profits that should be set aside for a local development fund is also uncertain. It is at present not known whether any company actually provides a share of its profits for this purpose in accordance with the judgment and, if so, who decides how it is spent. In Andhra Pradesh, this is particularly relevant in the case of the sizeable coal mining operation undertaken by Singareni Collieries, a subsidiary of the national state-owned company Coal India. Furthermore, since the judgment does not apply to other economic sectors, state-owned enterprises in the forestry, agriculture or tourism sectors can continue to operate in the Scheduled Areas without having to provide such local benefits or to involve tribal people in their management beyond the requirements of existing reservation policies, and have so far tended to include Adivasis only at lower levels of employment, if indeed at all. Finally, the state still has the right to undertake large-scale projects for the greater benefit of 'society' by using the powerful *Land Acquisition Act 1894* and its various amendments up to 1998. The Samatha judgment does not say how the state's right of eminent domain should be applied in relation to tribal land protection, and the Andhra Pradesh Government has thus been able to move ahead with the enormous Polavaram dam, which is expected to dispossess and displace more than 200,000 people, most of them Adivasi, which is more than the number displaced by the controversial Sardar Sarovar dam in Gujarat.

The immediate reaction of the Government of Andhra Pradesh, as well as the national government, was to appeal the Samatha judgment to a larger bench of the Supreme Court, but the judgment was upheld in 2000 (India 2000a). Attempts were then made to remove the basis on which the judgment stood by amending either the Andhra Pradesh Land Transfer Regulation or the National Constitution (Balagopal 2007a). An internal brief from the national Ministry of Mines took the latter path:[13]

> The impasse created by the Samatha Judgment can perhaps be resolved only through an amendment of the Fifth Schedule to the Constitution as opined by Attorney General. One way could be to add the following explanation … The regulations framed under paragraph 5(2) shall not prohibit or restrict the transfer of land by members of the Scheduled Tribe to the government or allotment by government of its land to a non-tribal for undertaking any non-agricultural operations including reconnaissance or prospecting or mining operations under the provisions of *MMDR Act 1957* [*Mines and Mineral (Development & Regulation) Act, 1957*] (India 2000b: para. 18).

The central government's Planning Commission was also worried about what the judgment would mean for future mining operations, warning that it would be 'necessary to make … amendments to overcome the hurdle placed in the way of private mining in notified tribal areas by the Samatha Judgment' (India 2001c: 44).

13 The briefing note was widely disseminated in the Indian press (e.g. Mitta 2000).

The national government's plans for constitutional change bear witness to the powerful interests working to open up the Scheduled Areas to private economic activity. Nevertheless, high-level voices in favour of the Samatha judgment were also articulated. President K.R. Narayanan's Address to the Nation on Republic Day, 25 January 2001, included the following observation:

> In eastern India, the exploitation of minerals like bauxite and iron ore are causing destruction of forests and sources of water. While the nation must benefit from the exploitation of these mineral resources, we will have also to take into consideration questions of environmental protection and the rights of tribals. Let it not be said by future generations that the Indian Republic has been built on the destruction of the green earth and the innocent tribals who have been living there for centuries (India 2001d).

The 'Campaign to Prevent Amendment to the Fifth Schedule', supported by civil society organisations across India, showed that it was possible to mobilise resistance both nationally and locally, within the state of Andhra Pradesh. The constitutional amendment was abandoned, and the final draft of the Tenth Five-Year Plan made a less controversial statement.

> To enhance the indigenous mineral resources, intensive exploration is required. An enabling environment must be created to attract new investments through private sector participation with modern technical and managerial expertise for finding new deposits and develop them sustainably in the Tenth Plan (India 2002a: 742).

While the contestation over the interpretation, and possible implementation, of the Samatha judgment was still going on, a new case came to national attention as the Government of India sought to privatise Balco. If successful, this could be seen as a transfer of Scheduled Area land from the government to a private, non-tribal entity, and that is something that is also banned in the land transfer regulations of Chhattisgarh, where Balco operates. The trade union representing Balco's employees took the Government of India to the Supreme Court, again using public interest litigation, to challenge the sale on the grounds that it contravened the *Madhya Pradesh Land Revenue Code 1959*, which had been inherited by the new state of Chhattisgarh when it was formed in 2000. However, the court allowed the sale to proceed because '[t]he land was validly given to BALCO a number of years ago and … even with the change in management the land remains with BALCO to whom it had been validly given on lease' (India 2001e). By stating that Balco was still the same company, and thus the same user of land, even though it had been privatised, the judges managed to reach the conclusion that the case involved no transfer of land and was therefore consistent with existing legislation. The Balco judgment also restricted the application of the Samatha judgment by stating that the latter 'is not applicable in the present case because the law applicable in Madhya Pradesh is not similar or identical to the … Regulation of Andhra Pradesh' (India 2001e).[14]

Following the Samatha judgment, the Government of Odisha set up a special committee to review its potential implementation in that state. The stakes were even higher there than they were in Andhra Pradesh, since the local economy relies more heavily on mining and its tribal population accounts for a much larger share of the total population. In 2001, shortly after the Balco judgment was handed down, the committee concluded that the Samatha judgment did not apply in Odisha (Yadav 2003). The most senior government official, Chief Secretary P.K. Mohanty, was cited as saying that 'the law in Orissa is not the same [as in Andhra Pradesh], although it does ensure ample safeguards for tribals' (cited in Mohanty 2003).[15] No further legal challenges have been made in favour of tribal land rights, anywhere across the Fifth Schedule states of central India, since the Balco judgment. Balagopal (2007a) has argued that the National Constitution should be sufficient to prevent mining across all of the Scheduled Areas, but this possibility remains untested in a court of law.

Since the Samatha and Balco cases were settled, activists working on mining and Adivasi land rights across India have either eschewed legal activism or combined it with other strategies such as mass mobilisation, lobbying of decision-makers and media campaigns to affect public opinion. Attempting to get justice from the courts is risky at the best of times, and when the scope of a judgment like that made in the Samatha case has been dramatically reduced, a preference for other strategies reduces the risk of this judgment being overturned completely by a new set of judges.

14 The question of how different the two laws actually were did not arise in the Balco judgment, nor did the validity of the provisions of the National Constitution, the second leg on which the Samatha judgment rested.

15 The laws cited in support were the *Orissa Scheduled Areas Transfer of Immovable Property (Scheduled Tribes) Regulation 1956* and the *Orissa Zilla Parishad (Amendment) Act 1997*.

3. The Formation of a Public–Private Alliance

With the Samatha judgment only making allowance for mining by public sector and tribal cooperatives in Andhra Pradesh, and the cancellation of a bauxite project proposal by Dubai investors in the state in 2003, it might have been assumed that no further attempts would be made to exploit the state's bauxite deposits of the state, at least for a while. But once the Congress Party returned to power in 2004, both nationally and in Andhra Pradesh, it was only a year or so before a new memorandum of understanding (MoU) was signed, this time with Jindal South West (JSW).

At the time, this project was but one of many of similar size and importance to the state's economy, and since measures to attract private-sector investment had been the norm for a number of years, there was nothing extraordinary about the government signing an agreement with a private company. What was crucial, however, was the fact that this was a proposal for industrial development in the Scheduled Areas, and this was an issue that had been contested for many years, resulting in strong protective legislation and a vigilant civil society. From the outset, the MoU had to be drafted in a complicated manner to ensure that the ore could be exploited in collaboration with a private company that was not allowed to operate in, or even be seen as to benefit directly from resources contained within, the Scheduled Areas. If the MoU did not comply with the land legislation, it was obvious that civil society organisations would challenge it in courts, and the challenge would have a good chance of being successful.

The starting point for a closer examination of the conflict over the proposed bauxite project is to detail the way in which it was planned and the identity of the proponents. From there we can proceed to an examination of the distributional outcomes by looking at the potential public benefits to be derived from the agreement.

Project Formation

With the Essar, Jindal and Birla conglomerates already involved in the aluminium industry or planning to enter it, the Tata Group was the only one of the major domestic metal producers not currently pursuing the bauxite ores of central India (see Table 3.1). As many as 12 bauxite mining and refining projects were at various stages of development in Odisha (Reddy 2006), with three in Andhra Pradesh, but the only recently opened bauxite mines anywhere in India were the two with low grades in Chhattisgarh and Maharashtra and one with non-metallic grades in Gujarat. However, a number of aluminium smelters had been constructed in areas without bauxite deposits, and some of the older refineries had recently been upgraded or expanded to accommodate new technology without the acquisition of additional land, thereby avoiding controversies related to displacement. An increase in the ability and interest of mainly Indian big business to establish an aluminium industry was countered by the strengthening of resistance on the part of oppositional groups in civil society who were able to mobilise across geographical scales. Between these two positions were state and national governments that had increasingly, but not invariably, supported industrial interests.

Table 3.1 Alumina refineries in central India.

Operator or proponent	Location	Commencement
Hindalco	Muri, Jharkhand	1948
Hindalco	Renukoot, Uttar Pradesh	1962
Balco (Vedanta since 2001)	Korba, Chhattisgarh	1965
Nalco (Government of India)	Damanjodi, Odisha	1986
Utkal Alumina (Hindalco)	Kashipur, Odisha	1992
JSW Aluminium	S. Kota, Andhra Pradesh	2005
Vedanta Aluminium	Lanjigarh, Odisha	2007
AnRak Aluminium (Penna Cement and Government of Ras al-Khaimah)	Makavarapalem, Andhra Pradesh	2007

Much about the way that the JSW bauxite project came into being remains unknown, but it must clearly have involved a significant planning effort due to the size of the investment and the complexity of the land situation. As far as is known, there was no tender process for the investment, though discussions were held with other potential investors, including Nalco (Andhra Pradesh 2005a). It would have been difficult for members of the state government to initiate plans just when the Congress Party had unexpectedly returned to power after 10 years in opposition. In any case, a generally poor level of state government capacity makes it harder for local bureaucrats to pursue plans that necessarily combine complex technical, economic, political and legal aspects. The Jindal Group, headquartered in the north Indian state of Haryana, which until now had been almost exclusively a steel producer, did not have any major operations in Andhra Pradesh, making it a somewhat unlikely investment partner. For these reasons, the project was seen by some parties as a central government initiative rather than a state one.

The project proponents and their consultants were able to plan and formalise their cooperation in a business agreement without engaging in public debate on a known issue of concern, and yet the Land Transfer Regulation could not be changed. Instead, the 2005 agreement explicitly accepts the special protection of tribal people's land affirmed by the Samatha judgment. It even includes a reference to an old government ruling from 1975 to further justify the supply of ore by a public company to a private investor:

> Whereas, the State of Andhra Pradesh is having rich bauxite deposits in Visakhapatnam and East Godavari (EG) Districts, consisting of about 550 million tonnes of metallurgical grade. Keeping its importance in view, the GoAP have reserved the entire deposit bearing areas available in EG District and Visakhapatnam District through [Government Order] No. 999 … 25/10/1975 for exclusive exploitation by the public-sector undertaking. Further, all these areas are falling under reserve forest as well as notified tribal areas. As per the AP Land Transfer Regulation 1959, transfer of these areas to non-tribals is prohibited. Further the Hon'ble [sic] Supreme Court of India in Samatha vs. State of AP case gave ruling that the state-owned Corporation can mine these areas and in case state owned Corporations are involved in mining, it does not amount to transfer of the areas to non-tribal. Considering these facts, GoAP is looking after a highly competent and financially sound entrepreneur who can establish value-added industry to produce end-products, based on these valuables, mined by APMDC Ltd (Andhra Pradesh 2005b: 1).

The MoU specified which deposits would be mined by the state-owned Andhra Pradesh Mineral Development Corporation (APMDC) to produce the ore required for about 30 years of alumina refining:

> GoAP shall direct APMDC to supply bauxite from out of the areas applied by them in Araku (Galikonda, Raktakonda & Chittamgondi) & Sapparla Groups, consisting of approx. 2446 ha. and containing approximately 240 million tonnes of bauxite ore (Andhra Pradesh 2005b: 2–3).

The MoU also specified that the privately owned refinery must be located outside of the Scheduled Areas in order to comply with the Land Transfer Regulation. The agreement states that JSW Holding Ltd (JSWHL):

> or its subsidiaries undertake to incorporate and promote a company … which will set up an alumina and aluminium refinery and smelter to produce about 2.5 lakh [250,000] tonnes of Aluminium per annum initially, with a provision for suitable expansion, in the State of AP. at the locations other than the scheduled areas mutually agreed to by the two parties and with a capital outlay of about Rs 9000 crores [90 billion rupees] (Andhra Pradesh 2005b: 2).

The proposed operations might seem to follow the law, since the government would be allowed to mine in the Scheduled Areas and the refinery would be built on non-scheduled land. However, the terms of the proposed cooperation between them are crucial, since the Land Transfer Regulation not only prohibits direct ownership of the resource by a non-tribal entity, but also the so-called *benami* operations undertaken in the name of a tribal entity but for the benefit of a non-tribal entity—in this case a private company. The MoU contained no detailed discussion of the benefits of the proposed project, or indeed of who would be planning, financing and undertaking the actual mining operations that must legally be confined to the public sector. But a number of passages appear to cast some doubt over the existence of any public benefits, or even any public involvement. The MoU made it clear that APMDC would not be able to bear the costs of mining, and might also need the expertise of JSW to prepare its plans, as illustrated in these extracts from the MoU:

> JSWHL or its subsidiary company shall bear all the expenditure in preparation of mining plans, cost of afforestation, net present value being payable to the Forest Department, etc.) …
>
> APMDC shall take the expertise of JSWHL or its subsidiary in preparing the feasibility reports, mining plans, etc. required for getting clearances from MoEF [Ministry of Environment and Forests], Govt of India for further leases …

> JSWHL/subsidiary shall provide machinery required for mining lo APMDC on hire basis. The hire charges shall be fixed by a [government-appointed] Committee …
>
> JSWHL/subsidiary shall provide cost of infrastructure required for development of mines as fixed by the Committee constituted by GoAP (Andhra Pradesh 2005b: 3–4).

Apart from allocating the ore to the private investor, the state government had one specific role to play in the agreement, which was to acquire land on behalf of the company.

> JSWHL … shall identify suitable land other than the land in scheduled areas. The same will be acquired and handed over to JSWHL … by GoAP/Collector (ibid.: 3).

Despite the legal terms of the agreement, and the anticipation of a three-year implementation period, progress on the ground was very slow. The refinery was approved and land was acquired after two public environmental hearings, but the mining operation had not undergone the environmental clearance process by 2012. A public hearing was promised in October 2009 but this was later cancelled for unknown reasons.

In February 2007, a second bauxite project was announced, replicating the earlier arrangement with JSW. The private-sector partner in this project was AnRak Aluminium, a joint venture between the Government of Ras al-Khaimah, one of the United Arab Emirates, and Andhra Pradesh–based Penna Cements (see Figure 3.1). This project has not only moved much faster and overtaken the APMDC–JSW project, but has been openly described as a 'Congress Party project'. Evidence pointing towards a local Congress Party connection was initially somewhat slender, since emphasis was placed on the foreign investor, but it turned out that Penna Cements, a company owned by the treasurer of the Andhra Pradesh State Congress Party, had made an investment in a cement plant in Ras al-Khaimah a few years earlier (Ras al-Khaimah 2006). Interviews conducted in 2007 and 2008 identified the same treasurer as an investor in AnRak Aluminium itself, along with other Andhra Pradesh Congress politicians. In 2012, the AnRak Aluminium website made it clear that Penna Cements was the primary investor in AnRak Aluminium; and interviews at the almost completed refinery revealed that Penna management was mainly responsible for day-to-day operations (Oskarsson 2012). The importance of political connections in the award of mining contracts was thus reaffirmed.

Figure 3.1 Construction of AnRak Aluminium's alumina refinery in Visakhapatnam District.
Source: Photo by author, July 2012.

In 2009, after many years of negotiations, Nalco was announced as the investor in the last remaining bauxite deposits available in Andhra Pradesh. However, this project has made no progress since the announcement.

The Government of Andhra Pradesh

The political component of the bauxite alliance initially involved a small circle of top state Congress politicians. Of paramount importance was Chief Minister Y.S. Rajashekhara Reddy ('YSR'), a powerful factional leader from the southern Rayalaseema region of the state, who had managed to unite the Congress Party and remove the seemingly unbeatable Chandrababu Naidu of the Telugu Desam Party in 2004 (Balagopal 2004). Virtually all decisions of economic importance apparently needed his approval, and minutes or notes of meetings about the bauxite project confirm that he was present. Chief Minister Reddy also played a key role in the state government when acting as its spokesperson on economically important projects and lobbying for administrative approvals from the national government. As one journalist put it: 'The CM is acting like a public relations officer for the companies when he comes to Delhi' (interview, Delhi, 2 May 2008).

While nominally belonging to the same governing party, the politicians seen as crucial in the formation of the bauxite alliance were of mixed regional, caste and class backgrounds, with the Reddy caste in a dominant position. For the purpose of alliance formation politicians only need to have a shared interest in the implementation of one major project. Allegations of favouritism in awarding contracts have been particularly common in the case of irrigation and mining projects in Andhra Pradesh. According to one local investigator:

> All irrigation projects are [implemented] by politicians but there are also some TDP [Telugu Desam Party] contractors. Congress said openly that we are also giving you contracts so stop complaining. They will all cooperate on this and also did [under] earlier governments (interview, Hyderabad, 28 February 2008).

An investigator in Visakhapatnam agreed:

> things move only through favours and you need political support which is unfortunate. The CM's son gets things done super fast (interview, Visakhapatnam, 7 February 2008).

Any major investment is given preference in a state where economic growth is high on the agenda, but certain investors with direct links to the state government are given special priority. As K. Balagopal, a well-known commentator on politics in Andhra Pradesh, expressed it at the Southern Regional Strategy Meeting on Special Economic Zones held in Chennai in 2008:

> In Andhra Pradesh all the developers are relatives of the Chief Minister. Tata and Jindal come second in the state.

We might thus expect that Jindal's bauxite project would be given somewhat lower priority if other investors with closer personal relations to the state government also needed support. One such would be AnRak Aluminium.

This is related to the fact that many—if not all—of the most powerful politicians in Andhra Pradesh are also businessmen these days. The chief minister's son, Y.S. Jagmohan Reddy, oversaw the development of a major business empire during the period from 2004 to 2009, which included a state-wide newspaper and TV news channel called Sakshi, a cement plant associated with a limestone mining lease, and information technology parks. Meanwhile, the former treasurer of the Andhra Pradesh Congress Party, P. Pratap Reddy, another relative of the chief minister, was the owner of Penna Cements and hence an investor in AnRak Aluminium.[1]

The promise of land set out in the MoU for the Jindal project was such as to ensure that select members of the legislative assembly (MLAs) from the project area would be actively involved. For example, it was the housing minister from Vizianagaram District and the commercial taxes minister from Visakhapatnam District, rather than the mining or industry ministers, who were recorded as supporting the project in minutes of meetings about it. On the other hand, the MLA for the tribal reserve of S. Kota, including the proposed mining area of Araku, does not seem to have been involved in the decision-making process, but did not voice any opposition to plans that were unpopular among his constituents. Being part of the circle around the chief minister and in control of personal networks of influence at the project sites seems to have been more important than nominal responsibility for portfolios like industry, mining or tribal welfare.

Of course, politicians are not only—or even mainly—concerned with making money, since they also need to maintain favour with the voters in order to get themselves elected or re-elected. For this purpose, a pro-poor image is essential since the poor make up the majority of voters. In Andhra Pradesh, the promotion of business is never presented as something opposed to poor people's rights to land and livelihoods. However, key politicians from the southern parts of the state are not especially aware of the important role that tribal land rights legislation plays in the Scheduled Areas. One senior administrator, who attended a high-level meeting in Hyderabad during the period when the bauxite project MoU was being finalised, commented as follows:

> YSR was talking about so-and-so much money being spent on tribals and I got a bit agitated. I said I wanted to speak to give a reply. I told the CM, 'Look Mr Chief Minister, for heaven's sake don't keep talking about this. Because the money you spend in the tribal areas goes to contractors and intermediaries; it doesn't really reach the tribals. What the tribals need is not money; they want their rights. The problem is that as soon as some officer tries to transfer land [back] to tribals you will transfer

1 They were connected to the central government through the federal mining minister, T. Subbarami Reddy, who has been involved in road and dam construction through the publicly listed company Gayatri Cements, notionally run by his own son.

> that officer. Your government will not allow land to be restored to tribal people. Basically what they want is the right to be recognised. They want the ability to supervise their own schools, their own hospitals. Give them the chance to become involved. Not money.' You know the reaction of the Chief Minister? I was sitting at a table with the Chief Secretary next to me and then the Chief Minister. The Chief Minister was whispering in the ear of the Chief Secretary. He was asking, 'What is this land transfer regulation?' (interview, retired Indian Administrative Service officer, Visakhapatnam, 20 October 2006).

An important part of the ability of top politicians to influence outcomes lies in their ability to exert pressure on the bureaucracy. This was evident in one meeting of senior state bureaucrats organised by the chief secretary, where the secretary of the Forest Department failed to make an appearance on the grounds that 'all the decisions are made by the CM anyway' (interview, retired Indian Administrative Service officer, Hyderabad, 26 February 2008). Since politicians could not hope to know the intricate details of the many procedures involved in formulation and implementation of the MoU, it was even more important for them to know the administrators would do what they were asked to do. Throughout the planning and implementation of the project, there were few if any noticeable disagreements between them, despite what appears to be a significant level of uncertainty about rule-bound governance, including a number of recent corruption scandals in the state that were related to mining and industrial development.

This was how the political side of the bauxite alliance appeared to be configured during the period of my fieldwork, but after the elections of 2009, and despite the return to power of the Congress Party, both at state and federal levels, the bauxite alliance underwent significant changes. To understand this reconfiguration, it is important to show how politicians might appear to be in a superior position when they are elected, but ultimately have to be concerned about how voters perceive them or else risk being voted out of power.

The project's main promoter at the federal level, the mining minister, lost ministerial office despite remaining as a nominated *rajya sabha* (upper house) MP. One of the main local spokesmen for the project lost his seat in the non-tribal part of Visakhapatnam District and thus his position as state minister for commercial taxes, but Chief Minister Reddy, before his untimely death, strengthened his position after the 2009 elections, and even managed to get his son elected to the state parliament. In addition, Vizianagaram District moved even more firmly into the hands of housing minister Botcha Satyanarayan's family, and hence the Congress Party. Apart from his government ministry, they now accounted for three of the district's seven state MLAs, while Mr Satyanarayan's wife was now a federal MP.

The most important change, however, took place in the central government, where the Congress MP Jairam Ramesh, who had expressed his concern for the future of the Araku coffee growers, became the new environment minister after this position had been held by the Tamil Nadu–based Dravida Munnetra Kazhagam Party in a succession of previous administrations. A stronger enforcement of environmental laws therefore seemed to be forthcoming, most importantly with the prospect of no further environmental approvals for mines across the country until the new Forest Rights Act had been implemented (India 2009a). While the new minister was likely to be placed under pressure to approve the bauxite project by fellow party members in Andhra Pradesh, this was clearly not what local Congress Party representatives had expected when the party strengthened its grip on power after the elections (Anon. 2010a).

Andhra Pradesh Mineral Development Corporation

The state mining company, APMDC, was on the verge of being closed down completely in the 1990s after it had incurred mounting losses. Since then, it had gone through a process of drastically scaling down the number of its own employees while taking part in a growing number of major investment deals. Its own mining operations were confined to a black marble mine in the southern district of Kadapa. With only 230 employees and strict limits on recruitment, the many new mining projects that had been proposed in its name did not indicate any actual increase in mining activity.

It is the mine planning section of APMDC that has taken on a more important role in recent years. Given its close connections to the state's Mines and Geology Department, with which it shares a managing director, the mine planners are in a prime position to apply for leases over new deposits, which are allocated on a first-come first-served basis, when these became available. Once a lease has been secured by APMDC it is usually sold on to a private company. The terms of the transaction, including the selection of the buyer and price charged for the asset, are open to political manipulation, and this has resulted in some of the state's biggest political scandals in recent years. As one Hyderabad-based journalist put it:

> APMDC invites for contracts but what we understand is that these are mafia style decisions. The close links between politicians and the industry and the pricing of ore is strategic (interview, Hyderabad, 25 February 2008).

Another journalist summed up the situation by saying that 'the government always get the contracts for own players when in power while the opposition protests' (interview, Hyderabad, 25 February 2008). It seems clear that political priorities have a significant influence on the way that the APMDC conducts its business. This impression was only strengthened by the arrest of three key state government bureaucrats who were accused of not following state regulations when allocating land and mineral resources to the private sector.

Figure 3.2 APMDC's office in a business centre in central Hyderabad.
Source: Photo by author, March 2008.

However, this method of allocating mining contracts to private companies could not be applied in tribal areas because of the ban on private investment. While smaller deposits have instead been auctioned on condition that only tribal people can apply for leases,[2] the bauxite project was deemed to be too large for this kind of arrangement. An authoritative source with insights into the operations of APMDC explained the situation as follows:

> Basically due to the Land Transfer Regulation in Andhra Pradesh the government has to do the mining in the state. APMDC is a very small organisation and as a government organisation it is difficult to run it efficiently. There will be political interference and we cannot hire competent people because of various rules (interview, Hyderabad, 9 April 2007).

This implies that APMDC is a rather empty public-sector operation that mainly exists on paper in order to supply private ventures like the JSW refinery. Or as one investigator put it: 'Whether public or private, ultimately it is the contractor who will carry out the work' (interview, Visakhapatnam, 7 January 2008).

Having circumvented the Samatha judgment by using APMDC as a front, the APMDC-AnRak Aluminium environmental impact assessment report for the Jerrila bauxite mine in Visakhapatnam District was confident enough to bypass APMDC in reserving a role in mine management for what for what it called the 'mining contractor' (ICFRE 2008: 164–70). This entity was not defined anywhere in the report but, given the activities assigned to it, could only be the company engaged to do the actual mining while APMDC retained responsibility for oversight. But it was still not clear that APMDC had the capacity to perform this function.

In the case of the JSW project, the role of the contractor would not be confined to the funding, planning and implementation of actual mining operations. The minutes of an APMDC board meeting also detail a range of social activities that APMDC itself planned to carry out in the proposed mining area with funding provided by JSW, though without any mention of the extent to which JSW would receive any public recognition for doing so.

> [A]bout 200 tribal youth will be trained in the mines of the Corporation at Barytes Mines, Mangampet, Galaxy Granite quarries at Chimakurthy etc. The total expenditure for imparting training to 200 tribal youth for a period of 2 years would be about Rs 2 crore as estimated. Further the Corporation would be providing mobile clinics at an estimated cost of

2 One example of this was the advertisement of sand mining leases in the riverbeds of tribal Visakhapatnam in *The Hindu* and *Sakshi* newspapers on 31 March 2008.

> Rs 10 lakhs. The Corporation will also provide the distribution of school uniforms to about 2000 school children by providing 2 pairs of uniforms, boots, and tie at an estimated cost of Rs 15.00 lakhs. The Corporation will also provide potable water initially for 2 villages i.e. Bisupuram and Nandivalasa which are near to bauxite deposits in Rakthakonda, Galikonda and Chittamgondi. The Corporation will also undertake public awareness programme by sending the public representatives to Nalco Project at Damanjodi, Orissa and conduct Gram Sabha [village assembly] and other meetings with villagers at a cost of Rs 5.00 lakhs. The total expenditure incurred on the above programmes will be reimbursed by M/s Jindal (Andhra Pradesh 2007a: 8).

One retired officer of the Indian Administrative Service confirmed that this was a widespread practice designed to create a public facade for private mining operations.[3]

Jindal South West

India's big business families have confronted very different operating circumstances in the last two or three decades. Some have been unable to deal with new sources of competition while others have diversified out of the sectors in which they were traditionally protected (Kochanek 2007). It is was therefore no surprise to see JSW, a subsidiary of the Haryana-based O.P. Jindal Group, move away from steel production, not only into aluminium but also to cement and power production.

From the operation of two small pipe manufacturing plants in West Bengal and Haryana in 1952, the Jindal Group had expanded into steel production as recently as 1970, and had since grown into a US$10 billion conglomerate, which by 2008 had made the Jindal family as the 12th richest in India, with an estimated fortune of US$2.9 billion (Karmali 2008). By then the group had 12 steel plants in India and two more in the United States, but was already divided into four main sub-groups—JSW, Jindal Stainless, Jindal SAW and Jindal Steel and Power—each controlled by one of the sons of the group's founder, O.P. Jindal. When he died in 2005, his wife Savitri Jindal assumed the role of group chairman.

3 The only exception may be found in the state of Gujarat, which has the only state mining corporation that is able to carry out large-scale mining operations on its own account.

The four Jindal brothers had substantial political and business connections between them, although they kept a lower profile than the heads of other business groups like Reliance, Tata or Birla. Naveen Jindal, the head of Jindal Steel and Power, was elected as a Congress MP from Haryana, and was said to be part of the group of young Congress MPs who were close to Rahul Gandhi. The JSW chairman, Sajjan Jindal, was the head of the Associated Chamber of Commerce, one of the top three business peak bodies in India, when the bauxite project was proposed in Andhra Pradesh.

JSW Steel was not only the main subsidiary of JSW, but also the biggest company in the entire Jindal Group, having grown to become India's largest domestic steel producer, just ahead of Tata Steel. While the group's headquarters were in Delhi, JSW was based in Bombay. As of 30 June 2009, its 8,500 employees were operating in a number of locations across India, with a major presence in the state of Karnataka. Two of its subsidiaries—JSW Steel and JSW Holdings—were already listed on the Bombay Stock Exchange, with JSW Energy planning to follow suit (JSW Energy 2008). Two other subsidiaries—JSW Cement and JSW Aluminium—were then planning to start operations in Andhra Pradesh.

The company's new projects would place considerable pressure on its finances. Steel and power investments alone were expected to require Rs 40,000 crore (about US$8 billion). The cement division of the company announced it would look for a partner for its limestone mining and cement plant in Andhra Pradesh (Kalesh 2009). Twenty-five per cent of the Rs 4,000 crore required to finance the alumina refinery would reportedly come from internal company sources, with the balance supplied by a domestic bank consortium (Rama Raju 2009), but an announcement of this arrangement was accompanied by another media statement saying that the plans would be put on hold until the market picked up (Joshi Saha 2009). It was not clear whether this was a strategic move designed to speed up the approval of the bauxite mine or whether the financial constraints created by an economic downturn warranted a greater focus on steel production and power generation, especially when power supplies were crucial for the company's other operations.

The MoU with the Andhra Pradesh Government chose to emphasise the capabilities of JSW in general rather than its knowledge of aluminium production:

> The [JSW] Group has rich experience in mining, ore transportation, metallurgical processing, refining, smelling, rolling of metals (ferrous and non-ferrous), power generation, port operation and industrial gases … It is clear that the Jindal group has the financial capacity, the organizational strength and the operational experience to set up large capacity, value addition plants of refining and smelting of bauxite ore (Andhra Pradesh 2005b: 2).

JSW did recruit some experienced staff, including the chief executive of JSW Aluminium, R.C. Swain, a former assistant vice-president with Vedanta Alumina, but most of the preparatory work was undertaken by consultants. The company even chose to operate without a permanent office in the area, instead using a few rooms in the housing estate built for employees of the Jindal Ferro-Chrome factory on the outskirts of Visakhapatnam city. A local consultancy undertook the land surveys for both the refinery and the mine, and one of its employees later became the site manager (and only on-site employee) at S. Kota. The tasks of site preparation and plant construction were also outsourced to other companies.

Regardless of who actually carried out the work, JSW Aluminium was credited as the author of the official land acquisition map for the refinery (JSW Aluminium 2007a), despite this being a task that the government was supposed to perform under the terms of the MoU. It was likewise JSW that supplied copies of official government documents to the consultants engaged in the environmental impact assessment of the mining operation, as evident in the company's office fax number on the top of each page (ICFRE n.d.). JSW thus appeared to function like a back office that processed and distributed information between government agencies and private consultants or suppliers engaged in various administrative tasks. An activist in Delhi claimed that this mode of operation was common practice amongst private mining and metals companies in India.

> Basically all these mining companies do the same; they stay away from doing actual work. Vedanta has contracted an Australian company to build their refinery and will then subcontract the mining to smaller companies. They only manage the money (interview, Delhi, 11 December 2007).

Apart from operational concerns, this poses questions about how social and environmental concerns could be handled properly with such limited experience of bauxite mining and alumina refining on the part of both of the main partners in the public–private partnership.

For the opponents of the bauxite project, JSW was a name without a face, a company coordinating work behind the scenes without ever revealing itself. The portrait of a 'highly competent and financially sound entrepreneur' in the MoU is thus of a company venturing into a new line of business, with limited in-house experience and a limited presence in the state, but an ability to mobilise the required economic, technical and political resources. At least that was the case until the economic crisis of late 2008 changed world market prices and the prospect of financing the project (Joshi Saha 2009; Rama Raju 2009).

Distributional Outcomes

Planning for large-scale mining and refining of bauxite ore in an ecologically fragile and economically poor region is a very complex matter that needs to take social, environmental, cultural, technical and economic costs and benefits into account. While the environmental and social impacts are discussed in Chapters 4 and 6, we can now consider the distributional outcomes of what was being proposed from an economic point of view, despite the difficulty of doing so when the proponents had presented broad visions rather than detailed plans. The MoU was based on a 'vision to augment growth and development in the State of Andhra Pradesh' (Andhra Pradesh 2005b: 1), while meeting minutes recorded that plans were being made 'in the interest of development of the area and tribals' (Andhra Pradesh 2005c: 2).

The project plans had to take account of material circumstances as well as the choices made in the creation of a business agreement. The fact that the bauxite ore was only present in certain locations in tribal Visakhapatnam District was impossible to ignore, but beyond this a range of different choices had to be made. An economic interest in keeping the refinery as close as possible to the mine in order to reduce transport costs had to be combined with the need to find an area of flat land on which it could be built, sufficient water to process the ore, specific methods of transporting millions of tons of ore and alumina each year, and a competent production workforce.

Given the choices that were made, it seems that the proponents opted for a complex project design that would deliver narrow economic outcomes. Had the actual goals been to augment public revenues or support a wider process of industrialisation, other choices would have been more appropriate. The evidence for this is not only the low level of forecast revenues and employment, but also the existence of a counterfactual alternative in the form of the public-sector company Nalco. Had Nalco been allowed or encouraged to invest in the project, public revenues would have been higher implementation would have been more straightforward because a public company can own land in the Scheduled Areas.

Meagre State Income from Mining

The first problem for public revenue is the low level of compensation that state governments receive directly from mining. A mineral royalty is levied on all forms of mining across the country, and determination of the royalty rate has been an ongoing issue in federal–state relations for many years. Although the states are recognised as the owners of what are known as major minerals, including bauxite, iron, coal and zinc, the royalty rates have been set by the national government. The state governments have protested, because they have to deal with the social and environmental costs of mining under severe budget constraints, but they have only been able to gain fairly modest increases in recent years (India 2006a).[4] The national government has not agree to higher increases because of its interest in supporting industrialisation and energy generation and, at least in the past, because this would reduce the profits that could be made by its own public-sector companies like Coal India or Nalco. While Andhra Pradesh has a more diversified economy than central Indian states like Odisha, Jharkhand and Chhattisgarh, and is therefore less dependent on revenues from mining,[5] it has come up with similar responses when attempting to find other ways to increase such revenues.

Aside from royalties, there were three main ways for the Andhra Pradesh Government to raise revenues from this bauxite project: by making a profit on the sale of ore to the refinery; by taxing the refinery itself; and by imposing additional taxes and fees on the land used for mining. Of these, the first two were ruled out by provisions of the MoU that set the price of the ore as 'the price as fixed by a committee formed by Govt of

4 The royalty on bauxite has notionally been tied to the world market price of aluminium but was roughly Rs 80 (less than US$2) per tonne during the period under discussion.

5 Even though Andhra Pradesh is the second biggest mining state in India in terms of royalty collection, its income from this source was only Rs 865 crore (about US$190 million) in 2004/05, or roughly 3 per cent of the state's total revenues. Odisha and Chhattisgarh received Rs 664 and 695 crore respectively from the same source (Bhushan and Zeya Hazra 2008).

AP, based on cost of production' (Andhra Pradesh 2005b: 2–3), and that declared the refinery to be a Special Economic Zone with wide-ranging tax exemptions.

Selling ore without making a profit might have necessary to attract JSW's interest in the project. The problem (for the promoters) was that the Samatha judgment required 20 per cent of profits to be set aside 'so that the constitutional objectives of social, economic and human resource empowerment of the tribals could be achieved' (India 1997: para. 114). If the profit was less than the market price for bauxite ore would have provided, then it could be argued that the bauxite project was in contravention of the judgment. A high-level committee of the Andhra Pradesh Government, with advice from PricewaterhouseCoopers, spent a significant amount of time trying to figure out how it could sell the ore at cost price to JSW, as promised in the MoU, while making it appear as if the price and the profit shared with tribal groups were both based on market conditions. The committee's solution was not to determine a market price directly, but rather to sell the ore at 1.25 times the royalty rate. Since the royalty rate was based on a formula that took account of the international price of aluminium on the London Metal Exchange, it could then be said that the ore price was based on a market price (Andhra Pradesh 2008a).[6]

The prospects for securing revenue from a land tax were unclear. The *Andhra Pradesh Mineral Bearing Lands (CESS) Act 2005* was meant to yield additional state government revenue from this source, but its effectiveness was thrown into doubt when a steel company took the government to court over the proposed tax of Rs 100 per tonne of iron ore being levied on top of the royalty of Rs 20 per tonne (Venkateshwarlu 2007).

The prospect of raising state revenues is not the only reason for a state government to encourage investment in an alumina refinery. There is also the prospect of investment in infrastructure, and other facilities that come with its construction, and the potential creation of additional employment. The problem for state governments is that there is no legal basis for demanding additional local industrial investment as

6 This approach was first established when the Ministry of Environment and Forests (MoEF) gave its approval for the Jerrila bauxite mine in 2008, despite admitting that 'the Expert Appraisal Committee has no idea about the reality' of whether 20 per cent of market-based profits would be made available for tribal welfare (India 2008c). I am grateful to Bill Lockhart (personal communication, March 2009) for his insights on this issue.

a precondition for mining. Such demands have been seen as barriers to trade within the country and have generally been struck down by the courts. Without a resolution of the federal–state conflict over how to compensate the resource-rich states, future deals between state governments and private investors are likely to continue to include combinations of mines and plants, despite an effort to limit such deals in the 2008 National Mineral Policy (India 2008d). This is all but guaranteed to cause more delays because of the increased complexity of planning for two projects instead of one and the increased risk of litigation and controversy. However, the separation of related projects may have some benefits for their promoters. In the case of bauxite, for example, where the mines are the focus of controversy, the establishment of a refinery can increase their power to bargaining for the subsequent approval of a mine (Kohli 2006).

Another aspect of this problem is the lack of incentives for states to cooperate. Bauxite ore located in the northeastern corner of Andhra Pradesh will not be processed in nearby Odisha even if the latter has better railway connections to the source or more readily available water or energy supplies. Similarly, ore from Nalco's Panchpatmali mine in southern Odisha is very unlikely to be transported across the border to Andhra Pradesh to avoid the need for new mines in the ecologically sensitive Araku Valley, no matter how technically and economically feasible this might be, since it would reduce Odisha's state revenues. It is possible that Nalco, as a major producer and exporter of alumina, could have supplied alumina to several smelters in Andhra Pradesh, but no plans have been made along these lines (Sivaramakrishna 2007). Indeed, given the interest that Nalco had shown in development of the Andhra Pradesh bauxite deposits, before any other agreements had been signed, we might conclude that an increase in government revenues has not been a high priority for leading politicians in the Andhra Pradesh Government.

Non-Tribal Industry Excluded from the Scheduled Areas

The Andhra Pradesh Government insisted on a combination of mining and refining, but the existence of tribal land rights forced what could have been one bauxite and alumina refinery project in the public sector to become two projects. Several project components caused additional difficulties when it was necessary to obtain bureaucratic approvals and acquire land for two projects instead of one. There was also the question of timing. The Andhra Pradesh Government would insist on the private investor making the first move, but the private investor would be worried that the mining lease or something else would not receive bureaucratic approval, thus creating an issue of trust between the two sides.

What made the chosen setup especially strange is that a superior alternative was already available to the state government. If Nalco had been chosen as the partner, all the facilities could have been located in the Scheduled Areas, since Nalco and APMDC are both public companies.[7] Nalco has been very profitable in recent years, operating one of the largest alumina refineries in the world.[8] It clearly has greater knowledge of bauxite mining and alumina refining technology, and of the particular operational conditions of the tribal areas of central-eastern India, than could be claimed by JSW or AnRak Aluminium.

Nalco had shown an interest in the Andhra Pradesh deposits for many years but had never been awarded a contract, nor had a valid reason for this denial ever been made public. Meeting minutes reveal how the company was willing to invest Rs 46,000 crore (about US$9.2 billion) in April 2005.

> The Chairman & Managing Director, NALCO … expressed their interest to establish industries to produce alumina/aluminium by making use of quality bauxite deposits of Jerrila area. They intend to establish Alumina refinery at Krishnadevapeta (KD Peta) and smelter at Visakhapatnam (Andhra Pradesh 2005c: 1).

The minutes suggest that the state government was agreeable:

> The Hon'ble [sic] Chief Minister instructed that APMDC will take up mining operations and supply the material to NALCO by fixing a reasonable price which includes cost of excavation and 20 per cent profit margin (ibid.: 4).

But despite these undertakings, contracts were signed with JSW and later (in 2007) with the government of Ras al-Khaimah. During this time, Nalco continued to make media statements about its intention to

7 Several public companies operate in the Scheduled Areas of Telangana, including Singareni Colleries and Sponge Iron India Limited.

8 Nalco's annual reports declared after-tax profits of Rs 24 billion (approximately US$520 million) in 2006/07, Rs 16 billion in 2007/08, and Rs 13 billion in 2008/09.

invest in Andhra Pradesh, and in early 2008, the federal mining minister announced that Nalco would soon be awarded a contract (Anon. 2008a), yet none was forthcoming.

Throughout this period, the Andhra Pradesh Government insisted that APMDC should be the mining vehicle, not so much because of tribal land transfer issues but 'for monitoring environmental and tribal welfare issues effectively' (Anon. 2006a). It was never explained why APMDC would be better at monitoring these things than Nalco would, given that Nalco was the company with actual experience of bauxite mining. Only in 2009 was Nalco granted mining leases over the last remaining deposits in the state. These are located on the border of between Visakhapatnam and East Godavari, making them the least accessible of all the state's reserves, and with the highest risk of security threats from the Naxalites. So far as is known, Nalco has not since been able to secure the crucial environmental approvals and move towards mining these deposits.

Where Were the Public Benefits?

Although Nalco's investment plans were frequently discussed in the media, and further details were available in the minutes of government meetings, it is possible that some unknown concern prevented an investment agreement. However, when seen in light of other dubious mining deals, the generally unfavourable position of public companies in Andhra Pradesh,[9] and the lack of public revenues forecast from the APMDC-JSW project, questions about the overall public benefits of this project were only intensified. When these questions could not be answered, the project could only be explained as an example of the rent-seeking behaviour that has often been associated with big mining projects.

The way the bauxite project was organised, with public-sector mining by a mining company that is unable to mine, and a private investor funding the whole project, suggests a legal arrangement designed to circumvent the tribal land transfer legislation that functions as a barrier to the bauxite industry. But a decision to circumvent rather than change the law could only add legitimacy to the continued demand for tribal land

9 Another public company, Vizag Steel, was not allowed to build a port on land it had already acquired, despite the prospect of lower transportation costs, and the privately owned Gangavaram port was instead developed on the same land. Vizag Steel also lost out to the new but politically well connected private company, Brahmani Steels, in its bid for an iron ore mining lease.

rights. At the same time, the legal manoeuvring seems to indicate that were significant limits to the power of the bauxite alliance, which would be open to challenge when the state proved unable to either operate or finance the mine.

Another aspect of the project design was the need for a significant level of trust between the company and the state government. It is not entirely clear how this trust was established or how it was reaffirmed over several years of slow implementation. For example, the company had to make significant up-front payments for the refinery, including the land on which it would be built, before any progress could be made with the mine. Given the history of bauxite mining as a major source of political conflict, what could explain the investor's confidence? Could the investment be seen as a way of securing future access to the ore deposit? If senior politicians were aware of the risk of lengthy delays, over a period in which elections were to be held and potentially lost, how could immediate dividends have been obtained from the unproductive work of securing the MoU and starting the process of land acquisition? Was it possible to secure the benefits of patronage well before the refinery had started production?

Those hoping to prevent mining could have used the prospect of limited public benefits to claim that this project would not contribute to wider economic development, either at the local or the state level, but would only benefit a small number of people. The well-known need for politicians to spend large sums of money in order to win elections could then have been connected to this lack of public benefit with the implication of rent-seeking motives. However, as we shall see in Chapter 6, the protests avoided the distributional issue, as if negotiations for improved economic compensation would have made the discourse on the dangers of mining seem less sincere. If some quantum of monetary or other benefits could compensate for all the negative impacts on Adivasi culture, then concerns about these impacts might not be taken so seriously.

4. Livelihoods at the Two Sites

The use of land for mining and refining in the Jindal South West (JSW) bauxite project would be in direct competition with existing livelihoods across two different sites and would impose other changes in surrounding areas. These changes would depend on the type of activities undertaken and the technical and other choices made as part of the planning process. Furthermore, open-cast bauxite mining on top of certain hills in the Agency would have implications that were very different from those of the industrial process of alumina refining on agricultural land in Vizianagaram District.

The ability of land-dependent rural communities, whether tribal or not, to cope with external changes brought about by industrialisation depends on their capacity for adaptation. Successful change could entail a movement into industrial employment with higher incomes, but for this to occur a wide skills gap would have to be bridged, and this would have to be done in competition with many better educated people from nearby cities. The many displacement-inducing projects in past and present tribal India have been particularly problematic for tribal groups, whose members have not been able to make this move into new activities or adapt to a new setting (Fernandes 2009).

Instead of assessing new employment opportunities, a more viable approach is thus to examine whether existing livelihoods could be maintained alongside the bauxite project, what forms of compensation were being offered in exchange for the loss of land and other resources, and whether people who were dispossessed had capabilities that would allow them to establish new livelihoods. There were also many people who depended on common property resources that might no longer be accessible, and others whose livelihoods would be compromised if assets on which they depended were damaged by industrial pollution or water consumption.

Compensation for Land and Livelihoods

At the time when the project was being planned, compensation for land acquired for industrial projects was still based on the arcane *Land Acquisition Act 1894* and its various amendments.[1] This legislation empowered the government to take over land for a public purpose and pay compensation according to an estimated market value, which included the value of the land itself, buildings, crops and other assets. This legislation had been subject to heavy criticism for its general deficiencies, but with specific concerns related to the Scheduled Areas.

The valuation of land is clearly a very complicated procedure, and over the years much effort, including court litigation, had been dedicated to providing more accurate assessments. This has been further complicated in recent years by sharply escalating land prices across India, while officially recorded prices have been understated in order to avoid stamp duties. For industrial projects, the market value is set at the date of notification of land acquisition and does not therefore take account of expected price increases due to the industrial development and the associated influx of people, nor the fact that people in the surrounding area may raise the price of agricultural land in anticipation of growing demand. In tribal areas, the market value may be especially hard to assess because the existing market is restricted to tribal people and land is often held informally or illegally (Singh 1986; Herbert and Lahiri-Dutt 2004; Fernandes 2007; Iyer 2007; Sampat 2008). To deal with these dilemmas, companies or state governments frequently offer higher levels of compensation than those required by the law, but this happens on a case-by-case basis wherever the opposition is strong enough to be taken seriously (Newell and Wheeler 2006).

Beyond the question of whether land valuations are fairly applied to all affected people, social movements across India have been built around the inadequacy of providing purely monetary forms of compensation.

1 This was subsequently replaced by the *Right to Fair Compensation and Transparency in Land Acquisition, Rehabilitation and Resettlement Act 2013*.

The Narmada Bachao Andolan movement has been at the forefront in highlighting the difficulties that people face when they are uprooted from the land, water and forests on which they have depended for generations (Baviskar 1995; D'Souza 2002). There are also important concerns of class, caste and gender amongst the affected groups that further shape individual outcomes (Lahiri-Dutt 2011). It has gradually been accepted across India that displacement should involve rehabilitation, including land-for-land compensation (Iyer 2007). The continued delay in passage of a national rehabilitation bill has meant that the Andhra Pradesh Rehabilitation and Resettlement Policy of 2005, with various amendments, has been applied to all large-scale land acquisitions, which means those affecting at least 100 families in the plains or 25 families in the Scheduled Areas.

This policy importantly defines displacement as the loss of a house plot for those living in the plains, but shows more official concern for tribal people by allowing the loss of any type of land, including agricultural land, in the Scheduled Areas to count as a form of displacement (Andhra Pradesh 2005d). A second important benefit for people displaced in the Scheduled Areas is contained in an amendment to the policy that makes land-for-land compensation mandatory (Andhra Pradesh 2006a). For people on the plains, new land is only provided if government land is already available for this purpose. This has been an obstacle to the rehabilitation of those who are displaced when it means that the government would have to acquire new land, thus creating even more displacement (Iyer 2007; Nathan 2009).

Mitigation of so-called externalities from industrial operations, including pollution and water consumption, is a process completely managed by government agencies, despite mechanisms like environmental public hearings that are intended to take public concerns into account. The main tools for mitigation are environmental impact assessment (EIA) reports and the mining plans included in applications for mining leases. State Pollution Control Boards (PCBs) exist to ensure that various prescribed pollution measurements remain within specific limits, while the Indian Bureau of Mines (IBM) monitors mining operations, so there can be some duplication in the monitoring of things like water pollution. However, PCBs and the IBM have both found it difficult to carry out their respective mandates due to severe shortages of staff and other resources (Bhushan and Zeya Hazra 2008). It has thus been difficult or impossible to demand retrospective compensation for proven evidence of environmental degradation.

The Bauxite Mineral Industry and Land Use Change

To understand how bauxite mining and refining is likely to affect Adivasi lands in Andhra Pradesh, it is possible to draw on a range of Indian and international studies. Much of the technology has been standardised, especially in the refining of alumina. However, it is necessary to combine a knowledge of mining, environmental management and land compensation practices in India with the specific environment of the Eastern Ghats in order to anticipate actual rather than theoretical change.

The formation of bauxite ore in central India has taken place over millions of years of seasonal heavy rain (1,100 to 1,900 mm per annum), followed by hot sun, which has exposed the hills of khondalite rock in much of eastern India to the phenomenon known as weathering. Minerals in the rock have slowly leached out to leave high concentrations of bauxite ore as caps on the top of particular hills in the region, including some in Visakhapatnam District, at elevations of 900–1,420 m. The depths of these bauxite deposits ranges from just a few metres up to a maximum of 54 m. They can be relatively small in area or up to several square kilometres. The east coast bauxite deposits of tribal Odisha and Andhra Pradesh account for 80 per cent of metal-grade bauxite ore in India, which explains why this region has come to be a focal point of the industry and its opponents (Rao and Ramam 1979).

Mining on an industrial scale in Andhra Pradesh is restricted to the handful of locations where sufficiently large deposits have been found (see Table 4.1).[2] A decision on whether these can be mined will largely depend on the feasibility of investments in transport infrastructure such as railways and ports (Bunker and Ciccantell 1994). The Araku deposits have the advantage of proximity to existing port and railway facilities constructed by an Indo-Japanese iron ore project in the 1960s, but they could not support a mining operation for more than 10–15 years. Thereafter, the more remote Sapparla deposit, currently without a railway connection, would have to be exploited.

2 Bauxite mines in eastern India are usually planned to excavate more than 3 million tonnes of bauxite per annum, which is enough to feed an alumina refinery with an output of about 1 million tonnes per annum.

Table 4.1 Bauxite deposits of Andhra Pradesh.

GROUP	Deposit size (m.t.)	Mine area (ha)
Araku		
Galikonda	14.5	61
Raktakonda	8.6	42
Chittamgondi	28.5	152
SUBTOTAL	51.6	255
Chintapalli		
Sapparla	186.3	1513
Gudem	38.4	263
Jerrila	246.0	1350
SUBTOTAL	470.7	3126
Gurtedu (East Godavari)	42.6	180
TOTAL	564.9	3561

Source: Rao and Ramam (1979).

Each of the stages in the production of aluminium has distinctive characteristics that determine its impact on local communities and environments as well as the overall cost structure of the industry (see Figure 4.1). The impacts on land, air and water quality are discussed in the EIAs undertaken for the Galikonda bauxite mine and the S. Kota alumina refinery, and in critical assessments of Vedanta's nearby Lanjigarh bauxite mine and refinery (Tingay 2010; Amnesty International 2011).

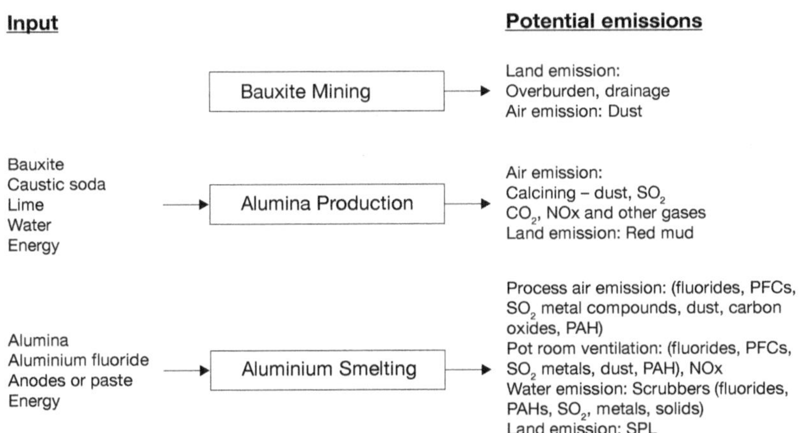

Figure 4.1 The stages of the aluminium industry and potential pollution.

Note: SO_2 – sulfur dioxide; CO_2 – carbon dioxide; NOx – nitrogen oxide; PFC – perfluorocarbon; PAH – polycyclic aromatic hydrocarbon; SPL – spent pot lining.

Source: Adapted by author from EIPPCB (2001) and BS Envi Tech (2008).

The energy required to produce aluminium metal is much greater than that required for other metals such as tin, copper and lead. While ore production accounts for between 77 and 83 per cent of the value of these other metals, the value of bauxite ore is less than 10 per cent of the value of finished aluminium (UNCTAD 2007). Since markets are usually far away from the deposits, and aluminium products are more difficult to transport than alumina, there are relatively few incentives for local aluminium production other than the interest of resource-owning countries to increase their own revenues. Aluminium smelters therefore tend to be located where low-cost power supplies are available, often from hydro-electricity (Barham et al. 1994). However, a recent trend in India and China has been to fuel smelters by means of thermal power, necessitating proximity to a coal-mining area to minimise the cost of coal transport.[3]

Bauxite Mining and the Environment

With many minerals washed away in the leaching process that originally formed the bauxite deposits, and with little or no topsoil remaining, it is common to find that the top portions of Indian bauxite hills are largely without forest or other vegetation beyond grasses and shrubs, while the hillsides have dense forest cover. While there are other causes of variable forest cover, including government policies and local practices, this fundamental characteristic of the east coast bauxite hills is the cause of one of the most common disagreements about the consequences of mining. Those in favour of mining see a rich bauxite deposit on a bare hilltop with few signs of human habitation, while those against it see a forested hill with springs flowing down its sides throughout the year to provide vital livelihood support for tribal communities further downhill.[4]

Open-cast mining of hilltop deposits entails extensive land disturbance, even when there is little in the way of overburden in the form of soil and rocks above the deposits themselves.[5] In Odisha, the flatter and more extensive bauxite hills make mining operations more straightforward

3 Northern Odisha has become the favoured location for smelters in India, with two smelters located next to the Hirakud dam and one in Angul.

4 In Andhra Pradesh, official planning documents favour the tree-free position (BS Envi Tech 2008; ICFRE 2008), while other observers have seen the forested hillsides (Moody 2007; Pattanaik et al. 2009). The national Ministry of Environment and Forests (MoEF) lists five bauxites deposits in Odisha with little or no hilltop vegetation but with forested hillsides (India 2008e). See Oskarsson (2017) for further analysis of this controversy.

5 The overburden is rarely more than 10 m in depth, with 4 m being the average at Galikonda (ICFRE n.d.).

from a technical point of view since the mining can proceed on top of the same hill for many years. In Andhra Pradesh, the topography is different, with smaller but thicker deposits on top of steeper hills. Initial steps in bauxite mining operations, other than the construction of the transport infrastructure, involve the clearance of vegetation, where necessary, and removal of any overburden. The actual mining typically consists of a combination of blasting with explosives and cutting of the rock with specialised machinery, followed by the use of mechanical excavators and human labour to load to the broken rocks onto trucks—or possibly a conveyor belt—for transport to a nearby railway station.

In the present case, there was a plan to mine Galikonda Hill at a rate of roughly 1 million tonnes per annum, which meant that operations would last for about 13 years. Since the refinery would need 3 million tonnes per annum, several other mines would have to operate at the same time (India 2008e). With several smaller mines operating for relatively short periods of time, it would be difficult to put in place long-term infrastructure such as conveyor belts in order to minimise the disruption caused by trucks transporting ore through villages (ICFRE n.d.).

The mining of Galikonda Hill would involve the excavation of a succession of relatively small blocks, each about 20–30 hectares in size (ICFRE n.d.). In this type of operation, blocks that have already been mined are supposed to be backfilled and revegetated, but it is doubtful if this has ever happened in any bauxite mining operation in India. The EIA report said that it was necessary to plant trees to prevent landslides and soil erosion but gave little detail of how, when and where this would be done other than to recommend the use of indigenous species of trees and pass responsibility to the Forest Department.

The overburden would be stored somewhere on top of the hills for later backfilling into the blocks that had been mined. The overburden would be moved at a rate of 50,000 tonnes per annum for the first five years of operation, much lower than the planned rate of mineral extraction. While this would alleviate the project's waste storage problems, it would also limit the capacity to backfill the mined-out area and the availability of soil for the planned tree plantation program.[6]

6 Whether it was indeed desirable to plant trees was an issue not considered in the EIA. It might be that the current grasslands on top of Galikonda contain unique environmental values that ought to be preserved, like those in the state of Maharashtra investigated by Dixon and Watve (2015).

Unlike many other forms of mining, bauxite mining does not involve the use of chemicals, but the drilling, blasting, crushing and transportation of the ore would generate significant amounts of dust, posing direct health risks to local people and potentially reducing agricultural productivity in the immediate surroundings. The EIA report proposed to suppress the dust with water sprinklers, and recommended that drains be dug to contain the run-off. This was likely to be a challenge in a region with as much as 1,900 mm of annual rainfall.

However, the main concern for the activists was the prospect of change to the overall hydrology of the bauxite hills affecting the availability of water for Adivasi and other local farmers, but also for city dwellers in the wider region, since several of the rivers of coastal Andhra Pradesh originate in the bauxite-bearing hills. This type of impact is technically hard to assess, and evidence from one site might not be valid for others since '[b]auxite is a heterogeneous mineral that is difficult to define accurately. It occurs in many different forms, and its physical properties vary greatly, even within single ore beds' (Gendron et al. 2013: 1).

Studies in Australia, the world's biggest bauxite-mining nation, with a correspondingly large body of research on the social and environmental consequences, conclude that bauxite does not retain water (Croton and Reed 2007), but studies of bauxite mining in Suriname suggest that it can sometimes do so (Goodland 2009).

Activists in India, lacking the capacity to conduct large-scale, time-consuming studies of the forestry, geology and hydrology of bauxite-bearing hills and the environmental impacts of bauxite mining, have simply asserted that some of the best remaining forests in Odisha are located on the sides of the bauxite hills and these same hills are important watersheds for both local streams and major rivers. It has been claimed that Nalco's Panchpatmali mine has caused hill streams to run dry (Patra and Murthy n.d.), and that the same thing has happened as a result of other forms of open-cast mining in the state (Kumar 2004). One Indian geologist has argued that bauxite mining would have this effect because the porous nature of the ore means that it possesses superb water retention capacities when compared to the underlying solid rock (Ramamurthy 1995). Other commentators have observed that '[b]elow the hollow crust on the summits, the layer of bauxite is like clay, holding moisture, letting it seep out gently throughout the year through streams which form all around the mountain's flank' (Padel and Das 2010: 7). Activists thus fear that if a bauxite hill is unable to retain water once it has been mined, the vital hill streams will run dry in the summer months, and this will result in severe hardship in the absence of any other sources of fresh water.

The idea that mining transforms local watersheds has been widened to incorporate the negative impacts on entire river systems. The regional dangers of bauxite mining have been most eloquently articulated by Arundhati Roy:

> If the flat-topped [bauxite] hills are destroyed, the forests that clothe them will be destroyed too. So will the rivers and streams that flow out of them and irrigate the plains below. So will the Dongria Kond. So will the hundreds of thousands of tribal people who live in the forested heart of India, and whose homeland is similarly under attack (Roy 2010: xii).

A counter-narrative claims that there is either no impact or the impact is even beneficial. According to a note released by the national Ministry of Environment and Forests (MoEF), bauxite mining can support the retention of water because blasting creates cracks into which the water can enter (India 2008e). This statement appears to be based on a scientific report by the Central Mine Planning and Design Institute at the site of Vedanta's proposed Niyamgiri mine, which found that the bauxite ore does not have much capacity to retain water, as measured by its low porosity, and could not augment the groundwater underneath the hill because of its low permeability (CMPDI 2006).

The Galikonda EIA report contained a contradictory account of the local hydrology by using arguments from both sides of the debate. According to the authors, some sort of water storage seems to take place in the hill, but this is due to the very thin—or sometimes non-existent—layer of soil and overburden, not to the bauxite ore itself. Since overburden can be stored and later replaced, mining need not therefore have a negative impact on water availability. In fact, mining operations combined with backfilling might improve the situation:

> [T]he groundwater recharge potential would not be negatively affected. In addition, due to the loosening of top material, after mining/during mining the recharge of ground water would increase (ICFRE n.d.: 121).

What seems clear is that bauxite mining would remove a significant part of certain hilltops and this would probably have some effect on the local hydrology. Backfilling could not possibly return the hills to their original state because the amount of overburden would be so much smaller than the amount of ore to be removed. The combination of high annual rainfall and soils that are already prone to erosion (India 2008e) suggest a need for careful planning and management if mining were to proceed, but there was little evidence that planners were taking local water needs seriously. The situation might be improved by reforestation, but if forest plantations can help to arrest soil erosion, they would also compete with local agriculture for the available water, as would the mining operation itself. The small springs around the hills provide essential water supply in areas with no storage infrastructure and only modest pumps or other means to access groundwater. The environmental impacts of mining would clearly not extend to the entire watershed, but there was still a desperate shortage of detailed studies of what they might be within the affected area. There was clearly a need for an integrated approach to water, forests and local livelihood concerns, but this was unlikely to happen because of the controversial nature of the topic.

Alumina Refining and the Environment

While much attention has been paid to the environmental impacts of bauxite mining, a number of reports suggest that refining poses the most significant environmental risks (Behera 2008; Nayak 2008; Amnesty International 2010). Refining alumina involves grinding and digesting the bauxite ore with the application of heat, pressure and a strongly alkaline solution of caustic soda. The alumina, the aluminium oxide in the ore, is dissolved during this process, allowing impurities like iron, titanium, lead and other heavy metals to be washed out. The alumina is then crystallized out of the liquid solution and purified at temperatures of up to 1,300°C. The final product is a white powder that constitutes the input to aluminium smelters (Bunker and Ciccantell 1994).

Modern alumina refineries are major industrial plants requiring investments of at least US$1 billion, with significant economies of scale, which can serve several aluminium smelters. One tonne of alumina typically requires about 2.9 tonnes of bauxite ore. Since a refinery must tailor its processes according to the particular chemical composition of the ore, physical and technological constraints encourage long-term supply agreements or even joint ventures between the mining and refining companies (Bunker 1994). Locating the refinery close to the mines reduces transportation costs but can expose already fragile environments to further pollution. Furthermore, in the Indian bauxite regions, where periods of heavy rainfall are interspersed with long dry seasons, water usage is more of an issue than in some other national contexts, and needs more attention than it has so far received in the international literature.

Alumina refineries need to be located close to an assured water supply because:

> [t]he reduction of bauxite to alumina is a wet process, requiring large quantities of water. This favours locations near rivers ... Proximity of refineries to large rivers greatly increases the danger of seepage and pollution and the cost of controlling it (Bunker 1994: 270).

The JSW alumina refinery would be constructed on a 540-hectare site in Vizianagaram District, and in this case the planned annual production of 1.4 million tonnes of alumina required a supply of about 3 million tonnes of ore. The refinery would need to take 8 million gallons (30,000 m^3) of water each day from a nearby reservoir, in direct competition with local farmers and residents of Visakhapatnam city (see Chapter 5). The resulting uncertainties over water consumption did create some controversy (see Chapter 6), though not as much as the mining proposal.

The waste material from an alumina refinery, known as red mud, is usually generated at a rate of 1 to 1.5 tonnes per tonne of alumina. Red mud is a toxic compound whose composition varies with that of the ore but contains caustic soda and a range of heavy metals (Bunker and Ciccantell 1994). If it contaminates groundwater or surface water sources it poses a risk to human health and that of agricultural crops. Red mud may not be as toxic as the waste from the processing of other metals like copper, lead or zinc, but the lead content alone in red mud from the Nalco alumina refinery was enough to prevent any form of plant growth (Rao et al. 2000). Fine red mud particles are also liable to be spread by wind, which necessitates a well-designed dust management plan (Tingay 2010).

Containing red mud is a serious challenge because of the large quantities involved and its continued toxicity after many years of storage. The EIA report on the JSW refinery proposed that a 90-hectare section of the site be set aside for red mud storage, with a subsequent expansion to 120 hectares. The storage pond would be lined with an impermeable sheet to prevent seepage, and would have high walls to contain the mud. Water would be removed from the red mud to create a thickened slurry, which would both reduce the volume of waste and the risk of seepage. In addition, the report suggested a system of water sprinklers to contain the dust, but gave few details about this would operate (Vimta Labs 2007). The report did not present a detailed account of existing groundwater or surface water bodies and how these would relate to the planned waste pond sites, which meant that the actual consequences of a spill were impossible to evaluate.

Current practices in the containment of red mud in India leave much to be desired, with deficient monitoring of the actual use of sprinkler systems in areas with high wind speeds and long dry summers that make it possible for particles to travel long distances. As much as 85 per cent of the red mud at the Nalco refinery was found to consist of fine particles that were easily spread in the locally windy conditions (Rao et al. 2000). The waste management system adopted at the Vedanta refinery in Lanjigarh did not use the thickening system for some unknown reason. This resulted in overflows from the storage pond, as well as ground seepage because of poor construction, with the consequent pollution of the interstate Vamsadhara River (Behera 2008; Nayak 2008; Amnesty International 2010).

Forest Livelihoods in Araku and Ananthagiri

A number of tribal groups have for generations made a precarious living in Araku and Ananthagiri mandals, both fully contained within the Scheduled Areas, on relatively unproductive land and under constant threat of eviction by the Forest Department. Farming with very few inputs in a rain-fed and densely populated area used to lead to seasonal food shortages and occasional cases of starvation. More recently, the food security situation had been improved by the provision of state government handouts and the diversification of agricultural activities. The practice of *podu* (shifting cultivation) used to be common, but nowadays most of the lower hill slopes have been converted to permanent cultivation, while the higher slopes are increasingly used for coffee plantations. Even so, tree felling and intensive *podu* on steep slopes, combined with a lack of soil conservation measures, have already resulted in severe land degradation (IFAD 1991). Forest products such turmeric, tamarind and jackfruit are still important for local livelihoods despite the generally poor condition of the forests.

Hopes for an escape from deeply entrenched poverty are linked to the unique climatic conditions of the Visakhapatnam Agency. The cool hills have proven to be highly suitable for coffee cultivation ever since the Andhra Pradesh Forest Department created the first plantations in the 1960s. Coffee yields incomes higher than any other potential alternative cash crop, and is grown in ways that require very little care or specialised skills on the part of the farmers. In addition, the Forest Department had secured the benefit of increased forest cover in the form of shade trees, while the Tribal Welfare Department gets more funding to support extension of the coffee plantations.

At the time of my fieldwork, coffee was being grown in 11 of the mandals in Visakhapatnam District by 60,000 farmers on 24,000 hectares of land. Interviews with local government officials indicated that each hectare could yield an annual income of Rs 8,000 for the farmer, with the possibility of some additional income if pepper were cultivated on the same plot. If the farmers could be certified as organic growers, their beans could be sold at a premium of 25 per cent (Naandi Foundation 2008). No wonder then that former national environment minister and Congress Party MP Jairam Ramesh voiced his concern over the possible impact of bauxite mining on coffee production (Anon. 2008b).

Figure 4.2 Tribal village with coffee growing in the shade of trees on the Raktakonda hill slope.

Source: Photo by author, April 2008.

Income from tourism was also increasing, as tourists from Visakhapatnam and Hyderabad would arrive for weekend trips throughout the hot season. Most of the hotels built to accommodate the tourists were run by the state-owned Andhra Pradesh Tourist Development Corporation, and all-inclusive packages made sure that very little of the income left the compounds inside which the tourists stayed and ate. Other hotels had tribal owners, and there was ongoing agitation, with support from political parties and non-governmental organisations (NGOs), to enable the sharing of revenues from visitors to the nearby Borra limestone caves. The villagers of Katiki had built a road to a nearby waterfall on the bauxite hill of Raktakonda, and were charging a fee for tourists to go there. Other villagers were looking to improve their income from coffee by selling it directly to the tourists from roadside stalls.

Figure 4.3 Paddy fields irrigated by canals.
Source: Photo by author, April 2008.

Villages in Araku and Ananthagiri mandals are mainly located in the valleys, where more flat land is available for the cultivation of wet rice (see Figure 4.3). A satellite photo of Galikonda Hill shows terraced paddy fields at the bottom of the valley, where water is captured from hill streams, with coffee plantations grown under tree cover on the hillsides (Figure 4.4). The plantations of the Andhra Pradesh Forest Development Corporation account for most of the tree cover, with a mixture of large tree species, while the more orderly patches of single tree species are in more recent and privately held coffee plantations. A distinct lack of vegetation can be seen on top of the hill, with only small trees and bushes more than halfway up the hillsides. Nevertheless minor cultivation is possible in the higher gullies, where some volume of water can be collected, and coffee plantations were still being extended further up the slopes.

Figure 4.4 Layered resources on and around a bauxite hill.

Source: Google Earth satellite image taken 24 December 2002. Available from earth.google.com (accessed 1 April 2010).

Official data is scarce regarding the villages in the immediate vicinity of the bauxite hills since most of them have long been considered as 'forest villages'—that is to say, villages that are seen as encroaching on forest land. This means that they are not located on 'revenue land' and thus fall outside of the administration of the Revenue Department and its many welfare services. One forest village that I surveyed contained a close-knit Nooka Dora community (with two Kondha Dora households) living on top of a bauxite hill, with only walking paths as a means of communication with the outside world, and in a seemingly precarious location (see Table 4.2). However, the setting was not as isolated as it might seem since the main Visakhapatnam–Araku road was relatively close and Ananthagiri town was within easy walking distance. There were close to 150 people in this community, which could seem surprising given the poor quality of the land and the lack of irrigation. However, large areas of land close to the top of the hill were being transformed into coffee plantations and there was scope for some additional agricultural activity. While the coffee plantations were reaching maturity, people could find work in the state government plantations nearby, as well as other wage-earning jobs in the area.

Table 4.2 Summary result of village survey in Ananthagiri Mandal.

Number of households	Official landholding	Unofficial landholding	Main crops	Farm animals	Literacy rate
31	---	111 ha	Coffee, rice	97 (cows + goats)	7 of 94 adults

Source: Survey by author, May 2008.

None of the land used in this village for coffee plantations, or the smaller patches where rice and other crops were grown, had officially recognised land titles, although the villagers had managed to establish a school with classes up to Grade 6. Claims had been made for titles to the coffee plantations under the terms of the Forest Rights Act, and each household reported the maximum allowable claim over 5 acres (or 2 hectares) of land.

In 2006, an NGO called Nature conducted a survey of villages in the immediate vicinity of the bauxite hills in the Araku group (Raktakonda, Galikonda and Chittamgondi) that were to be set aside for the JSW project. These were all tribal villages in the Borra panchayat (village council) area, with populations from the Kondha Dora, Nooka Dora, Bagatha, Paraja, Valmiki, Kondh and Kutiya Kondh tribal groups. Only three of the 14 villages had any formal land titles, but all were dependent on forest land (Nature 2006). These findings were confirmed by a subsequent survey (Reddy and Mishra 2010). The absence of formal land titles was clearly a major obstacle to the improvement of local livelihoods, despite the opportunities for expanding coffee production. Perhaps surprisingly, this was not only a problem on the steeper hillsides, but also in the valleys below, where the land was still classified as 'forest', irrespective of whether any forest, or even individual trees, could be found on it.

Agricultural Livelihoods in S. Kota[7]

Moving down from the hills, the Agency ends in a diffuse border with the plains, which seems to be largely unknown to people in the area despite its vital importance for questions of land tenure. Since it was located outside the Scheduled Areas, the proposed site of the refinery had a social context that was significantly different to that of the proposed mines in the hills of the Agency, despite their close geographical proximity. The refinery area, close to S. Kota town, had for some years seen an influx of outsiders who acquired the best land in what my informants described as a forested area that had been inhabited almost exclusively by tribal communities only a few decades previously. As one tribal villager put it:

> We have been here for a long time, earlier we used to go to [the] hills and depend on forest products. Once this land was uncultivable, but later we made it cultivable. With borrowing we dug bore wells and got water at 50–60 feet. We are farming this land with the help of loans. These coconut trees were planted in my childhood and now they are giving us some income. It took a lot of time to make this land cultivable and these trees to give us some income. At this moment some people came and asked us to give up these lands. They want to cut down these trees but, if this is done, how much time will it take to bring up new trees? (interview, S. Kota Mandal, 26 January 2008).

Some of the villages now about to lose land to the refinery had existed for generations, but for some reason were never included when the Scheduled Areas were demarcated, despite their inhabitants being recognised as tribal people and now having tribal caste certificates. Other tribal villages were displaced when the Tatipudi irrigation reservoir on the Goshtani River was built in the 1960s. At that time they were compensated with new houses and good (though forested) land only a few kilometres away from their original settlements. In 2007, this group of previously displaced villagers were once again facing displacement by the new refinery.

Some villages in the proposed refinery area had only tribal residents, while others contained a mix of people belonging to Scheduled Tribes, Scheduled Castes and Other Backward Castes. Villagers showed little awareness of how Scheduled Area land transfer legislation might help to keep more land in the hands of long-term tribal occupants or even make

7 See Oskarsson and Nielsen (2014) for a condensed discussion of this section.

it impossible to build the refinery. The local protest group never raised the issue of tribal land loss or displacement other than to highlight the unfairness in displacing some people for a second time.

The people who were due to lose land to the refinery officially lived in four 'revenue villages' recognised as such by the Revenue Department, but the 600 families were dispersed in roughly 15 smaller villages and hamlets.[8] A small village might contain about 100 residents, or 20 households, while hamlets only contained a few households. The composition of the local population was markedly different to that of the overall population of the mandal, in which tribal people are not very well represented. A survey of six villages by Reddy and Mishra (2010) found that 290 of the households to be affected by land acquisition belonged to Scheduled Tribes, 33 to Scheduled Castes (Dalits), 105 to Other Backward Castes, and 10 to other castes. By way of comparison, S. Kota Mandal as a whole had 74,500 residents in 2001, of whom 5,749 (8 per cent) belonged to Scheduled Tribes and 6,629 (9 per cent) to Scheduled Castes (India 2001b).

Of particular concern was the proposed acquisition of land from several Gadaba tribal villages. The 36,000 Gadaba people in Andhra Pradesh (India 2001a) form a small and almost exclusively rural community with a unique language only remotely related to other Dravidian languages.[9] Three out of the seven Gadaba sub-groups are officially defined as primitive and traditional hunter-gatherers. How and when members of this group came to settle as farmers in the S. Kota area is not well known, but interviews indicated that 10–12 of their villages had been present in the area since the 1950s, prior to the arrival of the dam-displaced settlers in the late 1960s. Official plans for the refinery did not recognise the presence of this particularly vulnerable group of people.

A survey of a sample of 19 households in the four revenue villages in 2008 showed that each household held slightly more than 1 hectare of 'assigned land' (see Table 4.3). Of the total of 23.6 hectares, less than 1 hectare had so far been acquired for the refinery, while another 11 hectares had been earmarked for acquisition.

8 Aside from the land to be acquired from the four revenue villages, 68 hectares of private land would also be required for the refinery, but evidence of its ownership is not available from government sources because negotiations were undertaken directly between JSW and the landowners.

9 They are also present in southern Chhattisgarh and Odisha.

Table 4.3 Summary of village survey results in S. Kota Mandal.

Number of households	Official land ownership	Main crops	Farm animals	Literacy rate
19	23.6 hectares	Rice, sugar cane, banana, sunflower	25 (buffaloes, cows and goats)	19 of 51 adults

Source: Survey by author, March 2008.

Official land use planning in the refinery EIA report was carried out by means of satellite imagery and secondary statistical sources. This analysis focused on the 10 km^2 study area prescribed by the MoEF, and not on the area proposed for the actual site. The conclusion was that 25 per cent of the area was double-cropped and 15 per cent was single-cropped agricultural land, 38 per cent was forest, while 16 per cent was classified as wasteland (Vimta Labs 2007).

However, the EIA report described land use on the plant site itself as 'waste land with agricultural activities in patches', while declaring that ownership was not an issue since the 'site near Boddavara village near S. Kota is selected and finalised as no Forest Land, approximately 85 per cent of total land is government/assigned dry land and marginal Resettlement and Rehabilitation (R&R) issues are involved' (Vimta Labs 2007: C1–2). With little valuable agricultural land, little displacement, no national parks or biospheres, wildlife sanctuaries or even forest land, the report painted a picture of an uncomplicated project site. However, official Revenue Department statistics, not presented in the EIA report, showed significant agricultural production in the four revenue villages (see Table 4.4).

Table 4.4 Agricultural land in the villages of the proposed alumina refinery in S. Kota.

Revenue village	Land area	Cultivated area	Rice (irrigated + unirrigated)	Sugar cane (irrigated)	Mango (unirrigated)	Cashew (unirrigated)
M.B. Vara	2,057	344	18 + 12	43	350	392
Cheedipalem	152	43	11 + 0	37	15	28
Chinakandepalli	292	72	28 + 9	76	13	0
Kiltampalem	645	368	33 + 0	782	55	0

Source: Andhra Pradesh (2008b).

Agriculture in the Godavari and Krishna river deltas in the southern part of the state has been subject to a major economic transformation in recent decades as a result of increased irrigation (Upadhya 1988; Damodaran 2008). Something similar has occurred amongst upwardly mobile communities in the S. Kota area, but to a lesser extent because of lower water availability. Directly east of the proposed refinery site, groundwater remained widely available throughout the year, largely due to the nearby dam and its associated irrigation canals. This made it possible to grow rice and sugar cane close to the dam, or to establish cashew nut plantations slightly further away.

Because of the way statistics are collected, it was not possible to distinguish the villages liable to displacement from others nearby, but it could be assumed that productivity would vary significantly between farmers depending on their ability to use various inputs. Overall, rice and sugar cane were the dominant cultivars in the mandal, and this pattern was most pronounced in Kiltampalem revenue village, indicating the greater availability of water (see Figure 4.4). M.B. Vara and Mushidipalli revenue villages had drier land, and their cashew plantations accounted for two-thirds of the cashew grown in the mandal. Much of the unirrigated land also contained mango orchards (Andhra Pradesh 2008b). M.B. Vara had 1,640 hectares of land classified as 'barren and uncultivable land', while the other revenue villages had little or no such land. Given that incomes from the drier areas, further from the irrigation dam, would be significantly lower, it is not surprising that people in the M.B Vara area were much less resistant to the prospect of land acquisition than those in Kiltampalem, although local social dynamics were also an important factor in their response.

During the course of my own fieldwork it became clear that the farmers were managing most of their agricultural activities without government support, by taking loans from private moneylenders to level the land and install wells, pumps and water tanks (see Figure 4.5). Indeed, they had never seen much of the government at all, as evident in the lack of schools, and several villages were without a single literate adult. They remained poor despite the strong potential for agricultural improvement, largely due to the high interest rates they had to pay on their loans,[10] but were still self-reliant and aspired to do as well in the future as their non-tribal neighbours in the adjacent villages, few of whom were liable to be affected by acquisition of land for the refinery.

10 In a survey of one village, it was found that each household had debts ranging from Rs 20,000 to Rs 100,000, with interest rates from 25 to 40 per cent. The size of the debt was generally correlated with the size of the landholding.

Figure 4.5 Pumps ensure that enough water is available to grow sugar cane in S. Kota.

Source: Photo by author, June 2012.

The non-scheduled status of this area had led many upwardly mobile agricultural communities to acquire land in recent decades. The cement houses, cars, motorcycles and agricultural vehicles present in their villages were in stark contrast to the assets present in the villages now due to lose their land, where one or two motorcycles were the sum of all capital goods, and only a minority of households had received any support from government housing programs or had received rather cramped housing as compensation for their earlier displacement.

In a survey of one of these villages, it was found that most people had few assets other than their small houses, with palm leaf extensions to provide a little extra space, and a few farm animals. Adult literacy rates were only slightly higher than in the Agency, but children and teenagers showed much more interest and capacity to continue their education. Despite their apparent poverty, local people expressed some pride in having ceased to be hunters who wore nothing but loincloths just a generation or two ago to become the landed farmers they were now. One of the benefits of having non-tribal communities as their neighbours had been the opportunity to learn from their agricultural practices, even if this entailed the precarious need for large loans that could be difficult to pay back in case of crop failure. There was no evidence of people migrating out of the area, or even venturing into nearby towns and cities, despite the apparent opportunities to take up construction or other paid work, given the existence of good and affordable public transport.

Many of the people in the proposed refinery area, like those in the Agency, thus had reasonably good hopes of improving livelihoods based on agriculture despite their present poverty. But in S. Kota, formal land titles were universal and much larger personal investments had been made in agriculture. If land was to be acquired for the refinery, the holders should at least be able to claim compensation for it, whereas the systematic denial of titles in the Agency made this more problematic.

Land Settlement and Dispossession

To understand the livelihood changes that would be caused by land acquisition for the bauxite project, and the potential compensation for those affected by it, we need to know the details of land use and tenure in both the proposed mining and refining locations.

Forest Land for the Bauxite Mine

Bauxite mining is associated with forest land in most parts of India (India 1998), but bauxite hills are not necessarily associated with good forests, as is evident in the lack of 'dense' forests in Visakhapatnam District (India 2005b), although detailed information about the quality of the forest reserves in Araku and Ananthagiri mandals is not available. There was also some uncertainty about the exact locations of the proposed mines. The official mining lease for the Galikonda mine was for an area of 97.5 hectares, but without precise coordinates or a map of the location (India 2007c). It was known that the Sunkarmetta and Ananthagiri reserved forests covered the whole of the proposed mining area, while the affected villages, agricultural fields and coffee plantations were not discussed in project planning documents. This is perhaps not surprising, given the history of these villages being labelled as 'forest villages', and their fields therefore being considered as illegal encroachments.

NGO activities and political mobilisation have in recent decades ensured that schools have been opened in these villages, and they have been included in programs to provide housing for the poor. The difference between forest and revenue and villages appeared fairly modest in practice, and yet forest villagers remained vulnerable to demands for bribes from forest officials in return for being allowed to continue cultivating the land (Anon. 2009a), and when rights to agricultural land are not recognised, there is no support from agricultural extension activities and the land cannot be used as security for a loan.

All land used for agriculture and other purposes in the village surveyed during my fieldwork was informally settled, which meant that the Forest Rights Act would be essential for security of tenure in the proposed mining area. However, recognition of new rights to forest land was uncertain, since the Mines and Geology Department and its business arm, Andhra Pradesh Mineral Development Corporation (APMDC), were aiming for permanent alienation, while other departments—especially the Tribal Welfare Department—were trying to settle it with tribal farmers. This was symptomatic of the complex nature of the bauxite project and the many uncertainties that prevented those affected from knowing what would actually happen to them. If other events stalled the mining plans long enough for private forest titles to be granted, the people of some villages would at least be able to stake a formal claim to some of the land. But while a title would surely be better than no title, even basic elements in the Forest Rights Act were yet to be specified, including the conditions under which such land could be acquired, by whom, and what compensation might be payable for its loss. If the mining project was not contested, then the land could be transferred within the state government, from the Forest Department to the Mines and Geology Department, or else directly to APMDC. This kind of transfer could give rise to internal government controversies, but it provides few benefits for the forest-dwelling peoples of Visakhapatnam.

The people in all six villages that I visited had applied for the maximum allocation of 2 hectares under the Forest Rights Act, with men and women making separate individual claims. However, no claims had been lodged over the much larger areas—up to several hundred hectares—that could have become community reserves. The unclaimed land stretched beyond the coffee plantations and was used for many different purposes, including the collection of minor forest products, as well as containing a shrine dedicated to the goddess of the hill. One explanation given for the lack of community reserve claims was that co-management of the reserves would invite the Forest Department back to the area to once again interfere with peoples' livelihoods. Successful forest rights claims in the proposed mining area would mean that the handful of hilltop villages would at least have a legal title to the land they were cultivating, which could make them eligible for compensation, but the many other villages below them, with hillside coffee plantations and customary usage of large areas beyond them, would remain outside of the mining licence and find it very difficult to make compensation claims.

According to its promoters, mining would lead to improved forest cover through mine reclamation activities on currently barren hilltops, while areas outside of the mining lease boundaries would be protected by pollution control techniques and would therefore not be affected. The distinct borders visualised in rehabilitation and resettlement policies were thus replicated in the engineered world of EIA documents, where local livelihood activities could persist in the valleys despite the introduction of excavation and blasting activities on the hilltops. Common property resource uses were not mentioned in the EIA report (Anon. 2006b; BS Envi Tech 2008), and the Galikonda mine would supposedly cause no displacement:

> Since there is no habitation on the mining lease area thus no households will be required to be displaced from their existing habitation, hence no Rehabilitation and Resettlement plan is envisaged for the present project activity. However, there will be indirect impact on the nearby villages and thus a community developmental package is proposed (ICFRE n.d.: 192).

Perhaps the mine promoters were planning to mine around the hilltop villages, or perhaps the villages did not appear on the maps they were using because the whole area was officially reserve forest. In either case, the approach to land acquisition bypassed the people of the Agency, despite centuries of struggles for the recognition of their land rights, and despite the new Forest Rights Act that was supposed to settle old injustices. At the same time, there was an admission of other 'indirect' (and unspecified) problems for those living close to the proposed mine, and hence a possibility of compensation, despite the lack of recognition of any loss of land or other resources, including potential pollution. Yet the compensation would take the form of uncertain grants, with no information provided about who would decide on the amounts or how the funds would be distributed.

Assigned Agricultural Land for Alumina Refinery

In the non-scheduled parts of the state, where land titles, as well as an awareness of the meaning of these titles and associated rights, are much more widespread than in the Agency, the bauxite alliance had to work out ways to acquire land without causing sufficiently strong protests to derail the entire process. It could do this despite significant civil society mobilisation and media coverage because it had control of the local bureaucracy and political influence through the Congress Party in all four of the affected panchayats in the S. Kota area. JSW was largely invisible in this process but provided support behind the scenes.

The JSW refinery would require space not only for the central ore refining activities but also for a thermal power plant, a housing site for its office staff and displaced people, and a significant amount of land for its two waste ponds (see Table 4.5).

Table 4.5 Proposed land use for the alumina refinery.

Activity	Land use (hectares)
Alumina refinery and co-generation (including storage and green belt)	300
Residue disposal area and ash pond	200
Township and miscellaneous	20
Railway lines	20
Total	540

Source: BS Envi Tech (2008: Figure 2.1).

The acquisition of fertile farm land, with the subsequent displacement of farmers, whether tribal or not, has become a very sensitive political issue, as well as an expensive proposition, throughout India. A few states have managed to avoid some of the controversy by acquiring large tracts of land for industrial parks, but Andhra Pradesh is not one of them. Instead, one method favoured by the state government is to find locations with a high proportion of so-called 'assigned land'. This category of land is the result of extensive land distribution programs intended for the benefit of the landless poor. Once assigned, this land cannot be sold like private land, only inherited. With 1.7 million hectares of land distributed since the late 1960s, assigned land represents a sizeable proportion of the state's total of 15 million hectares of cultivable land. Areas with large concentrations of assigned land, which on paper already belongs to the government, have come to be favoured as sites for industrial plants and other development projects (Seethalakshmi 2009). State acquisition of government land seems like a straightforward process, despite its disproportionate effect on some of the poorest people in the state.

The choice of an industrial site seems to depend on the ease of land acquisition rather than more tangible criteria such as the availability of infrastructure, labour, water or raw materials, or indeed whether the project satisfies environmental or social criteria. The potential alternative sites identified in the refinery EIA report (Vimta Labs 2007) were nearby locations with large concentrations of assigned land. Sabbavaram was the original site proposed for the JSW refinery before the S. Kota site was selected.[11] A report by the Land Committee of the Andhra Pradesh Government acknowledged that roughly one-quarter of all assigned land had ended up in the hands of non-poor recipients. A legislative amendment made in 2006 allowed the government to take such land back in order to allocate it to landless farmers, but the government still retained the option to use it for a different public purpose.

More assigned land becomes available for re-assignment from another clause in the legislation that requires land to be brought under cultivation within a certain timeframe. Since poor farmers often lack the equipment or the money to hire labour to help prepare the land for cultivation, much of the land assigned to them is at risk of not meeting this requirement (Andhra Pradesh 2006b; Balagopal 2007b). The government has claimed that it does not need to pay compensation for re-assigning land to a new public purpose, but this claim has been challenged in an ongoing court case. 'In practice the government pays or does not pay according to the pressure the landholders are able to put up' (K. Balagopal, personal communication, 2008).

Information about the actual type of land acquired for the JSW refinery was not readily available at the time of its acquisition. The EIA report failed to mention the fertile land and the mainly tribal villagers who were making a living from it. Of the 450 individuals who would actually lose land to the refinery, 257 (57 per cent) were Adivasis, 34 (8 per cent) were Dalits, 105 (23 per cent) belonged to Other Backward Castes, and 54 (12 per cent) to other castes (Andhra Pradesh 2007c). In 2001, only

11 In Visakhapatnam District, Makavarapalem is a site that was later assigned to the AnRak Aluminium Special Economic Zone, and Achutapuram has also been proposed as the site for such an entity. In Vizianagaram District, land was acquired in K.D. Peta Mandal for a glass factory that never became a reality.

8 per cent of the 74,500 residents of the mandal as a whole were Adivasis, and another 9 per cent were Dalits. The claim made in the EIA report was that '[t]he land identified for locating the Alumina refinery of 1,350 acres [546 hectares] consist of about 85 per cent government land and 15 per cent private land' (Vimta Labs 2007: C2–3). Since displacement would be 'minimal', affecting only 30 families, land acquisition was portrayed as unproblematic.

The Revenue Department was more precise in its internal instruction to acquire 368 hectares of assigned land, which was 68 per cent of the total area required, at a uniform price of Rs 500,000 per hectare. Another 84 hectares of government land was included in the same instruction, and this was also likely to have been cultivated since there is no vacant land in this intensely cultivated area. A significant but unknown part of the assigned land was in the hands of non-poor farmers with larger holdings, many of whom had already ceased farming on their own account and were living in nearby cities (Andhra Pradesh 2007b).[12] The remaining 68 hectares of private land, located in pockets between the assigned and government land, was acquired directly by the company, and there are no public records that identify the owners of this land or the compensation they would receive. Several of my own sources indicated that they would be compensated at significantly higher rates than the holders of assigned land, but the company suggested a smaller disparity in newspaper articles (Rama Raju 2009).

A detailed map showed that the refinery layout was split between three locations, with the main plant site and the two waste ponds separated from each other (JSW Aluminium 2007a). This was a peculiar choice, since the huge volumes of waste created by the refinery would clearly have been easier to dispose of if there had been one contiguous site. One reason for this design becomes apparent with the inclusion of nearby villages that did not appear on any official land acquisition maps. The locations of villages along the borders of the proposed site created the impression that project planners were attempting to cause a minimal level of displacement by acquiring agricultural land but not house sites. Another reason was that villages tend to be located close to water storage tanks that cannot

12 Land acquisition documents show that two relatives of the principal local politician, a major landowner in the area, had titles to assigned land.

legally be subject to compulsory acquisition. While 30 households would lose their house sites, which meant that they would be officially displaced, about 600 would lose agricultural land, and this type of loss would not be covered by the state government's rehabilitation policy.

A number of amendments were made to the land acquisition map, sometimes because it was found that ex-servicemen owned land parcels, though there does not seem to be any law prohibiting the acquisition of such land, or at other times because the land was found to contain or was adjoining a water tank (Andhra Pradesh 2008c). At yet other times, official documents simply stated that the land was either part of the refinery site or else excluded from it without giving any reasons (Andhra Pradesh 2008d, 2008e). If details of the planned land use were never clearly presented in the first instance, the many changes made with scant explanation only added to already significant levels of uncertainty.

Since proposed land acquisitions are meant to be advertised by notices placed in the local panchayat offices (see Figure 4.6), each change to the proposal risked spreading information that could create more awareness of what was being planned, and if people know what is being planned they can organise protests. In this case, the notices for the initial round of acquisition were never posted for public display to the villagers, and bureaucrats tried to conceal subsequent changes in the face of media and other pressure. This was done in early 2008 by amending the earlier government instruction for the land acquisition rather than issuing a new instruction that would require public notification (Andhra Pradesh 2008c). When local journalists found out and reported it in the local press, this did not result in more transparent government behaviour but an official government order, made a few weeks later, to make the changes more legitimate through compliance with various administrative procedures (Andhra Pradesh 2008d). Further delays meant that acquisition letters for the new land were only sent out a few months later (Andhra Pradesh 2008f) and, since no payments followed, the land portions were probably never acquired (Andhra Pradesh 2009a).

Figure 4.6 A deserted panchayat office close to the proposed refinery site.

Source: Photo by author, March 2008.

Some of the changes were linked to allegations of corruption. Local newspaper reports stated that the real reason for excluding some portions was not to exempt them from acquisition but to re-label them as areas of private land for which higher rates of compensation could be negotiated directly with JSW (Rama Raju n.d.).[13] But other changes did take some of the concerns of the poorest residents into account. A concession was made to one of the main demands of the refinery's opponents when 14 hectares of assigned land was excluded from the site because it belonged to tribal people who had previously been displaced (Andhra Pradesh 2008e).

The lack of clear information and the frequent changes made to the proposal kept many people on and around the site guessing whether their land was going to be acquired and, if so, what they might receive as compensation. Group discussions about the land acquisition map did not resolve the uncertainty. In one affected village, people felt that the government could make and change its plans at will:

13 There were also allegations of a Rs 100 million scam involving payments to non-existent farmers (LSP 2009).

> They can do anything. What they do today may not be valid for tomorrow. Today's collector will go tomorrow and most of the officials are transferred within a year. The new officers and the government are coming up with new schemes and procedures (interview, S. Kota Mandal, 26 January 2008).

The confusion over what was actually being planned made it difficult to create a mass movement that could put pressure on the bauxite alliance. But several people in the village that I surveyed indicated they had joined the protest group specifically because of the lack of information. They were protesting since they expected that their land, like that of their neighbours and relatives, would soon be acquired despite being excluded from the first two rounds of acquisition notices. Table 4.6 shows the losses projected at the time of my survey in March 2008.

Table 4.6 Projected land loss in a S. Kota village.

	Number	Landholdings (ha)	Projected loss
Households losing all land	2	0.81	0.81
Households losing some land	10	13.18	11.00
Households losing no land	7	9.64	--
Total	19	23.63	11.81

Source: Survey by author, March 2008.

Documents obtained more than a year later through the Right to Information Act showed that a total of 75 families were due to be displaced by the refinery, which was more than double the number indicated in the original planning documents (Andhra Pradesh 2007c). The reason for this discrepancy was not explained in any government document.

Compensation

JSW announced a special 'compensation package' for its refinery in addition to what the Andhra Pradesh resettlement and rehabilitation would have required. It offered one job for suitably qualified individuals from each of the estimated 600 families affected, irrespective of the type of land they would lose, or a one-off payment of Rs 300,000. Those displaced through loss of their houses, still estimated to be 30 families, would each receive a new house, a new cattle shed (valued at Rs 3,000) and transportation costs (up to Rs 5,000). So-called encroachers who could prove that they had been present in the area for more than five years would receive the same amount of compensation as those with valid land titles, but would not be entitled to employment on the project (Andhra Pradesh 2007d).

The kind of land compensation people could claim depended on the type of land they were cultivating and whether it appeared in the official records. The main strategies available for different types of land-losers are presented in Figure 4.7.

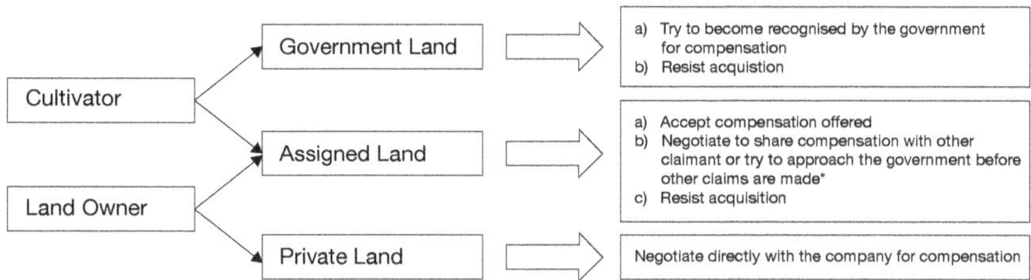

Figure 4.7 Typology of land compensation for the JSW refinery in S. Kota.

* Other potential strategies for particularly powerful individuals with assigned land were to try to get it excluded from acquisition completely or else to get it included in the private land negotiations for improved compensation.

Best off were those few landholders, less than 10 per cent of the total, who had private land titles, and who could negotiate directly with the company because they had the right to refuse to sell. Those cultivating or holding titles to assigned land could be fairly certain of receiving compensation, though the final amount paid would depend not only on whether their papers were in complete order, but also on whether they were aware of their rights under the proposed package.

Commissions could be extracted from illiterate people with faulty paperwork. Collaboration between bureaucrats and panchayat members across the four revenue villages, together with the local domination of the Congress Party, led to the suspicion that people higher up were demanding a share of such commissions. One of the prospective losers described the process as follows:

> They are offering 200,500 rupees per acre land. But they are cutting Rs 2,000 as land tax dues, they said we have not paid the land tax so far. Again they are cutting Rs 15,000 while drawing money. Altogether we are going to have loss of Rs 25,000 per acre land out of the offered compensation of 2 lakh so we will be paid only 1 lakh 75 thousand rupees (interview, S. Kota Mandal, 26 January 2008).

If the assigned land titleholder was not the actual cultivator, the two parties would have to informally determine how to share the compensation since the government would only base payments on the official records. According to a local journalist, this placed the titleholder in a better position than the cultivator, who had no legal way of contesting the payment or even of finding the actual titleholder (interview, S. Kota Mandal, 27 March 2008). The bargaining power of individuals was key to a settlement. A common proposal was to share the compensation equally between the titleholder and the cultivator, but some of the better off (non-tribal) farmers, who were able to access information about the land acquisition process, argued for a two-thirds share for themselves, leaving one-third for the titleholder. The cultivator of government land was in a similar position to the assigned land cultivator, since the lack of proper paperwork might completely exclude him or her from the receipt of compensation.

A sliding scale for compensation was thus created during the process of land acquisition for the refinery, from those with clear entitlements on paper and with knowledge of their rights, to those with unclear status or less knowledge of the government's rules, and finally to those who were paperless, landless and uninformed.

Many people were unhappy about the way the refinery had been imposed on them. As one older villager remarked: 'First they [the government] sold the land to Jindal. Next they will sell us.' To which a younger villager jokingly responded: 'Who would want to buy you? Land is useful but you are not' (group discussion, S. Kota Mandal, 26 January 2008). People's reactions varied between parts of the refinery site since there was little difference in the valuation of dry land (Rs 500,000 per hectare) as compared to irrigated land (Rs 560,000 per hectare). As a result, there was less resistance from the northwestern section of the proposed site, with its unirrigated land planted with cashew nuts. As one village head remarked: 'Earlier we got 10,000 per year from our lands and now we get 7 lakh in one go. Don't you think this is a good deal?' (interview, S. Kota Mandal, 19 March 2008).

Farmers without titles on government or assigned land were some of the strongest opponents of the project, since they were least likely to benefit from employment in the refinery. In a 2009 survey of the affected villages, it was found that half of the adults eligible for compensation had got temporary jobs on the minimum wage of Rs 2,200 per month, one-quarter was still hoping for employment, while the remaining quarter had decided to accept the cash payment of Rs 300,000 (Andhra Pradesh 2009b; Reddy and Mishra 2010).

Beyond making payment for the land being acquired, the company's efforts to 'develop this backward area' were quite ambitious (telephone interview, JSW employee, Visakhapatnam, 5 April 2008). The company aimed to transform farmers with no formal education into industrial workers in the course of one year spent in an industrial training centre. Even more implausible was a plan mentioned in an interview with one JSW employee to develop a call centre at one of JSW's subsidiaries in S. Kota town, where female farm labourers and housewives would be trained to become office workers with a salaries of at least Rs 20,000 per month. The company did not seem to be interested in helping people to continue the farming practices with which they were already familiar. The cash compensation on offer would be insufficient for anyone to rebuild an agricultural livelihood, since it was not enough to purchase land in the surrounding area.

Land Users out of Bounds

As has been shown, the direct compensation policies were tied to formal house and land ownership. However, the majority of people in the refinery area, as well as everyone in the mining area, were in the official 'project affected family' category, whose status was unclear. These included the many families in S. Kota Mandal who supported themselves as agricultural labourers, minor forest product collectors and livestock herders, or who were simply making a living just outside of the proposed refinery boundaries. In the poorly defined mining area, the situation was even more difficult because official documents did not acknowledge the existence of people living or using land within the proposed mining leases, despite the existence of fields, plantations and a few hilltop villages. As in the case of the refinery, being outside of the boundaries precluded any direct compensation claims.

What remained in terms of compensation at the mine site was general area support, such as the Samatha judgment's suggested investment of a share of the profits in a local development fund. The memorandum of understanding (MoU) stated that a 'minimum of 0.5 per cent of revenue [from the mining operations] shall be spent on the health, training, social infrastructure and welfare of tribals' (Andhra Pradesh 2005b: 4). No further details were provided, nor was it clear how much money would be available, given that most of the profits would come from the refinery, not from the mining operations. Only in the EIA report for the Galikonda mine was it proposed that Rs 58.7 million would be committed to a list of 'community development initiatives' that included entrepreneurship training, scholarships and general infrastructural improvements (ICFRE n.d.). Highly mechanised bauxite mining operations do not create many jobs (Bhushan and Zeya Hazra 2008), and first preference for jobs at the refinery would be given to those losing land in the S. Kota area.

Conclusion

In the two locations proposed for the bauxite industry, Adivasi villagers had long sustained themselves with marginal farming practices, but with a significant degree of self-reliance and some hopes for future improvement, either because of access to bore water for irrigated agriculture or through the establishment of coffee plantations. The limits to tribal land rights were acutely felt in both cases, since the proposed mine area was defined as forest, despite having many villages on the tops and sides of the bauxite hills, while the refinery area had been placed outside of the Scheduled Areas where tribal land legislation is applicable. Despite significant differences in the local contexts and the nature of the undertakings, very similar outcomes could be predicted when only cash compensation was offered to the few people who had formal land titles, excluding everyone in the proposed mining area and the many agricultural labourers and those depending on common property resources at the site of the proposed refinery.

In both cases, local people were left uninformed about what was being planned for the land and resources on which they depended for their livelihoods. At the proposed mine sites, people had virtually no information other than what they had been told by activists or journalists. At the refinery site, many remained uninformed about the extent of land acquisition, even while the land of their neighbours was being forcefully acquired. This was a sad result after decades of struggle, not only for land rights but also for the right to rehabilitation and participation in decisions about natural resource development. It seems Iyer (2007) is correct in stating that displacement policy in India has been returning to the earlier practice of only providing monetary compensation instead of attempting to make displaced people the beneficiaries of development.

While the framing of land tenure was found to be the main reason for inadequate compensation, the way planning was carried out further strengthened this tendency. Land acquisition took priority over social justice. The land tenure, compensation and mitigation policies were assembled by creative planners in such a way as to leave most people beyond their scope, or with only minimal compensation. In this manner, assigned land in the refinery area that was being cultivated by poor, mainly Adivasi farmers was reframed as government waste land of little value, while the proposed mining area was framed as uninhabited forest land, though not with actual forest on it, since that would have made it harder to obtain environmental approvals.

Additional land acquisition would be required for the planting of forests once the mining leases had been acquired, which raised the possibility of further dispossession. One forest plantation established to compensate for coal mining in the Scheduled Areas of Khammam District in Andhra Pradesh involved the acquisition of 10,000 hectares of land inhabited by Kondha Reddi tribals in West Godavari District, creating a form of double displacement (Sarin 2009). Likewise, 306 hectares of land for new forest plantations was allotted in Visakhapatnam and Narsipatnam districts to offset the operation of the Araku mines, and the prior use of this land was left unspecified in official documents (Andhra Pradesh 2005e).

There is no evidence that particular groups of people were targeted by ethnic or other criteria in the acquisition of land for the mine and refinery. The aim was simply to acquire land without creating protests that could completely derail the project plans. However, the distributional outcomes of this mode of planning are a matter of concern because the poorest of the poor were disproportionately affected. At the same time, there were instances where additional compensation was proposed, beyond what would have been strictly necessary according to government policies.

Unfortunately, several features of this process reflect the experience of other projects in central-eastern India. The layout of the alumina refinery for Vedanta Aluminium in Lanjigarh, Odisha, also left a number of villagers without their fields but living just beyond the boundary of the plant site, where they would face severe pollution (Amnesty International 2010). The land allocated to the nearby bauxite mine was likewise defined as forest land without any actual forest growth, leaving local people without compensation (Amnesty International 2011). Although mining project mitigation and reclamation are not very well studied in India, the risks created by the aluminium industry are not new, nor are those in charge of project planning unaware of them.[14] The problems created by outsiders coming to benefit from the natural resources of the Scheduled Areas are also well known (Vyasulu 1981; Singh 1986). The only new factor might thus be the opportunity for those affected to object to the plans.

14 See, for example, the debate between Srinivasan and others (1981) and Subrahmanyam (1982) on the establishment of Nalco, or the environmental survey of the aluminium industry by the Government of Odisha (Orissa 1996).

5. Government Mediation or Facilitation?

We have seen that concerns with Adivasi rights were relatively weak in the design of the bauxite project. Economic benefits would mainly be directed to the private investor, while Adivasi farmers would lose land to the project with only marginal compensation. While initial conditions thus looked unfavourable, implementation processes were still important. The way that the state government handled its multiple and often contradictory commitments, ensuring that due legal process was followed while facilitating project approvals and promoting private investment, became crucial in determining actual outcomes. The company itself was rarely visible in these processes, except at high-level meetings in Delhi or Hyderabad, but this was how the bauxite alliance had been formed. The state government was not expected to contribute any significant financial, technical or human resources to the actual establishment and operation of the project. Mediation is what the government, and especially top politicians, would do to justify a role in the alliance.

Mediation processes on the part of state and national government agencies determined the way in which the many existing concerns over what should happen to people, land, water, forests and minerals would be translated into actual outcomes. These took place in the complex system of regulatory control over investment approvals across national, state and local decision-making forums. At issue, though often couched in apolitical technical language, were power struggles over who should make decisions and who should benefit. The struggles over representation were not settled merely—or even mainly—in legal texts and policies, or even in the memorandum of understanding (MoU), but in these regulatory processes. This chapter therefore examines the extent to which democratically elected local bodies were able to make their voices heard, especially with respect to environmental issues.[1] If the mining and refining of bauxite ore were presented in technical reports as activities that would directly or indirectly affect local livelihoods, this could determine people's ability to demand inclusion in the decision-making process or their right to demand compensation from the result.

Recent Reform in the Approvals Regime across Federal India

India's federal government structure largely dictates the location of decision-making power with respect to mining investments. Since the Constitution says that land, water and minerals are all state matters, state governments should be firmly in charge. However, this has not generally been the case because the central government has had various ways of ensuring its own influence, initially through control of administrative licensing and funding approvals, and more recently through environmental and forest policy measures, as well as by virtue of its stronger financial position. In recent years, India's economic reform program has also involved significant changes to industrial and trade policies, with new openings for international trade and investment. This particular bauxite project would not have been possible without such policy reform, given its reliance on imported technology, some international funding and global markets for the end product.

Much attention has been paid in recent years to the transformation of India's interventionist state into a regulatory state (Rudolph and Rudolph 2001b). This has involved the setting up of independent regulatory bodies in sectors such as electricity or telecommunications in an attempt to avoid political interference. In other sectors, expert committees have been created to provide rule-based and 'scientific' forms of decision-making. The Ministry of Environment and Forests (MoEF) exemplifies this second form of regulation.

1 See Oskarsson (2015) for a previous version of this discussion.

The key government approvals for investment in mining and mineral-processing operations are those related to the environment, to forests and to land acquisition (India 2002c), as well the grant of actual mining leases (India 2006a: 2). Environmental impact assessment (EIA) was made mandatory for certain activities, including large-scale mining, in 1994 under the terms of the *Environment (Protection) Act 1986* and its subsequent amendments (India 2008f). Changes in the use of 'forest land' have to be approved by the central government under the *Forest (Conservation) Act 1980*, and proposals covering more than 40 hectares are examined by the Forest Advisory Committee under the MoEF (India 2008f). Licences to exploit 'major minerals', including bauxite, are covered by the *Mines and Minerals (Development and Regulation) Act 1957* and the National Mineral Policy of 2008 (which replaced an earlier policy from 1993). These three types of approval affect state government decisions to approve land acquisition, which may involve the exclusion of an industrial site from limits already placed on the extent of such acquisition, the re-zoning of land from agricultural to industrial use, or the removal of an industrial township from the jurisdiction of the local panchayat.

Examination of these approval processes in the present case suggests that the process of government mediation has limited utility. For all the plans and other documents that are produced, there is little mitigation of actual negative consequences for local people or their environments. Independent analysis of the issues is only really possible when activists pursue court cases or in those (rare) cases when media reports trigger further investigations. State government procedures are especially opaque and hard to follow.

Despite the economic reforms, the bureaucracy surrounding investment decisions has retained its complexity. In 2002, it was found that a typical mining project required 37 separate approvals at the central government level and 47 at the state government level (India 2002b). Existing regulations have been seen as major obstacles to investment and economic growth, even in official circles. A committee was already established under the Ministry of Commerce in 2002 with a view to speeding up the process and 'ensuring that scarce resources are deployed effectively' (India 2002c: 1). It was noted that 'while overall policy has been liberalised, reforms in institutional mechanism and procedural simplification to translate policy liberalisation into ease of doing business have generally lagged behind' (India 2002d: 7). Forestry and environmental approvals were found to be major stumbling blocks. The approval process might normally take about six months, but in some cases would take up to three or four years, which suggested a lack of procedural clarity and a case-by-case approach to regulation. The committee concluded that 'in order to simplify the procedures for grant of approvals, reduce delays and simplify regulation of projects during their operational phase, re-engineering of the regulatory processes … is an immediate necessity' (India 2002d: 15).

Over-regulation was also identified as the main problem to be addressed in the new National Mineral Policy, which could explain why 'the [mining] sector is unable to contribute to growth of the gross domestic product (GDP) of the country in any significant way, let alone up to its potential' (India 2006a: 12). The delays in procedures for granting reconnaissance permits, prospecting licences and mining leases under the Mines and Minerals Act became the main focus of the mineral policy committee, but this committee also stressed the need for the forest and environmental approvals to be 'speeded up' (ibid.: 2).

Nevertheless, much of the delay in the grant of mining leases was blamed on perceived state government interference. The federal mining minister, T. Subbarami Reddy, made this point at a conference of the Mining Engineers Association in Hyderabad in April 2007:

> Today it takes too much time to get all the licences you need for operations. There are too many clearances that act as hindrances. State governments have demanded value addition within their borders for granting of leases and this we want to limit. They will still be allowed to put up conditions but there will be time limits to how long this can go on before mining is freed.

Actual approval rates remained quite high during the period of national policy reform between 2006 and 2008. None of the 952 industrial projects, and only 10 out of 587 proposed mines, were rejected on environmental grounds (Dutta 2009). From 1998 to 2005, the MoEF had approved an average of 125 mines, involving 3,500 hectares forest land, each year, and the rate was now increasing (Bhushan and Zeya Hazra 2008). It would thus seem that delays in central government approvals were already having less of an impact on the development of new mineral projects. However, the push for reform was maintained in further committee reports (India 2008f), as well as in the 2012 proposal to set up a National Investment Board to ensure faster processing of especially large projects.

A closer reading of the actual legislation makes the regulatory changes seem less dramatic than the statistics on project approvals might indicate. The 2006 amendments to the Environment Act actually increased the scope and detail of the EIA regulations applied to the mining industry (India 2006b; Amnesty International 2011). This suggests that outcomes may have more to do with the changing priorities of decision-makers than with actual policy reform. Further evidence in this regard is the marked difference in the implementation of environmental regulations after the Congress Party's Jairam Ramesh became the responsible minister in 2009 and issued a note on the need to implement the Forest Rights Act of 2006 before any forest land could be used for industrial purposes (India 2009a). This had not been a concern for the previous minister, who had granted approvals for mining without regard to this legislation.

The terms of reference for the policy reform committees were not greatly concerned with the need to improve the quality of environmental regulation or take more account of the concerns of affected people. Nevertheless, the new mineral policy did include statements on the importance of sustainable development and support for Adivasi people:

> [A] framework of sustainable development will be designed which takes care of bio diversity issues and to ensure that mining activity takes place along with suitable measures for restoration of the ecological balance. Special care will be taken to protect the interest of host and indigenous (tribal) populations through developing models of stakeholder interest based on international best practice (India 2008d, para. 2.3).

State-level reform has proceeded with less debate in recent years, but along similar lines to the national process. For example, a 'single window clearance' office has been created for all investment applications in the Industry Department in Hyderabad, although this is only a case management office since approvals are still granted by each of the relevant departments. One informant told me that the main innovation consisted in the introduction of timelines and regular meetings to keep information flows moving between departments in order to prevent delays.

Despite the efforts of successive reform committees, central government legislation and regulations were still being added or amended at a fairly high rate, and the Forest Rights Act was one example that had a particular impact on the mining industry. State governments were operating in much the same manner, by amending existing policies and laws with 'government orders', such as those applied to compensation for land acquisition for the Jindal South West (JSW) bauxite project. Not only is it difficult to understand the overall policy intent of some of these changes, but frequent amendments at central and state levels have created a lot of uncertainty about what the law actually says. Civil society has shown some capacity to demand greater transparency in central government amendments, but changes at the state level have received less attention.

The uncertainty surrounding environmental regulations was compounded by legislative amendments in 2006 and 2008, additional ministry circulars, requirements contained in project-specific terms of reference documents, and the outcomes of court cases or the findings of special reports. For example, the controversial Lanjigarh alumina refinery and Niyamgiri bauxite mine in southern Odisha were together subject to at least seven special reports made on the initiative of the Supreme Court or the MoEF (India 2005a, 2007b; CMPDI 2006; WII 2006a, 2006b; Ramanathan 2010; Saxena et al. 2010). Additional reports on the JSW project included a watershed report (not made public) and a wildlife report (Azeez et al. 2008). As controversy has continued to follow bauxite projects in Adivasi parts of India, governments have typically responded by adding more and more information on which to base regulatory decisions, thus adding further complexity and opening opportunities for new challenges.

Public Consultation in the Approval Process

The only mandatory public consultation in the investment approval process is the environmental public hearing. This hearing, held at or close to the proposed project site, deals with information provided in the EIA report, but is only a source of advice to the ministry's grant of an environmental permit. However, wider public representation in matters of local natural land and resource use is possible under the *panchayat raj* legislation, with its vision of democratically elected local councils being part of a move towards greater decentralisation and self-governance. Although panchayats have been established in Andhra Pradesh since 1957 (Srinivasulu 2002), 73rd Constitutional Amendment of 1993 formalised the institution of *panchayat raj* as a mechanism of local governance in rural areas across the whole of India.

Panchayats operate in a three-tier system, from the village-level (*gram panchayat*) to the sub-district (*panchayat samithi*, known as *mandal parishad* in Andhra Pradesh) and the district-level (*zilla parishad*). At the village level, direct elections every five years hold panchayat members to account, but there are also village assemblies (*gram sabha*), comprising all eligible voters, that are intended to work as public forums for the maintenance of transparency and accountability (Johnson et al. 2003). Some panchayat seats are reserved for members of Scheduled Tribes, Scheduled Castes and Other Backward Castes, depending on their proportions amongst the local population, and 33 per cent of all seats are reserved for women.

Three main criticisms have been made of panchayat institutions over the years: states have been unwilling to devolve significant power to them; a resistant bureaucracy has limited their actual effectiveness; and local elites have influenced the outcomes (Srinivasulu 2002; Johnson 2003). In Andhra Pradesh, in recent years, the panchayats have often been bypassed in the allocation of development funds through the creation of a number of other institutions such as water user associations, self-help groups and joint forest management committees, while much of the actual control over development programs has remained with the bureaucracy. This was most noticeable during the rule of the Telugu Desam Party because the panchayats have traditionally been dominated by the Congress Party (Johnson et al. 2003).

The right of panchayats to be consulted over land acquisition was established in Andhra Pradesh after much protest and litigation, leading to a situation in which the gram panchayat and the gram sabha both had to provide their consent. However, once the right of consultation had been secured by litigation, the underpinning of the judgment could still be removed by changing the law, as happened in the High Court case over the construction of the Surampalem dam. According to Samatha activist Ravi Rebbapragada, the Andhra Pradesh Government introduced a resettlement policy that invalidated the earlier regulations.[2] In the case of the JSW alumina refinery, it was only thought necessary to consult the gram panchayat. Demands for the right of consultation have proven to be an ongoing struggle in which pressure has to be continually re-asserted.

The *Panchayat Extension to Scheduled Areas Act 1996* (PESA) was meant to establish panchayats in all of India's Scheduled Areas. The federal version of PESA gave priority to the gram sabha over the smaller gram panchayat, and empowered it to prevent land alienation, to be consulted on land

2 This assertion was made at a public meeting in Visakhapatnam on 26 March 2010.

acquisition, to have ownership rights over minor forest products, and the power to control local resource development plans and the grant of minor mineral leases. Section 4(i) of the Act stated:

> the gram sabha or the panchayats at the appropriate level shall be consulted before making the acquisition of land in the Scheduled Areas for development projects and before resettling or rehabilitating persons affected by such projects in the Scheduled Areas.

These provisions were stronger than those pertaining to land acquisition in non-scheduled areas, although the national legislation did not fully specify whether consultation actually meant seeking consent or simply an opinion from the gram sabha.

Actual implementation of the PESA has been weakened and varies by the requirement that specific legislation be passed by each of the states. The *Andhra Pradesh Panchayat Raj (Amendment) Act 1998* locates the process of consultation and planning at higher levels than the gram sabha. Consultation is supposed to take place at the sub-district level in the mandal parishad, while the actual planning and implementation of projects is coordinated at the state level. Decisions about the use of forests, water, land and minerals have never been fully devolved to the panchayats.[3]

Even this weaker Andhra Pradesh version of the PESA had questionable force, since the regulations required for it to come into effect were not published for more than 10 years (Dandekar and Choudhury 2010; Reddy and Mishra 2010). This legal technicality was not well known to members of the public who could see that panchayats exist, were participating in elections in the Scheduled Areas and were aware of the potential impact of the legislation.[4] The PESA regulations were finally made public in 2011, but by then the bauxite project plans had already been stalled for other reasons.

3 For example, the exploitation of minor forest products is still monopolised by the state government's Girijan Cooperative Corporation, with profit sharing but no real decision-making role for the panchayats (Reddy et al. 2004).

4 This type of technical delay is a tactic that had already been used in Andhra Pradesh, as it was with the Land Transfer Regulation of 1959, at least until a rebellion broke out in 1970 (Balagopal 1989).

The PESA legislation has not been implemented uniformly across central India. In Jharkhand and Odisha, panchayats are routinely ignored or else forced to agree to major land acquisitions by the presence of police (Bhaduri 2007). Saxena concludes that the legislation:

> has almost been forgotten and has not become part of mainstream political or policy discourse. … The implementation of the law has been severely hampered by the reluctance of most state governments to make laws and rules that conform to the spirit of the law. Weak-kneed political will has usually led to bureaucratic creativity in minimalistic interpretations of the law (Saxena 2005: 25–6).

The reluctance of the nine states with Scheduled Areas to implement the PESA has been explained by a former Madhya Pradesh chief minister, who said that '[i]ts implementation would put an end to mining projects' (Dandekar and Choudhury 2010: 18). However, such laws cannot be completely removed from the policy framework because of electoral pressure, and they remain as potential tools in political struggles to secure better representation for the poor.

Inter-Agency Disputes

While environmental public hearings have involved local people to some extent, the grant of forest clearance and mining permits has historically been the exclusive preserve of governments. However, this has not prevented contention between different levels of government or different agencies within them. As state governments have been given more freedom and responsibility to pursue their own economic development programs, disputes with the centre seem to have reduced in intensity, but they have not completely disappeared, as was evident in conflict over implementation of the new mineral policy.

A high-level meeting of key Andhra Pradesh state government departments was convened on 2 July 2005, the day after the bauxite project MoU with JSW had been signed. Attending this meeting were ministers and bureaucrats representing the Revenue, Forest and Environment, and Mines and Geology departments. Andhra Pradesh Mineral Development Corporation (APMDC) was also present and was given a key role in coordinating all activities to ensure that the necessary approvals would be forthcoming. This was important because of the record of previous conflict between the different agencies. The Forest Department had opposed plans to exploit the bauxite deposits ever since they were initiated in the 1980s, and had reiterated its opposition as recently as 2001 on the grounds that 'local people/NGOs [non-governmental organisations] were against plans; the proposed area is in notified tribal area; and the forest area is rich in flora and fauna' (Andhra Pradesh 2005c: 3). However, at this latest meeting, their minister reversed this position:

> The Hon'ble Minister for Forest informed that the mining of Bauxite will help in industrial growth of the nation and as bauxite capping is devoid of any forest, the Forest officials will immediately take steps for giving necessary clearances from the state government (ibid.: 4).

As tends to be the case with official documents, and despite explicit reference being made to the earlier conflict, no detailed reasons were provided for this reversal. Local people and NGOs were still opposed to the plans, it was still a notified tribal area, and it was unlikely that that any significant change to the local flora and fauna could have occurred since 2001. Nevertheless, the minutes of the meeting record that:

> It is decided that the Forest Department shall go through the proposals of APMDC submitted for forest clearance for Araku group of areas and accord clearance for the said areas and submit the proposals to the Government of India under Section-2 of the Forest Conservation Act 1980. If at all there are any procedural hurdles, the same shall be sorted out by way of direct interaction with the APMDC (Andhra Pradesh 2005c: 3).

An important element in the reduction of conflict between forestry and mining departments across India has been the principle of 'compensatory afforestation' established through the intervention of the Supreme Court. Application of this principle involves the payment of a calculated net present value for the existing forest and the planting of new forest elsewhere. Despite the many uncertainties surrounding its implementation, companies have seemingly been willing to pay the significant sums of money involved in order to allow their projects to move ahead, and forestry departments have been willing to exchange currently held land for new land somewhere else.

If forest clearance for the bauxite project mining had ceased to be issue within the state government, it became a problem when JSW was asked to pay for the net present value of the forest at the proposed mine sites. Two new MoUs were signed in 2007, two years after the initial agreement, to deal with this issue. The first required that the money should be paid 'upfront' (Andhra Pradesh 2007e), but the second, signed three months later, omitted the whole clause on forest compensation without further explanation (Andhra Pradesh 2007f). It is not clear whether the Andhra Pradesh Government had agreed to pay the costs itself, or whether JSW had agreed to pay on condition that there was no official record of its agreement. The payments could not simply be ignored or waived because the Supreme Court was monitoring the implementation of the compensatory afforestation principle.

In any case, the project come to a halt, from which it has not recovered, when the rare Blewitt's Owl (also known as the Forest Owlet) was reportedly sighted in the proposed mining area. As tends to be the case, a new study was commissioned by the government to find out whether the bird was indeed present and, if so, what could be done to mitigate the impact of mining on its habitat. The year-long study failed to find this owl, but 11 other species of owl were found instead (Azeez et al. 2008).

The most interesting aspect of this study was its limited frame of reference. For some unknown reason, it was restricted to the Araku Valley and the JSW project area, and paid no attention to the AnRak Aluminium project area, despite clear indications that the same owls might be present there.

> The Orissa Bird and Bio-cultural survey have undertaken an ornithological survey of the Eastern Ghats and … rediscovered the highly endangered bird 'Blewitt's owl' near Araku and proposed to designate the entire belt covering Sileru to Lammasingi, Paderu to Araku and Ananthagiri, etc. as an 'Important Bird Area' (IBA) of the country (Andhra Pradesh 2007g: 2).

The area designated in the Forest Department's terms of reference covered all the bauxite ore deposits, which implied that the new study should cover the whole of the Agency. The omission of the Jerrila area could have been due to some oversight, but the implications were significant. Since they were not covered by the new study, AnRak Aluminium's Jerrila mines were quickly granted their environmental permits in May 2009. The timing of this approval turned out to be crucial, just ahead of elections that enabled a new environment minister to take charge, with a more stringent interpretation of the law.[5] However, it has since seemed unlikely that the Jerrila mines would gain final approval for forest clearance.

5 This also occurred at a time when Vedanta's controversial Niyamgiri bauxite was making headlines nationally and internationally (Kumar 2014).

The Exclusion of Local Decision-Making

The opportunities for local deliberation over the JSW project came to focus on the proposed refinery rather than the mining proposals. That was partly because the Andhra Pradesh version of the PESA had not been made effective at the time, and partly because no environmental public hearings had yet been held for the mining proposals.

Land Acquisition and Panchayat Raj

As we have seen, the land required for the alumina refinery was spread over five panchayats in S. Kota Mandal and thus required separate decisions to be made for each one. Despite being named as a single village council, each of the panchayats in S. Kota consists of a number of independent villages and hamlets, none having more than a few hundred inhabitants and sometimes only a few families. Within each of the panchayats there was only a relatively small amount of land to be acquired, which meant that many of the panchayat members would neither be losing their own land nor be resident in the affected villages. Since the S. Kota area is non-scheduled, the elected panchayat members included a mixture of tribal and non-tribal people. The five panchayat heads (*sarpanches*), though not especially wealthy, were significantly better off than most other residents and were somewhat isolated from the demands of the villagers threatened with the loss of land. Perhaps more crucially, all five were non-tribal people aligned with the Congress Party, even though they were not meant to be affiliated with any political party, while many of the project's key opponents were supporters of the main opposition party, Telugu Desam.

Panchayat approvals were provided soon after the refinery site had been chosen. The first step was an administrative order that directed the relevant local government employees to organise panchayat meetings before the end of December 2006 (Andhra Pradesh 2006c). According to interviews I conducted in March 2008, the five panchayat heads presented almost identical resolutions to the five meetings, which had been drafted 'in consultation with' an influential Congress politician on the zilla parishad. The only difference between them consisted of the details of the land parcels to be acquired (KGP 2006; MGP 2006).

A tribal panchayat member from the village I surveyed during my fieldwork, who appeared to be drunk most of the time, said that he knew nothing of these plans, but admitted that (being illiterate) he usually put his thumbprint on any document with which he was presented. I was not able to find any signed and verified copies of the panchayat and gram sabha resolutions, and I am sure that none of the affected villagers had ever seen them either. One can only assume that the resolutions were adopted because the process of land acquisition and environmental approval actually moved ahead.

The long reach of the bauxite alliance into the refinery site had its roots in the control it exercised over local political institutions. The exact nature of this control is difficult to grasp but it involved the distribution of money and power and a measure of control over the local bureaucracy. The influence of the Congress politician on the district council was not only derived from his elected position but also from the fact that his family were the biggest landowners in the area. His influence in the district was closely linked to his relationship to the regional 'strongman', a Congress politician and state government minister at the time, who had direct access to the chief minister.

Had it not been possible to secure the panchayat approvals quickly and then conceal them from public view, a local opposition movement could have gained in strength. An interview with an agricultural extension worker, who was frequently sent out to undertake surveys for land acquisitions in the area, confirmed the way that these approvals were handled. Administrators normally keep out of the way while party workers and politicians figure out ways to deal with potential opponents. The prevention of meaningful deliberations over land acquisition is consistent with the broader Indian experience in which 'decentralisation has failed to prevent a local (and primarily landed) elite from controlling the local bodies' (Johnson et al. 2003: 2).

Bureaucratic interventions in land acquisition in Andhra Pradesh have thus tended to favour displacement with a minimum of local deliberation. The process of land acquisition for 'special economic zones' in Andhra Pradesh has been described as follows:

> The role of local revenue administration … is crucial in making or rather pressurizing farmers to concede without resistance to the establishment of an SEZ. Using their connections with the local pyravikaars [fixers] and the Panchayat raj functionaries, the subaltern bureaucracy of the Revenue Department could successfully spread the message that there was no point in resisting land acquisition as the government has supreme power to acquire 'any land, any where, any time' (Srinivasulu 2010: 13).

The author of this observation does not say whether the administrators were operating on their own initiative or at the direction of people above them, but in the case of the JSW refinery, local bureaucrats were rewarded for work that was controlled by politicians at higher levels who would make phone calls to various departments to make sure that land acquisition tasks were completed.

While it was possible for JSW to swiftly secure panchayat and gram sabha approvals through Congress Party connections that reached all the way to the proposed refinery site, much energy was also spent on avoiding the same procedures for the proposed mines in the Agency. It is not clear why it would have been more difficult to get the desired decisions in a similar manner for the mines, given that I found the Araku panchayats to be politicised in much the same way. Perhaps it was due to earlier difficulties encountered in attempts to convince members of the Tribal Advisory Council of the benefits of bauxite mining (Prasad 2000), or else because the uncertain status of panchayat regulations in the Agency created greater risk of messy discussions or negative newspaper coverage.

On several occasions, APMDC expressed the view that there was no need to consult panchayats before mining could be approved in the Agency, but gave different reasons on different occasions. At one point, the argument was that 'major minerals' like bauxite do not require consultation as the PESA only grants local decision-making rights over minor minerals (Anon. 2008c; HRF 2008a). A subsequent argument was that the environmental public hearing would be sufficient as a form of consultation. One unnamed 'senior officer' from APMDC was quoted as saying that '[a]s per the Mines and Minerals Regulations the outcome of the public hearing is construed as the consent of the people' (Anon. 2009b). These occasional statements from APMDC could be easily countered in the media by arguments that the PESA also grants decision-making rights over forest products and water bodies clearly affected by mining, while the environmental public hearing is based on legislation entirely distinct from the Mines and Minerals Act and the PESA. However, arguments made in the press did not lead to greater inclusion in the decision-making process, and so the protests continued (see Chapter 6).

Environmental Public Hearings

Since the refinery was seen as something that would pave the way for the more controversial mines, much of the discussion at the public hearing in S. Kota was about the mining proposal rather than pollution control measures at the refinery itself. About 1,000 people attended the hearing that was held on 4 June 2007, including party activists, NGO representatives and some of the affected people. The JSW representative gave a detailed explanation of the benefits to the government, to construction contractors and to local people, concluding with an assertion that 'there will not be any adverse environmental impacts in the surroundings due to the proposed industry' (Andhra Pradesh 2007h). The minutes of the meeting record that some 40 people spoke, and 96 per cent of those attending were opposed to the project.

The environmental public hearing has only a consultative status, so there is no requirement for its recommendations to be implemented. However, it was not possible to completely ignore such a level of opposition. Further discussions on the environmental approval took place at a meeting of the Expert Committee of the MoEF in Delhi's central administrative district in October 2007. Representatives of the Andhra Pradesh Government and JSW had been invited to respond to questions about why people were opposing the project. According to the minutes of this meeting:

> Representatives of the Government of A.P. informed the Committee [that] [m]ost of the persons [who] attended the Public Hearing were outsiders and not the real stake holders and directly affected parties … [A]ll the local authorities concerned with the project whose consent is necessary and all the Sarpanches/Panchayats/Hamlets have supported the project without any reservation (India 2007d).

Once blame had been laid at the feet of protesters who were outsiders, the signatures of the local Congress Party sarpanches would be sufficient to verify that the *real* project-affected people were indeed in favour of the refinery. This was seemingly sufficient to satisfy the MoEF experts and the refinery was thus approved six months after the stormy public hearing (India 2007e).

Neither activists nor those losing land had any knowledge of such high-level meetings in faraway Delhi. Agendas for such meetings are usually posted in advance on the MoEF website, for those who can access it, but the minutes would at that time not normally be available until more than a month after the meeting had actually taken place. This gave the planners a significant time advantage. Land acquisition actually commenced only a few days after the environmental permit was issued on 18 December 2007.

No public hearing was held for the proposed mines during the course of 2007 or 2008, but indications of how it would proceed could be inferred from the hearing that took place in October 2008, in Chintapalli town, for AnRak Aluminium's proposed Jerrila mine. A large gathering of protestors arrived at the site of the hearing, but so did a large contingent of police, who stopped and checked all approaching vehicles for suspected Maoists. No discussions under the terms of the PESA had so far been held in that area, and although titles had been claimed under the Forest Rights Act, none had so far been granted. The distance of the hearing from the proposed mine site, combined with the obstacles placed in the way of people's attendance, resulted in a walkout by opponents who were present. That left the APMDC representatives and one university professor from Visakhapatnam. The hearing was seen to have been completed, and the environmental permit was subsequently approved in May 2009.

The environmental public hearing remains the only mandatory forum for public information and debate about major project proposals despite its inadequacies. In some cases, it has at least provided information about forthcoming land acquisitions that represents a risk for project proponents in case opposition builds. To avoid this 'risk', the Andhra Pradesh Government was able to acquire land for the AnRak Aluminium refinery without a public hearing by declaring the site to be part of an industrial park that would count as a 'special economic zone', where a number of companies would have to commit to an investment before its environmental impact could be assessed. In this case, it turned out that there was only one company in the park, but by the time that the hearing was held, all the required land was already in the hands of the government. The result was that there was really very little left to discuss at the hearing, other than the amount of money that local people should receive by way of compensation, and the environmental permit was granted in August 2008.

Water for the Refinery or for Visakhapatnam City?

Even the municipal councillors of Visakhapatnam city, the second largest city in the formerly undivided state of Andhra Pradesh, have found it difficult to withstand the influence of the chief minister over access to vital local resources. Water access is a very sensitive topic in this city because of frequent scarcity in the dry summer season. The JSW refinery would be located right next to the Tatipudi reservoir and would need as much as 30 million litres of water per day (see Figure 5.1). The water in this reservoir had so far been used for domestic consumption and local agriculture. The EIA report on the refinery did not clearly state how its water requirements would be met. It said that the water might be obtained from the Raivada reservoir, which was somewhat further away, 'or from such other sources or from any existing water reservoir with approval of Govt of Andhra Pradesh which have no impact on local environment' (Vimta Labs 2007: C2–3).

Figure 5.1 The Tatipudi reservoir next to the proposed JSW alumina refinery.

Source: Photo by author, January 2008.

On 28 May 2007, one week before the public hearing, JSW issued a press release stating that the water would be derived from a pipeline controlled by the Greater Visakhapatnam Municipal Corporation (GVMC), and not from the Raivada reservoir, 'in view of apprehensions expressed by some sections of people in the media' (JSW Aluminium 2007b). Meeting minutes from the chief minister's office reveal that this change of plan had been made at a high-level meeting in that had just been held in Hyderabad (Andhra Pradesh 2007i, 2007j).

This proposal would not be popular with the residents of a rapidly growing city that was already short of water. The water in question would have to be derived from the giant Polavaram dam across the Godavari River, but construction of this dam had been blocked by litigation for several years and, in any case, water from this source had already been promised to farmers who given up part of their share in water from the Raivada reservoir when its water was diverted to Visakhapatnam city in 1997 (Andhra Pradesh 2007k). Furthermore, existing sources were already insufficient for the future needs of Visakhapatnam city, whose domestic requirements were projected to grow dramatically from 304 million litres per day in 2007 to 614 million in 2021, while industrial requirements were expected to reach 1,151 million litres per day in the same year. In 2007, the daily supply was down to 54 million litres because of recent drought conditions. The Godavari water would add another 810 million litres per day, but this was a long way short of meeting the projected requirements (Andhra Pradesh 2007l).

Nevertheless, a water supply contract was signed with the Visakhapatnam Industrial Water Supply Corporation (VIWSC), a joint venture between GVMC, the central government company Vizag Steel and the private company Larsen and Toubro, with GVMC holding a 51 per cent majority stake. Newspaper accounts in the month following the public hearing revealed intense debate about the terms of the water supply agreement amongst the city councillors, which initially led them to revoke it (Anon. 2007a). Subsequent articles indicated that they were pressured to approve it after all, but did not indicate the nature of this pressure or who was exerting it (Anon. 2007b, 2007c; Patnaik 2007). A few weeks later, the mayor declared that the approval had been given (Anon. 2007d), but once again there was no explanation of this change of mind nor any account of how GVMC would manage to supply its different customers in future. One activist told me in an interview that the 'city council is just following what the [chief minister] wants whether there is enough water or not'(29 March 2008).

There was a further twist to this story when the MoEF's letter of approval for the refinery, written in December 2007, specified the Tatipudi reservoir as its water source. According to this document, the '[t]otal water requirement from Canal/Tatipudi reservoir will be 8 MGD (1400 m^3/h) and permission is accorded by the Greater Visakhapatnam Municipal Corporation (GVMC) [via] letter dated 28th May, 2007' (India 2007e: 2). To make matters even more confusing, both the JSW press release and the MoEF letter referred to the same GVMC letter to support their different versions of the project plan. The GVMC letter actually did specify the Godavari River as the source (Andhra Pradesh 2007m), but the MoEF letter appeared to have more authority than a corporate press release, so the uncertainty persisted in a new round of media debate (Anon. 2008d; Patnaik 2008). While the contract to supply Godavari water to JSW was technically still in place, the VIWSC allocated a further 38 million litres per day to the AnRak Aluminium refinery, further deepening the water supply conundrum (Andhra Pradesh 2008g).

This simply intensified the level of public protest. In 2008, the Telugu Desam Party, now in opposition, organised a major strike (*mahadharna*) over the issue, while activists resorted to litigation in 2009 (Anon. 2008e, 2009c). Meanwhile, the state government took no action, at least in public, to resolve the issue. Whether and how water would be provided to Visakhapatnam city, to local farmers or to the JSW refinery would seemingly depend on how much, if any, would be available from the Godavari River, and then on the balance of power between different groups of potential consumers at some point in the not so distant future. If the recent past was any guide to the outcome, it would most likely be the farmers who would lose out, while the elected politicians would find somebody else to blame for their own decisions or lack of decisions to deal with the problem of water scarcity.[6]

6 When water was diverted from the Raivada reservoir to Visakhapatnam city residents in 1997, then Congress Party opposition politician Konathala Ramakrishna went on a hunger strike on behalf of the farmers. In the period from 2004 to 2009, he was the most powerful state government minister from Visakhapatnam District and a strong supporter of the bauxite project. In 2008, Telugu Desam Party politicians were keen to highlight this paradox, but remained silent about the fact that, when in government, they were the ones who had originally decided on the diversion (Anon. 2007e).

Bringing People Back In

The story so far is one of state government attempts to curtail debate about land use and water access. However, this does not represent the whole picture, since there are different opinions on what should be done in the different arms of the government at both state and federal levels. Ongoing negotiations about public participation in decision-making show that new opportunities might emerge as soon as old ones are found to be blocked by vested interests that want to limit the debate.

The existence of internal disagreements in the state government became apparent when the Tribal Welfare Department was encouraging people in Araku to claim land titles under the Forest Rights Act (Andhra Pradesh 2007n), while the Mines and Geology Department was attempting to alienate the same land. Biodiversity conservation concerns focused on the endangered Blewitt's Owl suddenly halted the mining project in Araku and Ananthagiri mandals and offered another chance to settle the forest rights, but many uncertainties remained even if that process could be completed. What legal protection would exist against the acquisition of such forest rights as compared to private land titles, to what extent would people be consulted before such acquisitions took place, and how would compensation be calculated? The Forest Rights Act is silent on these issues, so it was likely that future litigation would have to decide the outcomes.

The most recent of the often bewildering changes taking place in the battle over local representation was the MoEF circular that required gram sabhas across India to be consulted before any land claimed under the Forest Rights Act could be used for other purposes, and also required a majority of members to approve the proposal and the compensation arrangements (India 2009a). The new federal minister's support for the legislation also appeared to support the implementation of the Samatha judgment. However, the fractured openings in an ever-changing and contradictory regulatory system mean that only some of those who might benefit from such openings would actually be able to take advantage of them. Making use of these openings would depend on their ability to access information about their potential rights and then find an appropriate way to approach the government, directly or indirectly, in order to exercise them. The people of the Agency were unlikely to be able to do this on their own, but since tribal welfare and mining issues are pursued by some of the most capable civil society actors in the state, they might end up in a better position than the tribal people on the plains of S. Kota.

Technical Exclusions in EIA Reports

Aside from the bureaucratic procedures that constrain panchayat deliberations, a technical approach to the avoidance of any public deliberation is to frame EIA reports in ways that render people invisible, and thus make all environmental mitigation efforts a matter of scientific rather than community concern. If people and their lives are seen to be affected, either directly from a loss of land or other resources, or indirectly by pollution from a proposed industrial project, this can trigger the application of various legal protections. But if such impacts are concealed, the affected people must first make themselves visible before they can fight for their rights.

EIA reports on bauxite mining in India have tended to discuss pollution as a matter for technical measurement and mitigation practices that are equally applicable in all locations, rather than something that needs to take local livelihoods and environments into consideration (Tingay 2010). Despite these deficiencies, EIA reports have long been the only detailed public documents dealing with this issue, and have therefore received much attention from activists across India, despite their lack of reference to local circumstances (Bedi 2013). While social concerns might be more usefully addressed in a separate social impact assessment, there was no legal requirement for such a process for many years. By 2006, the MoEF guidelines only contained a few clauses relating to social concerns, with a primary focus on the use of agricultural and forest land (India 2006b). Even then, detailed land use information was routinely absent from bauxite project EIA reports (Vimta Labs 2006; BS Envi Tech 2008; Global Experts 2008; ICFRE 2008), but this did not prevent regulators from granting environmental permits.

The task of the EIA process has mainly been confined to measuring existing levels of pollution in a given area, detailing the pollution control techniques to be implemented by project proponents, and then estimating the future pollution levels once the project has started. So long as the future pollution load is within the national limits for all the measurement locations within a 10 km radius of the proposed site, there are few regulatory options for withholding approval. But even with this narrow frame of reference, there have still been reasons to question the technical validity of the reports (Vimta Labs 2006; Bhushan and Zeya Hazra 2008; BS Envi Tech 2008; ICFRE 2008; Dutta 2009; Amnesty International 2011). These include the way in which general statistics are provided for the whole of the 'study area' rather than for the smaller area that is to be acquired and used. In addition, the discrepancy between planning and implementation is known to be a major issue (Behera 2008; Nayak 2008; Amnesty International 2010).

Refinery Impact Assessment

There were several ways in which plans for the JSW refinery planning rendered local people invisible, and the land acquisition process left them more vulnerable to pollution than was necessary. The 10 km radius study area contained a potentially affected population of 65,155, but as we have seen, there was a much higher concentration of tribal people in the area immediately adjacent to the site (Table 4.6), and this point was overlooked in all the official plans (Vimta Labs 2007). Furthermore, the stated goal of minimising the level of official displacement was really just an effort to circumvent house sites, leaving hundreds of people in the immediate vicinity of several potential sources of pollution without significant buffer zones. The waste ponds could spread pollution in three ways: as dust in the event of strong winds, as water overflowing the waste pond walls in the event of a flood, or as leakage into the groundwater if the ponds were not properly sealed. Living in close proximity to the waste ponds was thus likely to be a major health risk. Air pollution from the processing plant and the thermal power plant was also a major issue, and local livelihoods were indirectly threated by a reduction in the productivity of agricultural land.

Water and air samples were collected as part of the EIA process, but the chosen locations had no clear rationale from the point of view of pollution prevention or health risks to the local population. Groundwater samples were likewise collected at locations other than those of the proposed waste ponds. When the report stated all emissions would be within the prescribed limits, it was assumed that there would be no risks to human health and safety or to plants and water sources (Vimta Labs 2007).

The report did not even mention the fishing pond located between the main plant site and the red mud waste pond, nor the Chilikalagedda stream running along the border of the proposed fly ash pond. There was no mention of existing groundwater levels, which were likely to be shallow because of the site's proximity to the Tatipudi irrigation reservoir. No hydrological maps were included to indicate the location of other water bodies and their flows. It was therefore impossible to evaluate the risks involved in a potential spill from one of the waste ponds. The report gave the general impression that on all accounts the refinery was an opportunity for economic development with only minor risks:

> The proposed alumina refinery has certain level of marginal impacts on the local environment. However, development of this project has certain beneficial impact/effects in terms of providing the employment opportunities that the same will create during the course of its setting up and as well as during operational phase of the project (Vimta Labs 2007: C9–1).

Mining Impact Assessment

The Galikonda EIA report described an operation area for the mine where no displacement would take place (ICFRE n.d.). No mention was made of the one village that did exist on top of the hill and whose site would seemingly have to be acquired. By denying the existence of any displacement or compensation issues for local people, the report could be safely framed in terms of compensating the relevant government agency for any forest loss. The exact boundaries of the mining areas were not clearly presented in the EIA report, nor did the report consider the precarious locations of many villages in the valleys below the proposed mine site. Little consideration was given to the potential impacts of dust pollution, water runoff, falling boulders and other debris on agricultural productivity. It simply promised that pollution levels would fall within the prescribed norms.

While the report denied the existence of any measurable risks, it nevertheless stated that 'local people have the apprehension that their coffee plantation[s] may be disturbed' and they 'perceived that the water requirement for the Mines may reduce their water availability' (ICFRE n.d.: 192), but it did not provide a scientific assessment of these concerns. Instead, it proposed '[c]ompensation of local people for their disturbance of agriculture/plantation lands, and deterioration of soil quality due to soil erosion, landslides, flooding, loss of fertility etc.' and '[c]ompensation in terms of loss of agricultural crop/coffee plantations' (ibid.: 151). It seems as if the environmental experts were not willing or able to side with those who might suffer negative consequences, but were finding ways to recommend some remedies without acknowledging whether local people's concerns were justified or not. Compensation thus appeared as a form of local welfare rather than a right. Other mining projects might not be obliged to provide even this limited level of support.

Conclusion

Given the closed nature of government (and company) operations, the examination of mediation in this chapter has had to rely almost exclusively on public documents complemented by interviews with outside commentators. This certainly created challenges in determining the nature of top-level government interventions, but could not hide a pattern of political influence over state and federal government decision. The outcome was a pattern of facilitation that almost exclusively interpreted policies and framed interventions in favour of project implementation.

It is clear that, given the many social clauses in relevant legislation, it took a fair amount of effort for the bauxite alliance to facilitate the required investment approvals and avoid responding to outside voices that would not have approved of their plans. This facilitation took place in an extremely dispersed authority structure because of the federal nature of governance in India. Key leaders of the Andhra Pradesh Government were certainly influential within relevant state agencies and were a key part of the national coalition government, but their influence was not unlimited. When chief minister Y.S. Rajasekhara Reddy died in a helicopter accident in 2009, project implementation ground to a halt, since he was the one politician who could possibly have exerted sufficient high-level influence to untangle the complex web of investment approvals.

These complicated procedures did not themselves serve to allay concerns relating to displacement, environmental degradation and water use, and yet the fact that so many protective laws exist, and more continue to be added, indicate opportunities for wider concerns to be raised. There is thus a strong tension between the political efforts to facilitate investment on one hand, and the continued existence of policies that attempt to improve social justice on the other. And government action that mainly worked to facilitate private investment in this project generated a lot of opposition against what was perceived as the planning of unjust outcomes. The next chapter examines the formation of this opposition.

6. Oppositional Noise from the Fringes

Despite the pessimistic findings of the previous chapter, where government mediation overall showed little concern for upholding the social and environmental legislation intended to protect Adivasis, there were many actors who worked towards a broader and more inclusive perspective. Over the years, a large number of individuals and organisations have protested against bauxite mining plans on the grounds of a need to protect Adivasi land and the impossibility of properly compensating those who would be affected. For opposition to the Jindal South West (JSW) bauxite project to have a significant impact, it would have to open the government to engagement outside of the private sphere of policymaking and project implementation where issues were being addressed with select business interests. Meaningful mediation depends not so much on government capacity but on the amount of pressure civil society actors are able to exert.

The first challenge for opponents of the JSW bauxite project was to find enough grassroots support to allow for large-scale mobilisation at the proposed project sites. If large numbers turned out, this would give increased legitimacy to oppositional activities, but given their severe lack of resources, poor people in the remote hills of the Agency would find it very difficult to create and sustain an opposition movement. Nevertheless, tribal social movements have at times been very strong in Andhra Pradesh as well as in many other parts of India. For example, local people protested strongly against the proposed bauxite project in Kashipur, in the neighbouring state of Odisha. As one activist commented:

> Kakinada is the one place in Andhra Pradesh where there is a strong local movement against a project. People tend to look down on Orissa for being backward and say that in AP we have so many movements but this is not really true on the ground. In Andhra Pradesh there is not the same type of grassroots resistance … (interview, Visakhapatnam, 3 January 2008).

On the other hand, the weakness of local resistance in Andhra Pradesh was perceived as a sign of maturity by another activist:

> There is not the same strength of movements in Andhra Pradesh but also not the same domination by outside middle class leaders as in north India. You have to show you are giving real benefits rather than go on talking about the same old thing, whether this is the Samatha judgment or the Forest Rights Act (interview, Hyderabad, 22 February 2008).

A better explanation instead for the relatively low level of local opposition to the JSW bauxite project was the small size of the directly affected population. If the government had proposed to change land rights legislation across Andhra Pradesh, then a much larger opposition would have been expected. A representative of the Communist Party of India (Marxist) (CPM) in Visakhapatnam District recalled:

> TDP [the Telugu Desam Party] was outright trying to change the 1/70 Act [the 1970 Land Transfer Regulation] which was against the interest of all tribals and got massive protests until the deal was cancelled. The Congress says it is upholding the 1/70 but does mining. In this way, mining has become a local issue with less protests compared to earlier (interview, Araku, 8 May 2008).

There were also special challenges facing any potential social protest in the Agency. The continuous Naxalite presence since the 1960s had resulted in significant security operations by the state government, often restricting the scope for public activity. Encounter killings of suspected militants used to be rampant as part of the state government's attempts to combat the Maoists (Balagopal 2006). Naxalite activity in the Agency had declined over the previous decade, largely due to the presence of the special Greyhound police force. Nevertheless, people associated with the government, including some who expressed support for bauxite mining, had still been killed by the Naxalites (Anon. 2007f, 2007g, 2008f; Sreenivas 2009). Even a limited Maoist presence made it more difficult for political parties and non-governmental organisations (NGOs) to operate in the Agency, while enabling the government to frame opponents as Maoists. On the other hand, while local members of the (mainstream) Communist Party of India (CPI) were jailed for agitating against bauxite mining during the period of my fieldwork, mainstream parties did not seem to be overly restricted in their abilities to organise public meetings or move between villages. A former Naxalite supporter had even been elected as member of the legislative assembly (MLA) for Paderu, the constituency next to the proposed Araku mines in the Agency.

Only one example was found of an independently organised local group opposed to the bauxite industry. This was the Adivasi Vimukti Sangathan (Adivasi Liberation Organisation), also based in Paderu. Its members were young people from the first generation of educated Adivasis, who had chosen to stay in the smaller towns of the Agency rather than migrate in search of better job opportunities on the plains. Other groups called themselves 'community-based organisations', but were actually dependent on external funding from larger NGOs or were related to an established political party. One example would be the Andhra Pradesh Girijan Sangham (Tribal Organisation/Movement), which was the local wing of the CPM. When money gives voice, the voice is ultimately that of non-tribal people.

The village leaders[1] whom I encountered in the Agency were largely non-committal on whether they would join a bauxite mining protest movement or not. Since no activity was evident on the ground at the time, they had seemingly adopted a wait-and-see strategy. People in one village indicated their willingness to send a few people to protest rallies, despite their recognition of the importance of Congress Party contacts. Another village had seen internal strife when a few educated villagers argued against the village head's support of the mining project. Yet other village leaders around the same bauxite hill already had roles as members of parties and/or NGOs who were strongly opposed to the project. Despite the ambivalence shown in my interviews, the general sentiment against the mining proposal was sufficiently widespread to make government officials warn us against venturing into the villages.

It appeared that the lack of local mobilisation was a cause of some concern amongst the activists who had been making good use of the courts. One said that the project 'will come through [move forward] but

1 Responses to my questions indicated that the village head's traditional authority is rarely questioned, but the extent of this authority is likely to vary between villages.

right now the tribals of Vishakhapatnam are resisting. It is ultimately the physical resistance which counts. When the bulldozers come, are you going to remain standing?' (interview, Hyderabad, 7 March 2007).

The low level of mobilisation did not necessarily mean that local people were passive. They just did not have the means to voice their opinions, so waited until a tangible target presented itself. As one said:

> They [JSW] did not ask to give our land to them. They did not know people's opinion, there is no agreement with [the] gram sabha. All this was done in [a] secret manner. They are working [surveying the land] when we are away from the fields. When we see these people working on our land, we catch them and beat them and give the information to newspaper reporters. We have done this two to three times (interview, S. Kota Mandal, 26 January 2008).

I found no evidence of government workers or surveyors being beaten up, some people were able to display survey equipment that they had confiscated, and newspaper reports had certainly been written.

People in the Agency, like those in the S. Kota area before them, would use 'weapons of the weak' (Scott 1985), such as acts of sabotage or other disruptive activities, against any visible targets. These were the only means available to them when most of the project planning took place in inaccessible government and business offices far from their place of residence. It was also clear that more violent action could result in people getting arrested when the government could claim to have followed the law.

The Opposition to the Bauxite Project

When the level of local mobilisation was limited, campaigning by non-tribal organisations and parties took on crucial importance. A number of NGOs[2] and left-wing parties formed the core of the opposition. The Bharatiya Janata Party and the Telangana Rashtra Samithi Party have virtually no presence in coastal Andhra Pradesh, so have never taken a position on the issue. All other parties opposed to the Congress

2 The idea that NGOs constitute a kind of financial enterprise has created a situation in which many activists refuse to apply this label to their own organisations, but the term is used here to signify a wide range of organisations working on social issues, including those that would reject this label.

Party were also opposed to the JSW project, though with varying levels of intensity. Several communist parties had campaigned strongly against bauxite mining for many years.

Although opposition to the project was not particularly well coordinated, opponents were still able to highlight the immediate threat of displacement for tribal people, and shared a wider concern over what would happen to natural resources and livelihoods if mining started. There was a tacit agreement among this diverse set of actors that the risks were too great and so the project had to be stopped. Since they were based mainly outside of the Agency, they had greater freedom to operate, better resources and education, and better access to media and the courts than local tribal actors.

Many of the organisations had been engaged with the issue for more than a decade, which meant that there was ready support for a new campaign as soon as the bauxite project was announced in 2005. A set of strategies that had proven successful in blocking previous projects could be deployed again. Agitation against bauxite mining had become sufficiently widespread to attract interest from mainstream political parties, which came with its own opportunities as well as risks. Certainly, the opposition was not a grassroots movement with a local base, so most of its activities were directed to raising public opinion and using the courts as an alternative to the political system represented by the state assembly or the national parliament.

Opposing Organisations

The opposition was very active during the period of my fieldwork, both in the Agency and in parts of coastal Andhra Pradesh. Many of the media and policy activities took place in Visakhapatnam city, while mass meetings and other outreach activities centred on the proposed project sites. The 'legal' activities shown in Table 6.1 involve filing cases in various courts of law, but occasionally also trying to make use of various government institutions such as the Andhra Pradesh Human Rights Commission or the Central Vigilance Commission in order to highlight certain kinds of injustice. 'Media' activities involve writing articles or providing information to journalists to raise public awareness. 'Grassroots' work includes public meetings, production of information leaflets and booklets, and the organisation of foot marches (*padyatras*) that are a common way for politicians and party workers in Andhra Pradesh to disseminate messages by walking like common people.

For political parties, 'political' work involves raising questions in the state assembly or national parliament or otherwise engaging democratic political institutions, while for NGOs it involves making representations to politicians who might support their cause.

Table 6.1 Main organisations in opposition to bauxite mining.

Organisation	Strategy	Collaboration
NGOs		
Samatha	Legal, media, political	CPM
Sakti	Legal, grassroots	None
Human Rights Forum	Legal, media, grassroots	CPI, CPM, CPIND
Political parties		
CPI	Grassroots, political	CPM (state-level)
CPM	Grassroots, political	CPI (state-level), Human Rights Forum, Samatha
CPIND	Grassroots, political	Human Rights Forum
Revolutionary		
Naxalites	Violence, media	None*

Note: * Collaboration with the Naxalites is illegal.

The three most active NGOs opposing the bauxite project all had histories of working on social issues in the area that dated back to the 1980s. Sakti and Samatha could both be said to have mining and tribal rights as part of their core agendas. It was therefore rather strange to discover the absence of collaboration between these three organisations, despite the fact that they were familiar with each other's work and shared a common goal. The left-wing parties opposing the project included the two parliamentary parties already mentioned, the CPI and the CPM, and a 'semi-parliamentary' party, the CPI (Marxist-Leninist) New Democracy (CPIND), as well as the revolutionary Naxalites. The Telugu Desam Party (TDP) is not shown as an opponent in Table 6.1 because its earlier history while in government made opposition to the project seem more like a populist ploy than an act of genuine conviction. However, there was occasional collaboration between the left-wing parties and the TDP in order for the former to make use of the latter's superior resources.

Samatha was founded in the late 1980s, and was being led by a couple, Ravi Rebbapragada and K. Bhanumathi. It was able to expand significantly after winning the Supreme Court judgment in 1997. Like other NGOs, it grew by establishing a set of offices and employing regular staff, and winning national or international grants to work on tribal welfare, mining and related issues. A number of smaller NGOs in the coastal Andhra

Pradesh region were receiving most or all of their own funding through Samatha, even though they otherwise operated independently. From time to time, Samatha headed the national network known as 'mines, minerals & People' (mm&P), which meant coordinating the work of NGOs and activists on mining issues at a national level. The organisation was thus able to act at local, state and federal levels.

Sakti was being run by Dr Sivaramakrishna, an academic with knowledge of tribal folklore and an understanding of the many injustices faced by tribal peoples. Years of fieldwork, especially in East and West Godavari districts, has made him an expert on settlement patterns of land and the means of engaging with the government and the courts. However, he also held office in the right-wing World Hindu Council (Vishwa Hindu Parishad), which made him a controversial figure for the left wingers in the opposition. Sakti had been active in the advocacy of tribal rights since the early 1980s. Like Samatha, it had been taking court action against mining and other non-tribal commercial activities in the Scheduled Areas of the state, whether these were sponsored by the government or by private companies.

The loosely left-wing Human Rights Forum (HRF) was an offshoot of the civil rights movement, specifically the Andhra Pradesh Civil Liberties Committee. It was a self-financed group of middle-class activists operating in both of the Telugu-speaking states, Andhra Pradesh and Telangana. Its members had regular salaried jobs, many being lawyers, teachers or journalists. A core concern of the HRF was to ensure that the state government followed the law, including the use of fair trials rather than violence when dealing with the Naxalites, while urging the latter to stop using violent tactics themselves. The HRF had got involved with bauxite mining proposals as part of a widening agenda on economic and social rights. The organisation was headed by K. Balagopal, a human rights lawyer and prolific writer on social issues, until his untimely death in October 2009.

The CPM, like the other left-wing parties, did not have a uniform presence in the tribal areas of Visakhapatnam, but worked in a few places where it did have a local support base, mainly in the Araku Valley. District and mandal party officials were very active in staging protests known as *dharnas*, speaking at public hearings and conducting padyatras. At the time of my fieldwork, the CPM had been subject to a lot of criticism because of the way that the Left Front Government of West Bengal had forcefully acquired land and injured a lot of farmers in the process of developing industrial projects in Singur and Nandigram (both of which were later cancelled). Since West Bengal was the home state of all the senior national CPM leaders, it was very difficult for the Andhra Pradesh branch to distance itself from what was going on there. The party was able to take a clear stand against mining in defence of tribal rights, but did nothing in the proposed refinery area other than object to the refinery's encouragement of mining.

The CPI worked in similar ways to the CPM, but was focused on the western parts of Visakhapatnam District, where the AnRak Aluminium project had been making strong headway. I did not encounter CPI members as often as CPM members during the course of my own fieldwork.

The CPIND is one of several 'Marxist-Leninist' parties active in coastal Andhra Pradesh, as well as in other (relatively small) areas across India. These parties have abandoned the cause of revolution, at least temporarily, in order to join in electoral democratic politics. As such, they are ideologically close to the Naxalites, with little faith in parliamentary democracy, but still participate in elections and retain a legal status, with no known organisational connections to Maoist groups. CPIND members had been active in trade union work but became engaged with the issue of displacement by the JSW refinery when other opposition groups focused on the mining proposals.

The history of the Naxalite movement in India can be formally traced back to the rebellion in Naxalbari, West Bengal, in the late 1960s, from which its name derives. However, this coincided with the Srikakulam rebellion in coastal Andhra Pradesh in 1969, which points to the established presence of violent left-wing insurgency groups in the Scheduled Areas of the state (Reddy 1977). The Naxalites became a single force through the merger of the Andhra Pradesh-based Peoples' War group and the Jharkhand-based Maoist Communist Centre in 2004. This meant that they had a presence across tribal central India, as well as in a few other parts of the country. It is estimated that Naxalites were present in 160 districts by 2005 (Banerjee 2006), but this did not necessarily mean control of actual territory.

The Visakhapatnam Agency used to be a core area of operation for the Peoples' War group, but its presence had since been much reduced (Balagopal 2006). A number of potential support organisations had to distance themselves from the Naxalites after the organisation was outlawed. Nevertheless, the Naxalites continued to make their presence felt in Andhra Pradesh from their bases in Odisha and Chhattisgarh, and had attacked a number of local politicians in the proposed bauxite mining areas. These attacks usually took place at night, with few traces left behind, but were reported in the local news as a result of pamphlets left behind after the attacks (Anon. 2007f, 2009d, 2010b; Narasimha Rao 2010; Rao 2010).

A number of other actors and smaller NGOs were also involved in protest activities. Foremost amongst them were journalists, especially those writing for the local Telugu-language press, but also those writing for the urban English-language newspapers. The so-called electronic media and mobile 24-hour TV news teams were also increasing their coverage. The influence of the media was sometimes hard to separate from formal politics, especially since the two most widely read Telugu-language newspapers, *Eenadu* and *Andhra Jyoti*, had a distinct TDP flavour, while the new one, *Sakshi*, with a related TV station, was established as a Congress Party counterweight, directly owned by chief minister Y. Rajasekhara Reddy and his family.

Claims Made by the Opposition

The issues presented in the previous two chapters, on tribal livelihoods (Chapter 4) and bureaucratic approvals (Chapter 5), became the basis for agitation against the bauxite project. On the other hand, claims about rent-seeking behaviour on the part of members of the bauxite alliance (discussed in Chapter 3) were largely absent. It seemed that any suggestion of giving a greater share of project benefits to local people would indicate approval of the project itself and point to the possibility of mitigating its negative effects. In other words, this would look like a sell-out when more important issues were at stake. The opponents whom I interviewed seemed to take corruption among top decision-makers for granted but believed that it was generally impossible to prove. As one opposition politician said about the chief minister and his suspected connections to the mining company Gimpex: 'They mix like water and milk. I can give information which leads to suspicions but not direct evidence against Gimpex' (interview, Hyderabad, 29 February 2007).

A CPM poster illustrates the type of claims being made by the opposition and also shows how the Agency and its people were viewed (Figure 6.1). The poster places a tribal man far up on the hill surrounded by nature, holding a spear that makes him appear somewhat primitive. The hill is covered in greenery, but it is not clear how anyone could make a living from these steep slopes with their degraded forest. A TDP poster represented tribal people in a similar light (Figure 6.2).

Figure 6.1 Anti-bauxite mining poster produced by the CPM.

Source: Photo by author, May 2008.

Figure 6.2 Anti-bauxite mining poster produced by the TDP.
Source: Photo by author, May 2008.

Chief Minister Reddy is placed at the centre of the CPM poster to signify his centrality in what was being planned, but also to make it clear that the poster is talking to the government when declaring that 'we will not sell our lands for bauxite'. The chief minister is equipped with devil's horns, possibly because he was a Christian, but more likely just to represent the sinister nature of his plans. Foreign-looking company representatives from JSW and AnRak Aluminium are placed at the bottom of the poster.

The impacts of mining on water availability were among the top concerns of the project's opponents. Claims on this subject were sufficiently widespread to be accepted as true by opposition members, despite not being recognised at all by the project's promoters. The HRF considered that '[i]t is a well established fact that the hills containing bauxite deposits have a good capacity for retention of water, which will be lost forever if the hills are opened up for mining' (HRF 2008b). While the loss of water would obviously have a negative effect on Adivasi farmers, the project's opponents could also present this as the reason for a wider audience, including the residents of coastal towns, to be worried about mining. The threat was described as follows at a meeting in Visakhapatnam:

> The rich forests of the Eastern Ghats in north coastal Andhra Pradesh, are the birthplace of many … blessed water resources that include rivers, springs, streams and ponds. It is these water bodies that have ensured that the region from time immemorial has remained rich and fertile with verdant forests, lush agriculture and a history of prosperity. It is these water resources that provided livelihood to diverse traditional occupations and gave bountiful water supply for the millions of people for drinking, irrigation and other uses … Now, there is a serious threat to the people of the region and their very survival as this life giving source is not only being tampered with, but also brutally destroyed by the very policy makers and the government whose primary duty it is to protect them as custodians of the resource under the Constitution of India (CGNAP 2007).[3]

A map made by Samatha illustrates the risk to water across northern coastal Andhra Pradesh if mining were to go ahead (Figure 6.3). It suggests that the rivers as a whole would be at risk if their watersheds were mined for bauxite. Since the rivers provide water to all the irrigation reservoirs along the coast, none would remain in the dry season, which would be bad for coastal farmers and city residents alike.

Samatha's watershed analysis was supported by Sakti, whose members also claimed that the loss of forest to bauxite mining would affect water availability in reservoirs: 'The hill streams originating from these forest ranges feed Eleru, Tandava, Varaha, Raiwada and Tatipudi reservoirs. These streams will be very adversely affected' (Sivaramakrishna n.d.).

The lack of authoritative information gave rise to a fair amount of rumour. One journalist I interviewed suggested that mining waste would fall down from the mountain and block the rivulets in the valleys, thereby depriving nearby coastal districts of water. The widespread agreement within the opposition on the dangers posed to water supplies can seem a little peculiar, given that there was only one bauxite mine operating in the region, which was Nalco's Damanjodi mine in southern Odisha. Even the impacts of this mine had never been studied in any great detail, although visitors and newspaper reports did frequently mention reduced water availability for farmers (Patra and Murthy n.d.). Even government reports on other proposed bauxite mines in the region tended to agree that risks to water were particularly serious and could not be mitigated (India 2005a; WII 2006a).

3 Signatories to this statement included representatives of Samatha, the TDP, the CPI and the CPM, but not Sakti or the HRF.

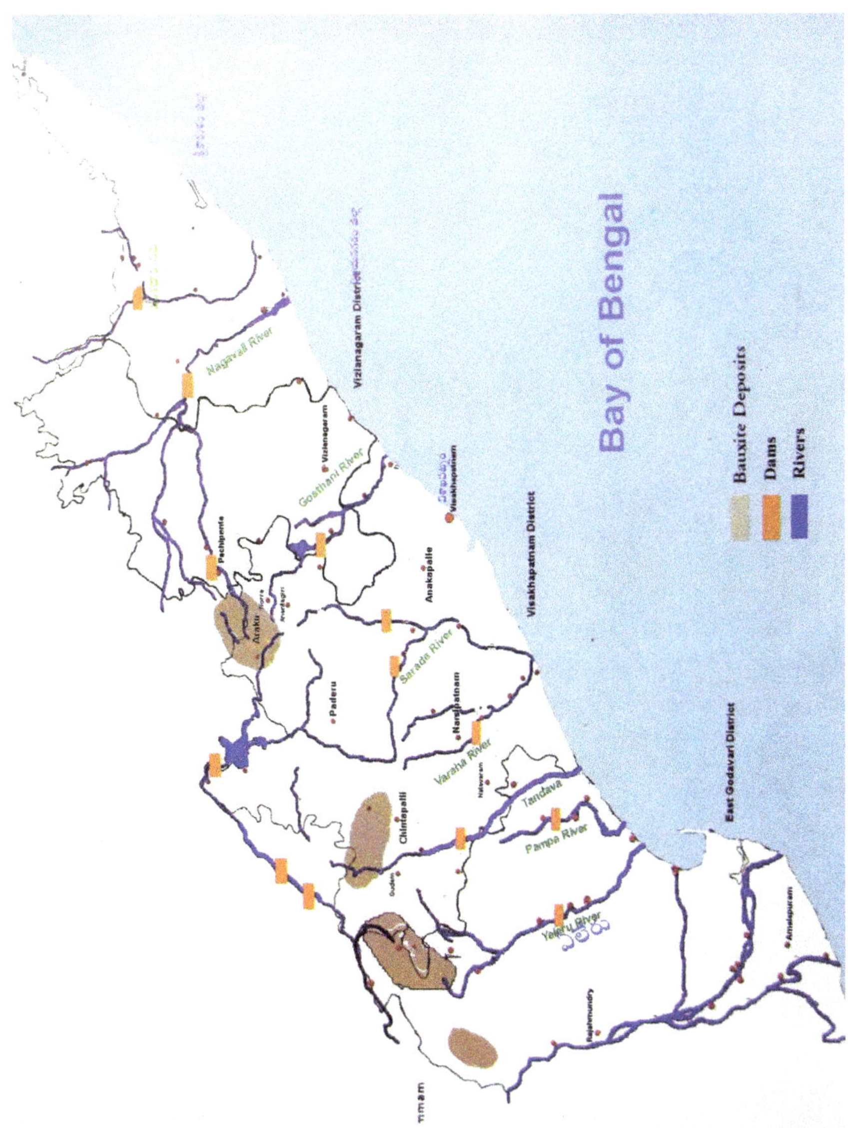

Figure 6.3 Map of bauxite mining and rivers in coastal Andhra Pradesh.

Source: Prepared as part of Samatha's campaign 'Health of the Hills is the Wealth of the Plains'.

Figure 6.4 Stream coming from Galikonda hill in Visakhapatnam District.
Source: Photo by author, April 2008.

In coastal Andhra Pradesh, the narrow strip of land between the Eastern Ghats hill range and the Bay of Bengal does not contain any major rivers. Instead, water flows down from the adjacent hills of the Agency area, which potentially makes the local rivers more vulnerable to drought because each has a relatively small catchment area. It is not clear how mining would change the availability and flow of river water across the region, given that the bauxite hills are only a small part of the total catchment (see Chapter 4).

The water loss narrative depended on changes to the hydrology of the hills to be mined, which would reduce their capacity to retain water in the wet season and slowly release it during the rest of the year. From this point of view, mining would not reduce the overall availability of water throughout the year, but would lessen the flow from mountain springs during the dry summer season. This narrative was not part of the original concerns about mining that were expressed in the 1980s and 1990s, but had become a concern of civil society by the 2000s.

Forest risks were described as equally serious to water risks in a poster produced by Sakti that included the following statement:

> Bauxite will be exploited by strip mining. A power shovel bites into the forests, soils, Laterite and Bauxite, piling up rows of soil and Laterite on one hand and Bauxite ore on the other hand. In this process the Eastern Ghats forest land will be laid bare (Sakti n.d.).

However, the same poster said that '[t]he bald hilltops indicate the Bauxite mineral reserves', making it less clear which actual area of forest would be cut down for mining. In one interview, a high-level member of the Andhra Pradesh branch of the CPM agreed that forests would be lost to mining, impacting the '32 rivulets [that] travel through the hills', but was more concerned that mining would open up one of the few remaining parts of the Scheduled Areas that were still predominantly tribal, since an influx of outsiders would create social problems and would drive tribal people off their land (interview, Hyderabad, 9 March 2007).

During the period of my fieldwork, activists in Araku were demanding to be heard through their panchayats, unaware that their state government had actually failed to implement the *Panchayat Extension to Scheduled Areas Act 1996* (PESA). One Hyderabad-based activist said that the Act 'has not been notified in AP so [the] Panchayat is not valid. The AP government says 20 households is too small so a proper decision cannot be made. It is sad we only learned this as of late' (interview, Hyderabad, 22 February 2008).

Some made a connection between livelihood risks and democratic deficits because common property resources such as water sources and forest land would be affected. This led to a legalistic argument in favour of local decision-making by the HRF:

> Under Sec 4 (d) [of the PESA], the power to safeguard and preserve the community resources, which is another name for common property resources, shall be with the Gram Sabha. Though the land being leased to APMDC [Andhra Pradesh Mineral Development Corporation] for mining is forest land, undertaking mining in that land will affect the water resources of the neighbouring hamlets since the water retained by the bauxite hills is the source of the rivulets and subsoil water that the people depend upon … The land proposed to be mined is also a source of minor forest produce such as thatching and dry twigs. It is a source

> of grazing for animals. The ownership of such minor forest produce is conferred on the Gram Sabha by Sec 4 (m) (ii) … and that right cannot be unilaterally taken away (HRF 2008b).

With all this attention given to the social and environmental impacts of mining in the Agency, it is interesting to see what links were being made to the proposed refinery. The CPM was of the opinion that 'the tribals are made to suffer in the hills for the mine and they are also made to suffer on the plains for the factory' (interview, Hyderabad, 9 March 2007). The CPIND's Bauxite Vyathirekha Porata Committee (Struggle Committee Against Bauxite) made the connection as follows:

> It is not the Boddavara [S. Kota] area that will be destroyed due to bauxite mining and Jindal refinery. In the 15-km radius from refineries, the land, water and the climate will be polluted due to poisonous drainage from the refinery. In the future, the rivers like Goshtani and Sarada which are providing irrigation water to Tatipudi and Raivada reservoirs, may be dried-up so the farmers depending on these reservoirs lose their land and livelihood. If the rivers [stop their] flow through Araku hills and valley, a number of reservoirs in Vizianagaram will be dried-up. Visakhapatnam city and Vizianagaram town will face drinking water problem. Therefore we have to resist bauxite mining which is questioning the sustainability of the human life (BTVPC 2008).

Sakti was likewise arguing that the application for an environmental permit for the refinery was premature, given the lack of clearances for the mine on which it would depend:

> As per the agreement, [the] factory is dependent on the ore to be supplied by APMDC. Since the APMDC did not so far get the necessary permissions, the attempts to push proposals on factory are premature. So I request you to stop further steps on the proposals on the factory forthwith (Sivaramakrishna 2006).

The HRF made a similar connection between the two project components:

> There is no independent and comprehensive EIA [environmental impact assessment] of the project that examines the bauxite mine, refinery, smelter, power plant and other components in a holistic manner. An alumina refinery cannot be run without bauxite. However, the project promoters and the state government are deliberately bifurcating the bauxite mining and refining portion. Instead of discussing the combined impact of all these projects, the promoters and the government have split the project into small parts where each is to be evaluated on its own, making it impossible to understand the overall impact. What is even more

> of a concern is that if the refinery is approved it will be used to blackmail a clearance for the bauxite mines in the Visakhapatnam Scheduled area (HRF 2008a).

Despite these connections being made, the main demand in relation to the refinery was for those losing land to be fairly compensated, while mining had to be stopped altogether.

From this discussion, it seems reasonable to say that opposition to the bauxite project was mainly based on social justice concerns, especially when environmental impacts were regarded as impacts on tribal people that could not be mitigated. The potential conservation values of the Agency were not such a major issue, even if they could be mentioned as another reason to protect the area. To improve the chances of wider public mobilisation, attempts were instead made to extend the size of the potentially affected area. The prospect of mine-related water scarcity in the coastal zone served this purpose, while refinery issues could not raise the same level of public concern. The concern with social justice did not extend to any discussion of the potential benefits of the project for tribal people because the opposition assumed that there were bound to be more losers than winners.

Competitive Mobilisation

The different messages of the opposition were promulgated through a form of competitive mobilisation. Ravi Rebbapragada, head of Samatha, explained this as follows:

> There only used to be us and the Birla case [that gave rise to the Samatha judgment]. We were there on the ground and could see what was happening. If the government passed an order we could see what was happening and make it become implemented. Nobody used to understand why we worked on these mining issues. Since [19]97 everyone talks about these things (interview, Visakhapatnam, 28 March 2008).

During the course of my fieldwork, padyatras to protest against mining were being organised by various political parties almost every week.[4] Frequent meetings were also held, sometimes with speakers invited from a cross-section of parties and NGOs. The CPM organised a meeting in the Araku Valley in early January 2008 that was reportedly attended by more than 10,000 people. This was a follow-up to a meeting held in the same area in November 2007 that was advertised with a banner declaring 'Let us fight against the government on bauxite', with central CPM party member and national MP Brinda Karat as the special guest.

The number of my informants who claimed to have taken 'the people', by which they presumably meant some of those who would be directly affected, on informational trips to the nearby Nalco bauxite complex in Odisha, made it seem as if most of their time was being devoted to such study tours. A number of people belonging to different organisations likewise claimed to have been responsible for ensuring that a share of the income derived from tourists visiting the Borra caves was distributed between the local villages. While taking credit for this benefit, those interviewed would uniformly fail to mention any of the others who had been part of the same campaign.

The bauxite alliance initially attempted to counter the intensity of oppositional activity. When the NGO Nature, based in Araku, produced a critical (Telugu-language) booklet entitled 'Bauxite for Whom?' in 2006, APMDC responded with a pamphlet titled 'Bauxite for You'. Samatha's documentary on mining was likewise countered by an APMDC documentary. JSW Foundation, the corporate social responsibility arm of JSW, made a sudden appearance in Araku, conducting health camps and donating ambulances (Anon. 2007h). Given the financial resources available to the bauxite alliance, it might have been expected to outspend the opposition, but a source with insights into APMDC's operations said that its outreach activities were quite insignificant because 'we don't have the budget for this' (interview, 9 April 2007). The reasons for this

4 The TDP held an 'Anti Bauxite Excavation Pada Yatra' in Araku and Ananthagiri mandals that started on 22 April 2008. The CPM held at least three padyatras during this period. One lasted from 19 February to 2 March, also in Araku and Ananthagiri, where many activists reportedly fell ill due to the poor water and food they were consuming. Two previous padyatras had been conducted in the Araku and Sapparla mining areas respectively. The CPI conducted one in AnRak Aluminium's proposed mining area between December 2007 and January 2008.

limitation are unclear, but no public promotion of the project came to my attention in 2009–10. The publicity contest was overwhelmingly won by the opposition groups.

The strength of the opposition was especially evident in the Agency, where surveyors or any other people associated with the project would be threatened on sight. One CPM representative explained this activity as follows:

> Surveys by Jindal and Al Khaimah are going on secretly. Nobody has seen them but they are ongoing. We saw some people in helicopter and opposed them. Other people came as tourists and under cover did survey two months ago. They were from SSSC [apparently a social science research institute] in Calcutta. They were warned and were never seen again. For the last year they have seen others come and go to secretly do surveys (interview, Araku, 8 May 2008).

Even air surveys were hard to undertake since helicopters would be chased away if they attempted to make a landing (Narasimha Rao 2008). There were similar limits on what the government or JSW could do at the S. Kota refinery site, despite their acquisition of most of the land and receipt of the environmental permit. Survey instruments and other tools had repeatedly been removed by local villagers who refused to hand them back. Both of the proposed sites were thus close to being no-go areas for the bauxite alliance, even while work proceeded on securing final approvals for the mine or making adjustments to the land acquisition for the refinery. It was as if the project's opponents, when not allowed to make their voices heard, believed that they could prevent the project from moving ahead simply by blocking its access to information about realities on the ground.

Despite the level of opposition to the project, it was evidently making some progress, albeit at a very slow pace. That the local opposition was even able to delay the project is noteworthy, given the lack of coordination of strategies or sharing of information by those involved. The NGOs had core ideological differences that obstructed any form of cooperation. Samatha could be characterised as apolitical since it did not subscribe to any particular ideology, at least when compared to the right-wing Sakti and the left-wing HRF. Sakti was difficult for others to engage because of its association with right-wing Hindu groups, even while it shared the HRF's goal of tribal empowerment and learning. The HRF and Sakti both criticised Samatha for receiving larger amounts of funding, and this perspective was shared by other project opponents. One activist who had no relationship to the HRF or Sakti referred to Samatha as one of the 'NGOs [that] have no resource constraints and so they corrupt local people' (interview, Hyderabad, 18 October 2006). Meanwhile, Samatha's members seemed to view the other organisations as intellectuals with too many ideals to be able to get real work done.

The fact that Sakti and Samatha had been pursuing separate court cases before the Samatha judgment was another issue hindering their collaboration. One activist complained that 'today PIL [Public Interest Litigation] has too many petitioners and this confuses the issue' (interview, Hyderabad, 12 October 2006). Another even thought that 'the government won the [Samatha] case since government corporations were allowed to do mining' (interview, Hyderabad, 12 October 2006). The receipt of recognition for success was one of the sources of division between the NGOs:

> The Samatha judgment gives credit to the organisation but we want tribal people to be in control. We want tribal youth to be our cadre for their own village and work for their own benefit (interview, activist, Araku, 9 May 2008).

Despite their differences, the NGOs had come to similar conclusions about the livelihood risks and social injustice that the project posed for Adivasis. None of my NGO informants doubted that the other NGOs were sincerely attempting to stop the project from going ahead. The political parties, on the other hand, were known to make periodic radical about-turns in their policy positions, typically when they moved from being in opposition to being in government. Nevertheless, the left-wing parties did a better job of working together than the NGOs, possibly because they already had to do this in the state assembly to combine the power of their few MLAs. Even so, it was also important for each party to be separately recognised for organising certain activities on the ground, depending on where each party had a supporter base.

The educational qualifications of the NGO activists and the local mobilisational reach of the political parties were sometimes a solid basis for cooperation between them. The NGOs had the ability to access information and make use of it in courts and in the media. They communicated in both English and Telugu, and often shared their communications with the political parties that were also engaged in protests against bauxite mining, to facilitate the spread of information to local villages. The parties had a greater capacity to organise meetings and demonstrations, with written material confined to brief pamphlets or posters that were sometimes reproduced in the newspapers (see Figure 6.5).[5] But while the parties and the NGOs were both able to recruit local Adivasis, the latter were commonly subordinated to non-tribal members in the decision-making process, which replicated the hierarchical nature of the wider society.

Figure 6.5 Public meeting on the S. Kota refinery proposal held in Vizianagaram.

Source: Photo by author, January 2008.

The larger membership of the parties meant that they could do more to reach out to villages in the Agency. One activist said that the CPM:

> did an excellent job in the tribal areas when conducting padyatras. They went to the different areas and spent a week in each proposed group [of bauxite hills]. After the padyatra they had provided so much information in the hills that even your average person who was not even particularly

5 The banner in Figure 6.5 reads: 'Do not build Jindal Factory that contaminates irrigation water and drinking water. Signed Telugu Desam, CPM, CPI and Samatha.'

> politicised was writing slogans on the walls against the project. They could have done something similar [at the refinery] in the plains (interview, Visakhapatnam, 13 March 2007).

Instead, the CPIND was inspired to leave its traditional base in Visakhapatnam city and take up the cause of those affected by the land acquisition for the refinery. This was a small group, seriously short of resources, and although it was supported by the combination of larger opposition parties, it did not make an appearance until after the environmental public hearing had already been held, and had insufficient knowledge about what was being planned to seriously hamper the land acquisition process. The environmental approval coincided with a dharna protest at the local revenue office that was aimed at getting some kind of clarity on the land acquisition and compensation plans. The subsequent arrest of 42 protestors in S. Kota town was widely covered in the press but had no real effect on the plans. By the time the protesters were released on bail in January 2008, dozens of hectares of cashew plantations had already been acquired and cut down, and there was no prospect of securing compensation beyond the uniform rate calculated by the government. Arguments on this score ran counter to the widespread political support for programs of modernisation and industrialisation outside of the Scheduled Areas, which was why the opposition focused on the prospective mines, and not on a refinery that was seen as just another industrial project on the plains (Oskarsson and Nielsen 2014).

Limited Resources Force a Turn to Mainstream Politics

When frequent public meetings and newspaper articles failed to have an impact on the project, the NGOs resorted to the courts, while the left-wing parties were more inclined to associate themselves with the mainstream parties—especially the TDP, but sometimes local Congress Party members—in order to get a result. Formal politics thus captured most of the space for protest. Those opponents who made the turn to mainstream politics could increase the visibility of their demands by holding bigger demonstrations, but the demands themselves were diluted by the need to deal with strong caste and class interests, so were more likely to be demands for better compensation than for outright cancellation of the project.

The TDP was by far the largest and most resourceful opposition party in Andhra Pradesh, but was not widely trusted because of the years it spent trying to implement bauxite mining projects when it was in power. Its enormous party office in the posh Jubilee Hills area of Hyderabad had a whole floor equipped with library and computer facilities that could not be matched by all the other opposition groups combined. During my fieldwork at the proposed project sites, it became clear that some of the most prominent activists had at some point been associated with the TDP. One sarpanch who had both TDP and NGO connections claimed, in typical fashion, that 'the party is nothing and people are important', yet it was unlikely that all activists would quit the party if it again proposed to open new mines (interview, Araku, April 2008). TDP members were clearly better off and better educated than those from other opposition parties, and some tried to explain the party's new approach to the issue. A local party worker from Vizianagaram District claimed in an interview that this was part of its efforts to reconnect with the masses once it was out of power. And one of the party's national MPs was tracking mining deals in what he claimed to be a fight against corruption rather than a change in party policy.

TDP mobilisation was sometimes large-scale and sometimes non-existent. There were somewhat surreal highlights, as when the former chief minister, Chandrababu Naidu, the so-called CEO of Andhra Pradesh (Suri 2005), rode in a bullock cart during one campaign against the AnRak Aluminium refinery. However, the capacity of formal politics to defend affected populations has repeatedly proven hollow, with the norm being populism in opposition and money politics in government. Some of the top TDP politicians attempting to lead the opposition were thought to have funded their own political careers from mining ventures. In some cases, like the AnRak Aluminium refinery, TDP politicians would only speak on behalf of the big landowners, and would renounce their opposition once these claims had been settled. In an increasingly competitive political system, the tension between bold promises and radical policy backflips is getting harder to manage because of the media coverage that makes it more visible.

There were very few opportunities for public debate between the project's proponents and opponents. The opponents had to seize such opportunities on the rare occasions when they were presented, such as when CPM activists stormed the stage in Araku Valley, the main city in Araku Mandal, when high-level state Congress politicians were holding a public meeting, or at a conference on bauxite mining organised by

Andhra University in Visakhapatnam city, when NGO members engaged in a heated argument with the head of APMDC (Anon. 2009e). These arguments produced as much (or as little) mutual understanding as the frequent stormy scenes in the state assembly, which was the only regular state forum for authoritative debate on the issue. On several occasions over the years, the opposition parties created turmoil in the assembly over the mining issue, with loud and extended arguments, sometimes complemented by walkouts or dharnas (inside or outside of the assembly hall), or by other forms of obstruction (Anon. 2008g, 2009f, 2010c). But despite their hard work, they seemed to lack the key informational resources that would enable them to support their accusations against the government. Even the well-documented evidence of corruption in the development of AnRak Aluminium's Jerrila mine only resulted in the promise of a central government investigation.

One typical response by Chief Minister Reddy was to declare that 'TDP leaders are indulging in mudslinging as they are jealous, shaken and perturbed over the rapid strides made by the Congress regime on all fronts, particularly [the] industrial sector' (Anon. 2008c). A more nuanced discussion of the distribution of costs and benefits was seemingly impossible so long as the chief minister could claim that industrialisation was proceeding along the lines proposed by the previous TDP Government.

NGOs and Legal Activism

The Samatha judgment shows that legal activism can be a successful strategy for mining activists in Andhra Pradesh. This strategy was supported by the increased role of the judiciary as an instrument of governance since the 1980s, and further encouraged by the introduction of public interest litigation by the Supreme Court in the 1990s. Active intervention by courts has been described as a 'massive expansion of civil, political, economic, and social rights as the court increasingly supported citizens' rights against arbitrary encroachments by the state' (Hardgrave and Kochanek 2000: 108). However, access to justice has been severely limited by cumbersome procedures and a massive backlog of cases waiting to be heard (Galanter and Krishnan 2003).

One serious problem with using the courts as instruments of social justice is the broad scope for interpretation afforded by the Indian legal framework:

> Indian laws are a labyrinth of contradictory ideologies existing simultaneously … Given sufficient ingenuity, the country's jurists can protect their laws in favour of justice; there is sufficient elasticity to interpret them in ways leading to fairness. But it also demonstrates that the very fluidity can spell disaster for these laws; it can allow vested interests to alter them in favour of injustice (Singh 1986: vii–ix).

Those seeking to defend Adivasi land rights could thus find many legal provisions in support of their case, but so could those intent on promoting industrialisation. One retired officer of the Indian Administrative Service commented on the politicised nature of the courts:

> There is no solution in India to evaluate different claims in a clear and critical manner. All statements become political and then it is difficult to evaluate the truth of claims. The courts are the only place where disputes are settled but they are the least equipped and do not have the time to study issues properly (interview, Hyderabad, 29 March 2007).

But some activists were more optimistic:

> The Supreme Court is leading the economic reforms in our country since the politicians need the vote to get re-elected. Judges don't need votes. Since 1990 when the structural adjustment started the parliament has not amended a single law to suit globalisation. All the necessary declarations of law have come from the Supreme Court definitions (interview, Hyderabad, 7 March 2007).

Allegations about the bribery of judges were common, but comments were also made about the way that some judges had bought into the corporate conception of development and were free to follow this conviction in ways the politicians were not. At a public meeting in Delhi, the well known lawyer Prashant Bhushan stated:

> the time may soon come when we completely will have to write off the judiciary as a means of getting justice. Still we may not have reached this stage but soon we may (20 December 2007).

All the NGOs contesting the bauxite project had the capacity to pursue court cases within the state, but only Samatha had the connections in Delhi that were required to challenge central government decisions. Once a case is accepted by the courts, it is virtually guaranteed to last for several years. Aside from attempting to reach a positive verdict, activists have several avenues of appeal that, irrespective of initial judgments, guarantee further delays. A case was initially lodged against the Polavaram dam in

2005 and was still being heard by courts of appeal until 2010. Similarly, the Niyamgiri bauxite mine in Odisha was held up in a Supreme Court case from 2004 to 2008.

Political parties have rarely filed court cases, possibly because the slow process of resolution entails the risk of taking on an issue that may not give them any clear electoral advantages. It is also possible that years spent in court might be wasted in case of a policy backflip in the transition from opposition to government. The CPM was exceptional in launching a court case against the environmental approval of the Jerrila bauxite mine, although this case was later taken over by the more experienced NGO Samatha.

Court Cases Related to Bauxite Projects

Cases against the JSW bauxite project, including appeals against environmental approvals, were launched at almost every possible opportunity. At times, there were even cases independently filed in the same court on the same subject by different actors (see Table 6.2). This is testament to very active vigilance and an almost completely disorganised approach to litigation.

Table 6.2 Court cases against bauxite projects in Andhra Pradesh.

Court	Petitioner	Respondent(s)	Issue(s)
AP High Court	Sakti	State government	Mining not according to land transfer rights.
AP High Court	Four tribal MLAs	Nine including MoEF, Ministry of Tribal Welfare, Andhra Pradesh Tribal Welfare Dept	Environmental hearings held without first consulting the AP Tribes Advisory Council. No gram sabha meetings in affected villages.
AP High Court	Samatha and Forum for a Better Visakha	State government	Water consumption by JSW refinery.
Supreme Court	Shoba Hymavathy, (former TDP MLA)	JSW Aluminium	Approval of mining and refinery proposals.
Delhi High Court	Samatha	MoEF/National Environment Appellate Authority	Environmental permit for AnRak Aluminium/APMDC mine.

Source: Andhra Pradesh (2009c).

The route taken by ordinary cases is through the lower courts to the High Court at the state level, and then on to the Supreme Court at the national level. For environmental matters, it was possible to appeal decisions by the Ministry of Environment and Forests (MoEF) to the National Environmental Appellate Authority (NEAA), also based in Delhi. This somewhat dysfunctional one-man entity operated for several years as plans for a new National Green Tribunal were being worked out.[6] Creative lawyers realised that decisions of the NEAA could also be appealed to the Delhi High Court, which has jurisdiction over the functioning of central government offices, and that is what happened in the case of AnRak Aluminium bauxite mine.

A case was launched by the NGO Sakti in the Andhra Pradesh High Court shortly after plans for the JSW project became public knowledge in 2006. The key issue in the case was whether the agreement between the state government and a private company violated the provisions of the tribal land rights legislation that only allow mining in Scheduled Areas to be undertaken by state-owned entities. After only four months deliberation, the case was dismissed on the grounds that the agreement could not come into effect until the central government had granted an environmental permit (Andhra Pradesh 2006d: 2). It appeared that the judges wanted to avoid taking a stand on this sensitive issue until the approval process had been completed, but by that time it would most likely be too late to obtain a different judgment, since the investment already made in the project would be used by the proponents as the basis for an argument that it should be allowed to proceed.

A subsequent case was launched against the JSW and AnRak Aluminium projects by the state tribal MLAs in August 2008 on the grounds of a lack of consultation with the Tribes Advisory Council. The government responded by saying that it had held such consultations in 2000. The council had already approved the Polavaram dam, which threatened to become a much more significant source of displacement than bauxite mining. I was unable to discover further information on how this case proceeded. The case over water allocation for the JSW alumina refinery, also lodged in the High Court of Andhra Pradesh, moved very slowly because the NGO activists who launched it felt that the judges were unsympathetic, so they relied on various procedural technicalities to delay the proceedings. Sooner or later the judges would either retire or be transferred elsewhere, and this might create an opportunity to secure a more positive outcome.

6 This tribunal was eventually established in 2010.

In March 2009, the CPM filed a case with the NEAA, appealing against the decision to grant an environmental permit of AnRak Aluminium's bauxite mine (Patnaik 2009). This was a routine procedure, but such appeals had almost as routinely been rejected.[7] The grounds of this appeal were that the public hearing did not ensure widest possible participation, the EIA report is faulty, and the environmental clearance will negatively affect the local environment. Six hearings were held before the appeal was rejected in August 2009 (India 2009b), and that is what prompted a further appeal to the Delhi High Court.

The CPM's argument about public participation included a point about the views expressed by the local gram panchayats, and thus invoked the provisions of the PESA:

> The Gram Panchayat[s] of G.K. Veedhi and Galikonda Mandal Parishad of Chintapalli have passed resolutions opposing the proposed activities of mining and transmitted those resolutions to the collector Visakhapatnam and to the member secretary AP Pollution Control Board (India 2009c: 4).

Although the environmental regulations do not require consultation with the panchayats, the APMDC responded by saying that it had indeed taken their views into account in the 2000, during the period of the earlier TDP government:

> The resolution dt. 19.02.2000, duly signed by 130 people, passed by the Jerrila Gram Panchayati conclusively expresses the intent of the local body in favour of the proposed bauxite mining. The said Gram Panchayat after considering the proposal made by this respondent [APMDC] passed another resolution dt. 02.10.2008 affirming its earlier resolution dt. 19.02.2000 (India 2009d: 5).

The record of the 2000 meeting contained a long list of names, accompanied by fingerprints, that was barely legible because of the poor quality of the photocopy. This was supplemented by a 2008 statement that purported to verify the earlier resolution. It is not clear how the NEAA in Delhi evaluated the relative validity of the local resolutions presented to it by the CPM and the APMDC, but evidently chose to believe the latter (India 2009b). At least this established a precedent for any subsequent

7 The NEAA had only supported the appellants in one of the cases brought before it, and that was an appeal against the permit for the Polavaram dam that was brought by the same activists who were now appealing against the bauxite mine, which suggests that they had learnt something from their experience.

case against the JSW project, since it seemed to establish some need for the gram sabha's views to be taken into account, whether or not environmental approval procedures or the state's panchayat regulations actually require this to be done.

Since the JSW project was stalled even before it could reach the critical environmental clearance stage, the process of appealing such an approval had yet to be explored by activists. A case could also be launched under the Forest Rights Act, since forest land was apparently being diverted to mining before the settlement process according to this Act has been completed, or even under the older Andhra Pradesh State Forest Act of 1967, since another court judgment had ordered a fresh process of determining land rights in the Agency's forest land under the terms of this legislation.

Given the number of current and potential future cases, the most appropriate description of the litigation strategy pursued against the JSW bauxite project would be that it consisted of a flood of cases pursued in as many courts as possible, in the hope that some at least would get support from the judges, or would otherwise lead to time-consuming deliberations that would slow down the rate project of implementation.

The Search for Procedural Errors

While legal loopholes have given policymakers some assurance that they can work their way around inconvenient legislation, the difficulty of following complex administrative procedures has also created additional opportunities for opponents to stall government projects. The entire field of land acquisition is filled with opportunities to question the consistency of land records, to ask whether proper surveys have been undertaken, or whether correct information in the prescribed bureaucratic format was presented to the public at the right time and in the right location. Further opportunities arise when forest land is involved, even if the forest only exists in outdated official records. Mistakes made in bureaucratic procedures have long been a very rewarding arena for litigation by activists, but success has often been tied to the timeliness with which information can be obtained. No court is likely to undo a process of land acquisition once it has been completed, even if errors can be proven after the event. The Right to Information process, which has its own lengthy appeal procedure, is therefore less helpful for this kind of litigation than information leaked by insiders.

In the case of the JSW project, a search for procedural errors could have seemed preferable to demands for better compensation for affected people, since the latter would seem more like a way of agreeing to the project. On the other hand, attempts to stall the project on technicalities, instead of seeking better compensation for displaced people or a chance for them to be heard through the panchayats, could encourage the proponents to argue that the activists were simply engaged in 'anti-developmental' activities. It was this kind of argument that was already reducing their opportunity to be heard in new policy forums where business associations are now normally included.

Uncoordinated Legal Activism

Legal activism was interpreted by a retired officer of the Indian Administrative Service as a large-scale failure to communicate:

> When I was working we did not have all these acts so basically litigation was not an option. People would come to us and we would listen to their complaints. Then we would look at the other side and see what truths there were in that initial statement. We wanted the projects to move on so would seek a solution that could take as many claims into consideration as possible. Today when you go to court you might win the case but the losing side who is forced to do a certain thing will feel let down and will only grudgingly implement the order and that too do as little as possible. There are serious problems with how this is done in India today however and it is only getting worse. People just do not listen to one another. The media tells one-sided stories and the courts cannot settle disputes it has no experience or time in dealing with (interview, Hyderabad, 6 April 2007).

The proliferation of courts in which to lodge appeals, and the ever-expanding number of laws on which they could be based, did seem to reduce the need for agreement among activists, or even a collective approach to the search for justice. However, it is not clear whether the older, and still popular, practice of seeking out top bureaucrats or politicians for favours rather than seeking to gain these things as a right by means of litigation would be preferable, given all the rent-seeking behaviour induced by the older practice over the years.

It has been shown that legal activism on social issues requires coordination and sharing of information in order to be effective (Epp 1998). The bauxite cases documented here suggest limitations on the resources or the willpower required to make legal activism a viable strategy to achieve long-term change, despite the hard and sincere efforts of many public interest lawyers and activists. Instead of working on coordinated strategies to deal with core issues, activists could be dismissed as opponents of 'development' because of the way that they had been using the courts to delay projects, by taking advantage of the poor flow of information between government departments. The ability of a handful of activists and lawyers working on mining and tribal rights was certainly impressive, but if it had been possible to focus on only a few cases, and if activists had campaigned jointly to put pressure on government agencies, as well as judges, there would have been a greater chance of achieving positive outcomes. It would also have helped if more information had been shared with directly affected groups at a local level.

Legal activism still offers the best opportunity to get the government to respond to allegations, since each party to a legal case is forced to submit verified documents in support of their respective positions. Court records with attached documents are far superior to newspaper articles or attempts to obtain government documents through the Right to Information process. In court, it is not possible for the government to deny that certain kinds of information exist, since the court can demand that it be submitted or, if it really does not exist, that it be created. Legal activists and litigants who can access information that allows for an initial court challenge can thus use the courts to produce additional information that may well allow for further challenges.

Missed Opportunities

Delays to implementation of the JSW bauxite project were only partially due to the activities of the project's political opponents. There were also planning failures, larger changes in political conditions and the sheer complexity of implementation issues. The refinery was delayed for more than a year by the selection of a new site, most likely based on the high price of land in the original location. The concerns over wildlife conservation delayed the environmental approval process for the mining operation. Once that got going again, a new central government minister was demanding greater compliance with environmental laws and forestry legislation before approval could be granted.

Two major opportunities did exist for the opposition to permanently halt the progress of the project, but a lack of strategic coordination seemingly prevented both from being taken. The first was to block land acquisition for the refinery since it was clearly linked to the viability of the mine and therefore should not have been treated as if it was a separate project. Had this acquisition not happened, the company would most likely not have been willing to spend more time and money to get the mine approved. Clear statements by NGOs to make the connection, combined with on-site demonstration by political party and other activists under the watchful eyes of journalists, might well have been sufficient to prevent the refinery from moving ahead. So far as is known, this strategy was never considered.

The second opportunity lay in the provisions of the Forest Rights Act that enabled large community reserves to be established in the proposed mining areas. Not only do community forest reserves give land rights to people who have been denied them for centuries; they also give them a right to representation, since the MoEF has made gram sabha decisions mandatory before any land claimed under this legislation is used for other purposes such as mining. It was more of a challenge to take this second opportunity because of the hurried introduction of the Act in 2007 and 2008, and hence the lack of information about what was required in order to make different claims. Furthermore, the MoEF circular that made gram sabha deliberations mandatory was only published in 2009. The implementation of forest rights land titles is still under contestation, which means it is technically not too late to demand community reserves in the areas proposed for mining, as is apparent by the Niyamgiri bauxite mine being denied its approvals in 2014.

Civil society attempts to mediate the implementation of the bauxite project focused on delaying or completely stopping it rather than mitigating or compensating for some of its effects. Civil society pressure certainly contributed to the government's production of additional reports on various matters of concern and seems to have also influenced stricter adherence to bureaucratic procedures, but the project's opponents made few if any claims about alternative actions or initiatives that would enable tribal people to escape their current situation of desperate poverty. At least the bauxite alliance had a plan of action, however flawed, that could instil some hope for a better future. The oppositional groups, by contrast, were content to simply oppose the plans.

Even when demands for local democratic representation were being raised, the main goal appeared to be to stop the project from being implemented rather than to promote an alternative form of development in which natural resources are utilised to improve the living conditions of tribal people. The existence of so many public forums where challenges could be made appeared to contribute to a lack of focus in the efforts of the opposition. This was particularly evident in the pursuit of alternative forms of litigation made possible by continual legislative amendments and the creation of special purpose courts. When a group like the bauxite alliance does not wish to engage in serious public debate, making noise might be the only strategy that remains. And yet there is:

> an irony to the noise of public controversy. Though it may be loud enough to set public agendas in the press and legislative bodies, it always carries the capacity to turn away those who hear no music in democratic disagreement and news-based social conflict (Simonson 2001: 407).

There is, then, a risk that conflictual opposition further reduces the likelihood of arguments for social justice being heard in the elite government–business forums where most decisions on development in India are made these days.

7. Habermas's Nightmare?

The previous chapters identified a number of information problems that have had an impact on the capacity of different actors to understand and take appropriate action related to the Jindal South West (JSW) bauxite project. The problems have ranged from the project's original conception, when an agreement was signed with no prior public debate and doubtful public benefit (Chapter 3), to the lack of information provided to affected people about what was being planned and how they would be affected (Chapter 4), to the government procedures that worked to exclude people from being seen as affected and from taking part in deliberations over the project (Chapter 5), and to the populist rhetoric and mass litigation produced by the project's opponents, which largely drowned out a discussion of genuine grievances (Chapter 6). This discussion has shown that people were simply talking past one another, leading them to occupy entrenched positions in oppositional discourses.

This chapter continues this discussion by detailing the information access and availability issues that I encountered during my fieldwork. The strategies used to uncover information further illustrate the depth and nature of the problems that prevented the creation of any common ground between the opposing discourses. Information is here seen not only as a vital resource to which access is determined by sheer power, but also as being uncertain, complex, full of contradictions and coded in languages that determine who can and who cannot access and make use of it. By situating the researcher as an active participant in the story, the importance of power dynamics and the partial nature of the informational resources available to any individual actor are also illuminated.

Accessing Information from the Government

It was not possible for me to contact the politicians and industrialists who signed the original agreement to obtain their comments on the project. Bureaucrats were easier to approach, as they are required to be in their offices, at least for some part of the working week, but bureaucrats do not like to provide information since that poses a risk to their work and their careers. One strategy to navigate this problem was to depoliticise the request by asking for official statistics and publications of a general nature rather than information more directly related to the project. In that process, I discovered an apparent ground rule that states even ostensibly simple statistical information was always available somewhere other than in the office where I happened to be searching for it. The Land Information Office in Hyderabad advised me to approach the joint collector of the project district, followed by the local head of the Revenue Department (the *tehsildar*), in order to obtain the relevant land records. At the tehsildar's office in the Visakhapatnam Agency, I was told that population statistics were available for all the mandals in the Visakhapatnam city office, but this advice was never tested, since another option was suggested by the head of one local revenue office: approach a local non-governmental organisation (NGO) and they will be able to provide you with the information you are looking for.

I spent quite a lot of time travelling between government entities in Hyderabad, talking to the planners in the Mines and Geology Department, the miners in the Andhra Pradesh Mineral Development Corporation (APMDC) and the MoU signatories in the Industry and Commerce Department, all seemingly part of the scheme, and ended up with only a few brief notes and a suggestion that I look for a copy of the documentary that APMDC had made to promote the bauxite project. I could find no library that even collected the gazettes where government orders are published. The availability of information seemed to depend on the status of the person seeking it, or of the organisation to which that person belonged, as well as the willingness of bureaucrats to part with it, and thus resembled a type of patron–client relationship.

There are indications of very limited information flows even between different branches of the same government.[1] It was not necessarily a simple matter for the state government's Industry Department to access information about land from the Revenue Department. On a number of occasions, JSW had to step in to ensure that information kept flowing from one department to the next, as shown by some of the fax messages that JSW sent to the environmental consultant producing the project's environmental impact assessment (EIA) report for APMDC (BS Envi Tech 2008). Otherwise, it seemed that the flow of information around industrial projects of special importance, like this bauxite project, was not even controlled by high-level bureaucrats in the relevant agencies, but by the chief minister and a small set of locally powerful ministers who were not necessarily connected to these agencies.

When I told a retired officer of the Indian Administrative Service how I had been struggling to get information from the government, and how I felt that everyone should have a right to access basic information about what was being planned, the otherwise forthcoming former bureaucrat suddenly became angry, exclaiming, 'Who are you to get information? Who are you?' His argument against access to information was apparently based on the risk that people could misuse it to create all sorts of trouble. Instead, he seemed to feel that a 'good' administrator should only be magnanimous enough to deliver information to people who were found to have 'genuine intentions'. Although he was aware that this attitude could lead to other problems, including an increased risk of corruption, this former official thought that such problems should be addressed by reforming the education of elite bureaucrats rather than opening up the flow of information. Another former official took a very different line by advising me to 'say in your report that nothing of the information you have was given by the government voluntarily'.

Despite the intense secrecy, the quality of the government's information production must still be questioned. How could government employees be expected to produce accurate information when they are working in early twentieth-century facilities with no proper equipment, and seemingly little relevant training in the use of modern technologies? And what kind of quality can be assured when government departments are making drastic staff reductions, as was the case with the Agriculture Department,

1 This is a crucial element in Chibber's (2003) explanation of the federal Planning Commission's inability to design appropriate plans ever since its inception.

which at times during my fieldwork seemed to work mainly as a land acquisition compensation assessment department, rather than providing support to help farmers produce better harvests?

Accessing Expert Knowledge

When interactions with politicians and bureaucrats proved largely futile, I sought to engage with outside experts to see if there were specific studies that could provide a better understanding of the aluminium industry and the local conditions in the area where the bauxite project was being proposed. General information of this sort was almost as difficult to find as the more contentious material directly related to the project, even though the experts were not under direct government control and worked in an environment where there was supposedly freedom of speech.

A professor at one local university denied the existence of any studies relating to the locations where mining was proposed, even though his colleagues at this same university had discovered the bauxite ore body in the 1970s. According to this professor, no one studied the area these days, and the university had no maps or any older material that was in any way relevant to my study, whether it related to biodiversity, forests, agriculture or any other topic. I was advised to use Google Earth to find satellite images if I wanted to know about forest cover, and to ask the NGO Samatha for additional information. Only later did I discover that this same professor had spent a lot of time working on forestry and wildlife issues in Visakhapatnam District, and had taken a number of relevant books and reports into his office at the university and, for some unknown reason, was unwilling to grant access to myself or to his own colleagues in the same department.

Another professor at the same university, who had a much smaller office, responded to my enquiries by saying: 'If you require information for research purposes I will give information but otherwise I will not.' I had assumed that my own credentials were already clear, since I had been introduced as a researcher by another employee of the same university. Once further papers and a business card from the University of East Anglia had been displayed, the professor handed over copies of a number of his own seminar papers, on which he wrote 'with best compliments'. One might have thought that any academic would want to distribute such material in the hope of getting it a wider audience.

Other academics would respond with a gasp when I informed them of my topic of study and exclaim that it was very contentious. But then, quite unexpectedly, other contacts led me to a few free-thinking members of the university's staff. It was those in the Geology Department who proved most open to discussion of the impacts and implications of bauxite mining, including the risks of pollution. This department had actually been marginalised by the politicisation of the bauxite issue, since their science no longer seemed to have any value. Not only were researchers in the department powerless in the face of an argument that 'national treasures' should be used for the public good; they could not even travel to the hills since people might mistake them for surveyors or otherwise associate them with the mine's promoters. There were a few academics in other departments who felt that the secrecy surrounding the project was ridiculous and were happy to let me copy maps of the area that are not available for sale to the public. They could not provide me with full-sized originals in colour since they would struggle to get new ones from the Geography Department, which had control of this particular asset. But I later found that this was no obstacle, since the maps had already been scanned and could be printed in colour from a regular 'Xerox' shop.

Another interesting aspect of information control in the university world was the library, which was only accessible by means of a letter of invitation. Once inside, the only things immediately accessible on the dusty bookshelves were ancient books of little relevance for my purpose (or possibly any other). Statistics from the national census could be accessed from cupboards that were normally locked. Once permission had been sought from the head librarian in her air-conditioned office, photocopies could be made if the Xerox machine operator was present in his own office, which was not the case on the occasion of my visit. Possession of a digital camera, and the authority to walk past the information guardians with it still in one's possession, was a partial solution to that problem, but only yielded a few pages of what in the end turned out to be not very useful 'public information'.

Even these tactics were insufficient as a means to access copies of the most useful information on the bauxite deposits, which was contained in doctoral theses on bauxite ore geology written in the late 1970s and early 1980s. These are kept in a separate section of the library, in a corner of the top floor with a librarian dedicated to guarding it. Here again, an invitation letter had to be produced, this time with the signature of the head librarian added to it. But in this case there was no point in looking for the absent photocopy operator, since the theses could only be read in the adjacent reading room. The explanation for this was that some theses are yet to be published and free access could ruin the prospect. When I asked the guardian for guidance to finding a thesis of particular interest to me, the result was a vague nod towards a disintegrating card index system.

The geological reports prepared by the Geological Survey of India in the 1970s, as advertised on its website, look to be more accessible, but still command a premium price. Reports on the bigger deposits cost hundreds of thousands of rupees (India 2008b). So that constitutes another kind of limitation on the flow of information.

The main characteristics of the aluminium industry, in terms of geological and operational characteristics, but also its negative consequences for local employment and the environment, were already known in the late 1970s and early 1980s. They had been evaluated in numerous committees and subjected to comparison with international experiences. And yet the same debates were continuing 30 years later, and with very little in the way of openly available information. The older reports that already existed had largely been forgotten or hidden away, so nothing was being learned from them.

The experts are impressively effective at keeping information under control, and that is partly due to the direct influence exerted by the government. A company that leaks information will find it difficult to win new contracts from the government, as indicated in a letter written to one environmental consultancy firm:

> [T]here are reports that the [company] officials at certain levels are providing information to outsiders, without maintaining the confidentiality expected of a professional organization and this has resulted in unseemly controversies at the public hearings organized in respect of Irrigation Projects (Andhra Pradesh 2005f: 1).

The government official who wrote this letter went on to advise the company to 'induct competent officials with professional expertise related to irrigation projects and possessing integrity and high standards of efficiency'.

Other forms of information control are exemplified by the case in which experts in environmental management altered their own findings to suit dominant interests. I was told about surveys undertaken to determine whether sand mining along the Andhra Pradesh coastline should be allowed or whether pollution levels for industries in the region were within prescribed limits. In both cases, information was collected and analysed according to prescribed procedures. But the expert author of the sand mining report then changed the crucial data in the final draft to reduce the number of turtle nests that had been found and hence to make sand mining seem a less harmful activity. Likewise, the pollution control laboratory applied a general procedure to ensure that measured test results would fall within the prescribed limits so that this finding could be used as the basis for a negotiation to have pollution control equipment installed, instead of leading to the denial of an environmental compliance certificate.

Individuals expressing opposition to the JSW bauxite project could expect visits from both government employees and representatives of the Jindal Group. However, since there was not much more that could be done to prevent those free from direct government or company patronage from speaking their minds, these visits could lead to an offer of benefits for those whose minds were changed. One NGO was reportedly approached by a representative of the JSW Foundation, the company's corporate social responsibility division, promising that 'anything you want us to do to avoid another Nandigram we will do' (interview, activist, Visakhapatnam, 4 January 2008).[2] Academics were also approached with offers of funding to host a conference on bauxite mining.[3] While support for the government could be rewarded with perks like these, the maintenance of an independent stance brought few personal benefits and could stall an academic career.

New Technology for Information Dissemination

New legislation and information technology (IT) offered some hope for improved access to information. The Andhra Pradesh Government has not only been keen to attract investment from IT companies but has also tried to use technology to modernise its governance. The government's IT projects have included the eSeva project set up at local offices across the state for the payment of utility bills (amongst other things), a new web portal with information on its various agencies (www.aponline.gov.in/)

2 Nandigram in West Bengal had recently been the site of violent clashes over land acquisition for a proposed petro-chemical plant.

3 The national seminar on bauxite mining in Andhra Pradesh and Odisha was held at Andhra University on 17–18 July 2009.

and an e-procurement website for public tenders (www.eprocurement.gov.in/). The central government has been even more proactive in its efforts to spread information through websites, and the Ministry of Environment and Forests (MoEF) has been at the forefront of this move. Right to Information (RTI) requests from the MoEF have, however, been denied on the grounds that the information is already available on its website. This is in spite of official websites being frequently inaccessible, and only a small minority of the population having access to a computer and the English-language skills required to navigate the site.

The Ministry of Corporate Affairs is another example of a ministry that has enabled the web to distribute information about registered companies all across India (www.mca.gov.in). However, this supposedly public information can only be accessed by users who are willing to pay Rs 10 per copied page and have a credit card to pay for it, and once the information has been ordered, the information seeker must visit the physical office of the Registrar of Companies in the state where the company is registered in order to obtain the copies. In the case of JSW Aluminium, this would be the office in Mumbai, even though the Jindal Group is based in Delhi and its project was in Andhra Pradesh. The service does not appear to be aimed at the public but at companies seeking information about other companies.

My experience of the limitations of IT as a vehicle for the spread of public information in Andhra Pradesh has been confirmed by Thomas and Parayil (2008), who found that access and use was much greater in the state of Kerala, not because of the size or quality of investment in IT, but because of people's ability to make use of information, and to some extent their interest in doing so. Nevertheless, there was still evidence of change during the course of my research on the JSW bauxite project. The many RTI requests received by APMDC may have explained why that organisation started to post all mining agreements on its newly created website.[4]

4 apmdc.ap.gov.in/Home/RTI (accessed 3 September 2018).

The Poor Quality of Official Information

In the controversies over access to information, it became apparent that government information was at the centre of the argument. In media debates and court cases alike, the government has been seen as the provider of the kind of information that comes from surveys carried out by authorised personnel and performed according to specific procedures that are deemed to give it legitimacy. But is this dependence on the government warranted by the quality and independence of the information it produces?

Government surveys of proposed industrial sites gave the appearance of being thoroughly politicised, as top Hyderabad bureaucrats and (at times) even politicians would bypass local (and usually unavailable) bosses and order local government workers to undertake them. This caused a great deal of confusion, since the workers had been trained to follow orders made in writing and passed through established bureaucratic channels, but there was no time for this when sudden phone calls were received. In what appeared to be uncoordinated pressure to get all the required surveys done at the same time, one Agriculture Department survey team was unable to complete its work because the Revenue Department had yet to produce the basic details of the land to be acquired. On the other hand, some government employees took great pride in the efficiency of their work on behalf of the corporate proponents. One such case was that of the Revenue Department official who bragged about finishing land acquisition for an earlier project in just a few weeks and thus getting handpicked to do the same for the more important AnRak Aluminium project.

The sheer complexity of local land tenure, and the poor information management skills of government employees who were largely stuck in a pre-computer era, with facilities dating from the 1950s, posed serious challenges to the quality of information production. Even though Revenue Department officials sometimes used satellite imagery to make plans for land acquisition, poor land records remained an obstacle to more detailed work at ground level. I witnessed a local surveyor involved in planning the JSW project take worn 1950s village maps from a steel cupboard in his otherwise bare office and repair them with a razor blade and tape. The result was an official land acquisition map labelled 'JSW Aluminium', rather than 'Government of Andhra Pradesh', even though the government was legally responsible for land acquisition.

The digitisation of such documents cannot compensate for the poor quality of the original data. The information contained on local maps had not been updated for decades, and thus failed to take account of numerous illegal land transactions. In the end, the government was not interested in providing compensation to anyone not present in its own ancient registers of title, as shown in Chapter 4. Even so, Revenue Department officials had to travel daily to the JSW project site daily by bus from their head office in Vizianagaram over a period of several months, even working on weekends, to sort out issues with the land records in order for the acquisition to proceed.

When combined with the deficiencies of the EIA reports discussed in Chapters 2 and 6, this indicates a basic lack of local knowledge about who might be affected by the project. There was simply not enough in the way of existing information about the local environment, nor any capacity to make up for this deficiency, to make plans for adequate compensation or mitigation. Even where relevant and reasonably accurate information did exist in the numerous and voluminous reports produced by the government and its various consultants, there was still uncertainty about the legal and regulatory standards that should be applied to it. This inevitably meant that the project would fail to demonstrate compliance with the best social and environmental practices.

Even though new to the aluminium industry, a company like JSW Aluminium would have known that the technical knowledge required to build a large alumina refinery is available in national and international markets, so it did not have to rely on its own resources or those of the government for that purpose. The international technology supplier could provide the equipment, an engineering group could prepare the site, and consultants could compile various planning documents. However, it seems that the company and its many consultants still did little to gather the social and environmental information that would have made it clear why so many people were protesting against it. Under these conditions, opposition actors and organisations will continue to find genuine reasons to object to bauxite mining and refining projects across central India.

Information from the Bauxite Project Opposition

The wide range of groups and individuals who had come out against the bauxite project included activists, journalists and political parties. Information about the bauxite project was actively pursued by each of these groups, albeit with widely varying degrees of success, and put to use for specific purposes.

Moneyed NGOs and Struggling Activists

The way that information collection and dissemination took place amongst NGOs and activists was typical of many other actors during the period of my fieldwork. There were only a few organisations working on the issue with sufficient people and funds to collect information on a larger scale, and it was on these organisations that many other organisations and individuals, including journalists, had to rely. Journalists would reward access to information in the form of publications mentioning the name of the organisation or party that provided it, or simply by writing stories on topics favoured by the NGOs. The greater resources of the moneyed NGOs that were the main repositories of information naturally created a fair bit of envy and resentment on the part of activists with smaller means, who did not have much to offer in return for it or who did not want to get involved in making such deals.

One of the most important documents about any industrial project is the EIA report. This is a document that people affected by a project are supposed to be able to read in their own language. It is supposed to be made available at a number of local government offices some weeks ahead of an environmental public hearing. It is also the only document that has to be made public, so the public hearing becomes the only venue where many aspects of a proposed project can be debated. According to one EIA consultant, the wide variety of concerns normally debated at such hearings have generally not focused on environmental issues because economic issues tend to dominate the agenda.

In coastal Andhra Pradesh, it has mainly been the larger NGOs that have the capacity to receive advance information about the timing and location of a public hearing and hence the availability of the EIA report. These organisations know their rights and are able to demand access to these public documents, which they can then pass on to experts across the country who can provide critiques of them. Other people with an interest in the report are then obliged to approach the larger NGOs in ways that are very similar to those by which people approach the local government for favours. While the NGOs need to show that they are doing good work in order to continue receiving support from their donors, their comparative wealth and perceived secrecy are sources of constant contention with other activists, who rightfully feel that a wider dissemination of information will help the common cause.

There is a perception that activists used to get information from bureaucrats, at least occasionally, on an informal and friendly basis, but that this space has since been closed. In recent years, with an apparent reduction in the contacts between activists and individuals working in the government, some have resorted to the Right to Information Act. Despite the many benefits offered by this legislation, the use of legal means to extract information is unlikely to close the gap in understanding between activists and the government.

The use of public interest litigation to obtain information requires even more resources, since information is already required before plans can be challenged, and the legal basis of the challenge also has to be established. For these reasons, NGOs need to combine their own knowledge of the law with an ability to persuade lawyers to take on their cases at little or no cost. This activity may yield more information than RTI requests because the litigant will receive all the information that the court asks the other parties to provide.

The Media: Active and Free, yet Ultimately Ineffective

Some very competent journalists operated out of the small towns in the vicinity of the proposed JSW refinery and mine. The limited interest of the English-language press in covering rural stories made it necessary for opponents to talk to the Telugu media, and especially newspapers like *Eenadu* and *Andhra Jyoti* that were (unofficially) aligned with the oppositional Telugu Desam Party (TDP). Journalists at these papers were hard at work to press the government on its accountability for programs and projects all over the state. The Telugu media had a readership keen on stories about corruption and poor people losing out as a result of economic development.

The state government responded to such reports by pursuing a few cases against the editor of *Eenadu*, but was otherwise largely obliged to allow the papers to publish what they wanted. Some saw the launch of the Telugu paper and TV station Sakshi, owned by the son of the chief minister, as a strategy to counter this critical press coverage.[5] Critical stories about the proposed refinery included one about the withholding of information about land acquisition from people who would be affected (Anon. 2007i), another about the secret (and illegal) alterations made to the boundaries of the area to be acquired (Anon. 2008h), and a third about the extraction of commissions from compensation payments made to local farmers (Anon. 2008i). English-language newspapers like *The Hindu*, *Deccan Chronicle* or *New Indian Express* only carried stories about the problem of water availability in the cities or reports of political party meetings, but *The Hindu* took a particular interest in tribal issues in the state.

Some exaggerations were evident in the press coverage, and the capacity to obtain and interpret government documents varied enormously from one journalist to the next. Some got their hands on maps and other government documents on which to base their stories, but would not say how they had done so. One journalist claimed that he had made RTI applications and travelled to Hyderabad to obtain some of his information, but journalists generally seem to have obtained government information informally from local sources. On several of my own visits to government offices, I came across journalists casually chatting with government workers.

The many stories covering various aspects of the JSW bauxite project seem to have had very little actual impact. One S. Kota journalist expressed his frustration by exclaiming that the stories were just 'cries in the wind'. This was not the fault of the journalists themselves but of the larger system. News stories spread information about the proposed bauxite project to an impressively wide audience in rural and coastal Andhra Pradesh, but they would not carry much weight in a court case, nor could they be used to initiate investigations since they were seen—perhaps somewhat unfairly—

5 Despite the recent spread and popularity of intensely competitive local TV news stations, the TV crews were rarely present in the locations where my fieldwork was conducted.

as being 'unscientific' and biased in favour of the political opposition. Even if the media did a good job at shaping local public opinion, that too had very little relevance for actual outcomes.

Political Parties

As discussed in the previous chapter, all the opposition parties quickly decided to 'be with the people' and against any bauxite projects in coastal Andhra Pradesh. They included the TDP, which had formerly favoured mining when it was in power, as well as a number of left-wing parties.[6] Opposition politicians were generally very keen on meeting a foreign researcher like myself. The left-wing parties had cells that operated only in certain locations, and this seemed to restrict the amount of information they could provide. Limited resources and a lack of experience of ever being part of the government meant they were not able to discover much about its plans or shed much light on the ways in which it operates. And even if the left-wing parties did have access to information, they would have had few ways of putting it to use aside from fuelling more news stories in a media space that was already full.

Many left-wing parties, active for decades in coastal Andhra Pradesh, preferred struggle on the ground to information collection and dissemination. There was even disdain for information, among the more radical groups, as something inherently bourgeois. Since, in their opinion, the government was invariably going to be wrong and had to be opposed, they doubted the point in spending time and effort to rediscover this fact. Unfortunately, their ignorance of relevant laws and procedures meant that those working to mobilise farmers to reject land acquisition at the refinery site, despite the impressive levels of self-sacrifice, were rather like the blind leading the blind. Party workers who were not even aware that the proposed refinery site was located just outside of the Scheduled Areas, which allowed for the non-tribal ownership of land, insisted that all the land was scheduled and the whole acquisition was therefore illegal.

The TDP, which had been in power since the 1980s before losing office four years previously, and which has significant financial resources, also had a clear informational advantage. With the former member of legislative assembly (MLA) Ashok Gajapathi Raju and a number of panchayat and

6 The policy turnaround has come full circle since the TDP returned to power in 2014 and once again came out in favour of bauxite mining (Anon. 2015a).

mandal parishad seats in the S. Kota and Araku constituencies, it also had a significant local presence. However, as we saw in Chapter 6, the party chose not to capitalise on its available resources other than to host a few padyatras and meetings in the Visakhapatnam area and to make noise in the assembly. It could most likely have gathered any information it did not already possess about the politics and economics of the JSW project, so it was no wonder that even a left-wing party worker would put me in touch with TDP members to assist in my own search for information. A visit to the TDP headquarters in Hyderabad revealed an impressive library and a number of staff working full-time on information collection, but the purpose of their doing so remained unclear. Like other parties, the TDP does not usually engage in the sort of litigation for which such information would be crucial. It could have used its own information when making its frequent objections to the state government's plans in the assembly, but this would have meant sharing the information with the left-wing parties that also have a few MLAs. It was perhaps more likely that the party was using its information in direct negotiations with the government rather than in public forums.

The Politics of Opposition and Information Control

As already indicated, my own interactions with activists and opposition party members were quite straightforward. There was not even much of a need for informal introductions, even when I was seen as being aligned with particular activists. Yet this does not mean that much information was being shared between the project's opponents. My interview with one NGO leader initially prompted a 15-minute rant against Samatha, since I happened to mention that I had previously volunteered to work for them. The antagonism was based on the credit the organisation had received for the Supreme Court judgment, despite its many imperfections. The head of another, smaller NGO went so far as to argue that Samatha was really working for the government, apparently because the government had mentioned the existence of the judgment in the development agreements it signed with private companies. Once activists had calmed down, it was possible to discuss the issues in greater depth, and frequently to access the information that they had taken pains to collect.

NGOs often do not get along due to ideological differences, and are in competition with each other to promote their own organisations and attract additional support. The political parties functioned in much the same way. The result was a lack of coordination in the gathering of information, as well as in actions that would have been more effective at achieving their common goal. A wide range of activists and political parties were invited to speak at meetings on the bauxite issue, but padyatras in rural areas were organised separately by each party, and if others were invited to join them, the timing would be such as to keep the organisers in the limelight. In one of the rare cases where NGOs combined forces, one NGO threatened to withdraw its funding from a joint activity when another NGO was thought to have taken too much credit for the campaign on its website.

The level of trust between parties and activists was also quite low. In one case, a local party worker blamed the head of a local NGO for being a 'cunning fellow' who was only interested in money, while the latter returned the favour the next day by accusing the party of sending out 'double messages'. Both seemed equally single-minded in their opposition to bauxite mining, but had somehow failed to understand one another, despite living in the same small town. Other activists saw politics as a necessary evil with which one had to engage in order to make an impact. It was only the parties who had the capacity to mobilise opposition on the ground, even though their support could be withdrawn as quickly as it had been created.

The result was that each NGO, activist, party worker or journalist involved in opposition to the bauxite project was working in a single local cell, and had only a small piece of the puzzle, usually confined to that particular location or the specific issue that they were following. Only a few individuals had some capacity to circulate information between these different actors. Several of the findings presented in this book thus constitute my own attempt to combine the results of fragmented and time-consuming information-gathering activities by different members of the opposition.

Greater Access to Information at Local Sites

Having searched libraries across the state and enquired at what felt like countless other locations, it almost came as a shock when I discovered that detailed statistics about people and agriculture could be swiftly printed out from a computer at a local revenue office, and then copied to a thumb drive when the printer stopped working. Otherwise, despite the right introductions, access to information was just as challenging at the proposed project locations as it was in government offices in Hyderabad. On any given day, it would be almost impossible to first find the tehsildar, the most senior officer in any given office, and then persuade him or her to authorise the right person to provide me with information. This would invariably require several visits, since the statistician or the surveyor would be absent on each occasion. In the case of the Agency, the problem was compounded by the fact that one statistician had information on the revenue villages and another on the forest villages. Only the person in charge of any particular document or map could bring this out of the locker for me or anyone else to see. On one occasion, a surveyor agreed to meet me on the day after a joint meeting with the tehsildar, but then immediately took leave, apparently without informing his boss.

The fact that I was able to gain any access to local government offices was nothing short of amazing to many activists. To put this into perspective, about six weeks before I sought information from one of the offices in December 2007, a group of 42 project-affected villagers, led by a group of politicians from all the major opposition parties, had spent four days blockading the same office, demanding to know the plans for land acquisition. The officials stayed away from the office until the blockade ended, when the police moved in and arrested about 30 people. The process of land acquisition actually started during the fortnight in which this core group of activists were being held in the Visakhapatnam jail. In the months that followed, the tehsildar refused to respond to letters objecting to the land acquisition notices, despite one such letter being handed over in person by the same set of opposition politicians in the presence of a large media gathering.[7]

While I was spending time at the proposed project sites, lower-level local government officials would actually call me to ask when we could meet and then show up at the appointed time. When doing so, they did make sure that they had political cover from a sarpanch and had consulted with local employees of the company before they would talk. The only thing that can really explain why it was easier to conduct my research at these sites, other than a general curiosity to meet foreigners, would have to be the altered power differential between the two sides. It was apparently harder to ignore a foreign researcher at this level than it was in Hyderabad.

7 A legal case was later launched against the tehsildar, but the land acquisition process continued.

Every single person I sought out at the various project sites, especially the villagers, turned out to be forthcoming. If not necessarily eager to respond, they were seemingly only unable to provide information when it was really not available to them. I showed the villagers maps with the refinery area outlined on them in an attempt to work out where their own plots were located. I was surprised that this did not create too much interest despite the fact that some of the respondents had been arrested only a few months previously when they were demanding more information. It seems that they did not regard maps as substantial and reliable sources of information because they could be drawn today and changed tomorrow, just like any government plans. Several local farmers indicated that they had not received land acquisition notices, but had joined the local opposition group in the belief that they would be affected by a second phase of land acquisition. They did not know that there would be a second phase, but could not see why their land would not be acquired if this was happening to other people's land. The documentation was of much greater interest to the teenage children of the largely illiterate farmers whose land had already been earmarked, yet their few years of poor schooling did not enable them to make much sense of the Revenue Department's technical jargon in English.

I did find one villager studying land acquisition maps and documents on the occasion of a visit to his home. This was a non-tribal man who had illegally bought land many years earlier, and was naturally tight-lipped about where he had been able to get hold of this information. Unfortunately, he also seemed to have little interest in sharing it with other villagers, even though he was nominally a member of the bauxite opposition.

The main problem with information collection in the villages was generally not people's willingness to discuss and share what they knew, but the fact that they simply did not know what was going on. Nor did local government officials in the proposed mining area know much more of what was being planned than what they had read in the newspapers. They had not even been called on to conduct surveys as part of the planning process, unlike those at the proposed refinery site, since this work had been contracted to a consultancy firm.

The surprising amount of information in circulation at the refinery site found little productive use other than in a few local news stories and for individual bargaining on the part of those being displaced. It was not being collected by the project's opponents in 'civil society', who preferred to stay in the cities and spend a lot of their time filing RTI requests. This acceptance of the government's authority as a producer of information does not seem to make much sense, given the poor quality of much of the information they were producing. Perhaps it was a strategy influenced by the demands of the courts, or simply based on their reluctance to travel to rural areas. Local villagers would have been better off if activists with the ability to access and interpret technical planning documents had come to explain what was about to happen, thus enabling the villagers to make more informed decisions on how to proceed.

Conclusion

The picture that emerges here is not one of an all-powerful alliance that has perfect information itself and the ability to prevent others from accessing it. Rather, the poor information flows seem to be the result of a widespread recognition of information as a valuable resource that needs to be protected and only released if something can be gained by doing so. This behaviour was found to reach far beyond the key state planning departments that the bauxite alliance could hope to control, not only to the rest of the government, but also to most of the other organisations and individuals that I encountered during my fieldwork, including researchers, journalists, opposition parties and NGOs.

The informational struggles were almost exclusively concerned with data produced by the government. This information was seen to be authoritative because of its supposedly high quality and the strict procedures that were meant to guarantee independence from political influence. However, my own observation cast doubt on these perceptions. Survey workers were found to be heavily influenced by senior administrators and politicians, and to be using poor facilities and methods to produce the information. Combined with the many site-specific information gaps found in the public documents and special reports examined throughout this book, the government's limited ability to produce truly authoritative information made it seem impossible to properly compensate land losers or mitigate negative environmental impacts according to principles of best practices. When mediation over land use change is impossible, future mineral projects are certain to generate continued protests.

I am not suggesting there is such a thing as perfect information or a perfectly transparent mode of organising society. Even with better access to information, struggles would still have to take place to ensure that there is justice. The very promising Right to Information Act was found to have many procedural issues that limited its usefulness, but recent improvements in access to information provide some reason for cautious hope for improved communication in the future.

For now, I can only conclude that the sum of many informational problems currently prevents any meaningful communication from taking place. This breakdown in communication, with very limited options for meaningful deliberations, could be seen as a Habermasian nightmare, since it seems to imply that contestations over mineral projects in tribal India are destined to end in paralysing stand-offs where little that is productive can be accomplished.

8. Conclusion

A significant body of research on resource projects in indigenous territories around the world has shown that vast disparities of wealth and power usually play out to the advantage of the promoters and developers, at best with some form of consultation and perhaps compensation or a share of revenues for the traditional inhabitants.

> [C]omplications and challenges … are almost always the same: environmental pollution and consequent community backlash; dislocation and relocation; new forms of poverty and inequality; and local-level grievances stemming from perceived minimal contributions to local economic development (Gilberthorpe and Hilson 2012: 1).

What is not quite so common in the literature, however, is a discussion of when and how an aggressive process of industrialisation is halted in its tracks. This book provides such an account, even if an incomplete one, since the pursuit of local self-determination remains unfinished and the development proposal is in limbo rather than being decided in favour of the local land users.

When the Jindal South West (JSW) bauxite project got stuck, the core conflict was over the question of whether the constitutionally protected Scheduled Areas should be used for mining rather than the low-intensity cultivation and extraction of forest products that constituted Adivasi livelihoods. Informational problems turned this dispute into something that no side was able to resolve. Examples included the serious problems with the land records available to the government, which did not allow for a swift and efficient process of land acquisition, and the reluctance of oppositional groups to share the information of admittedly poor quality with one another. The result was a *landlock*—a complete paralysis over the question of how scarce land and natural resources should best be put to use. This has wider significance, given the many similar conflicts that continue to linger in a state of uncertainty as a multitude of industrial projects have been proposed, without providing significant local benefits, in rural parts of India.

To explain the experience of deadlock between different forces, the analysis in this book has moved beyond a view of land conflict as something that involves exclusively material interests. If that were the case, then the state government and its private business partner would already have secured a decisive victory, given their superior access to resources. Instead, we have seen a long, drawn-out process of contestation, where the discursive resistance to Adivasi dispossession has strong historical roots and many active supporters. Since this particular struggle took place mainly in the arena of discursive claims made well beyond the proposed mining and refining sites, an account of governance processes allowed for a better understanding of the importance of informational problems in shaping the outcomes of the contest.

The chosen approach did admittedly entail the loss of a deeper ethnographic or socio-cultural account of the people who lived at the proposed project sites. However, it allowed for a wider appreciation of the way that India's geographically dispersed institutional landscape, and its many different actors, engaged with manifold controversies in a multitude of forums, and selectively interact in their attempts to influence outcomes. This has made it possible to produce a more general account of the way in which the all too common land conflicts across the country are negotiated in uncertain, frequently overlapping and even purposefully unclear processes.

The proliferation of groups with a capacity to contest major resource projects, and indeed the wider process of industrialisation, has been a significant phenomenon across India in recent decades. The inclusion of more voices speaks well of Indian democracy when the rights of certain groups of people are being denied, and yet there are significant challenges when each of these groups has different modes of engagement. One gets the impression that the overall debate takes place between multiple actors using different means of communication, indeed different technical and natural languages, across multiple forums. The result has been that people appear to be talking past one another, with a breakdown in mutual understanding. While the resulting deadlocks may protect some people from very harmful projects, they do not result in productive outcomes in the poverty-stricken parts of central India, as poor people are still threatened with the loss of their lands while investors waste their money in endless controversies.

Land Rights and Adivasi Livelihoods

In Andhra Pradesh, it is no longer possible to refute the argument that Adivasis need their lands and forests:

> Land and the produce of the forest remain their main source of livelihood, but [the] availability of land is restricted by forest reservation on the one hand and non-tribal encroachment on the other (Balagopal 2007b: 4029).

This book has attempted to show how strong support for land rights came to be institutionalised in the Visakhapatnam Agency, and to document the various past and present movements and actors who have ensured that such rights are recognised in law, and have since succeeded in blocking changes aimed at reducing their strength. The end result has been that the *Andhra Pradesh Scheduled Areas Land Transfer Regulation 1959* remains in force, although it might not have been applied to bauxite project proposals had it not been for the non-governmental organisation (NGO) interventions that led to the Supreme Court Samatha judgment in 1997.

Adivasi land has been subject to a 'precarious balance' (Balagopal 2007a) in recent decades, but attempts to reinterpret the land legislation through the use of a government proxy to allow private bauxite mining have shown the need for ongoing public awareness and pressure. Andhra Pradesh is in no way unique in demonstrating the inconsistency between formal Adivasi land rights and the reality of widespread alienation to commercial and other interests. Only a small amount of land is actually under tribal private ownership and control, given the alienation of agricultural land to non-tribal farmers and the vast stretches of nominally 'forest' land that is claimed by the government. Other loopholes include the many state-owned industries that continue to operate on Adivasi land, supposedly in the public interest, and the threats posed by the construction of mega-dams. Similar patterns of alienation have been observed in other parts of central India (Padel and Das 2010; Lahiri-Dutt et al. 2012).

Also important is the limited coherence of the Scheduled Areas, where any citizen is free to settle and work so long as no attempt is made to purchase or lease any land. The Visakhapatnam Agency is unusual in Andhra Pradesh, and more generally in central India, in having a predominantly Adivasi population, albeit with a great diversity of tribal groups, and a low level of land alienation to non-Adivasi people. The same level of tribal domination is not found in other Scheduled Areas for a variety of historical and demographic reasons, resulting in a mix of peoples that is far from the ideal of a protected region outlined in the Constitution's Fifth Schedule. Adding to the confusion is the existence of other areas containing non-scheduled Adivasi villages, such as those at the proposed JSW refinery site. While the ideal of distinct Adivasi territories remains on paper, government policies continue to dilute its actual meaning. The Forest Rights Act is one example, given that it allows non-tribal forest-dwellers to claim land rights based on long-term occupation of the land.

With so many loopholes and inconsistencies, it can be tempting to cast doubt over the need to persist with special land rights for Adivasis. It might even leave them 'tied to nature in a particular place' (Baviskar 2005: 5110), thereby reducing possible livelihood alternatives available elsewhere in the country. Nevertheless, throughout the period of national independence, including the recent period of economic reform, tribal land transfer laws across India have not been repealed or even reduced in strength. From time to time, state governments show some interest in amending the laws to create more space for private mining, forestry or non-tribal agriculture (Rao 2003; Balagopal 2007a; Kumar et al. 2005; Yadav 2016), but these efforts have been blocked. Some fundamental rights have become established to the point where it is very difficult to change them, and land for tribal people seems to be one of them, even if it does not have a very good track record in terms of improved human development in an economy where most of the prospects are outside of the agricultural sector.

In the case outlined in this book, the land rights legislation certainly played an important role. At the refinery site, the people affected were located outside of the confines of the Agency and their land could be acquired much like any other land on the plains. Indeed, the refinery case seems to show that the land held by Adivasi farmers, as compared to privately held land, was preferred by the project's promoters because of its weaker tenure, the confused nature of the many illegal landholdings, and the reduced capacity for protest on the part of the occupants. The blanket protection of Adivasi land in the Scheduled Areas was clearly preferable.

But how is this related to the level of civil society opposition to bauxite mining proposals? In the context of widespread land alienation, the strength of this mobilisation is somewhat surprising. Although the bauxite industry certainly comes with a number of social and environmental costs, it is not obvious that it causes more damage than other extractive industries, or that the negative impacts are harder to mitigate. Large-scale coal and iron ore mines, strongly toxic chromium mines and radioactive uranium mines would seem to need more attention, given their scale and polluting potential. Another striking feature of bauxite project contestations is the lower level of protest directed against the alumina refineries as compared to the mines themselves, despite the evidence that refineries generate more polluting waste and use up more precious water resources in their operations.

The strength of protests against bauxite mining can only be fully comprehended with reference to the location of the main ore deposits in tribal Andhra Pradesh and Odisha. It is as if this form of mining has come to be seen as an attack on the last green havens of the Adivasis. The lush forests of bauxite hills like Gandhamardhan and Niyamgiri in Odisha seem close to the ideal represented in the writings of Verrier Elwin in the early twentieth century, with strong remnants still present in activist and popular imaginations. This is in stark contrast to dominant accounts of Adivasi central India as a region of poverty and violence. The paradox in the cultural politics of bauxite mining becomes apparent when Adivasis have 'to perform their marginality, their vulnerability, and, ultimately, their Otherness, in order to qualify as candidates before the [Forest Rights Act] and its accompanying discourses of tribal empowerment and security' (Ramesh 2017: 173).

In such cases, the livelihood needs of the people themselves seem at risk of being forgotten. In our present case, if bauxite mining was prevented, thus allowing people the chance to stay on their land, how much would this help to reduce their poverty? While improved security of tenure could lead to poverty reduction, people in the Agency would still have to battle for their rights to forest land, while those in the refinery area would still struggle to pay off the debts accumulated in the preparation and cultivation of their land. Even if their rights were extended through the Forest Rights Act, what would this mean for their livelihoods? Land rights alone do not seem to be sufficient for Adivasis who often have significant areas of land under cultivation, if not outright ownership, and yet remain poor. Although the efforts to protect Adivasi land appeared to be well intentioned, failure to challenge the existing power structures that continue to shape everyday resource relations could mean that such struggles simply 'maintain a class system that further marginalises the poorest' (Shah 2007: 1825).

Irrespective of the outcomes of the struggle over bauxite mining and refining, land is a necessary but not a sufficient condition for lifting Adivasis out of poverty, since people lack the capabilities and resources to use the land more productively. Opponents of the bauxite project would therefore have done well to formulate alternative models of development that could provide solutions to the endemic poverty of the Agency. This should not have been impossible, given the increase in coffee cultivation that was already happening, as well as the tourism potential of the hills. To outline development alternatives is not only an imperative for future livelihood improvements once tribal land rights have been secured, but an essential instrument in claims for legitimacy in the ongoing struggles. The bauxite industry promoters, with their plans to industrialise the region, offered some hope for a better future, at least for educated village elites, despite the many flaws in these plans. A search for suitable development alternatives needs to become a key part of activist movements hoping to be taken seriously in future political debate about resource use and social justice in the hills.

State Intervention with Little Public Interest

India's economic reform process was supposed to open up the country to global markets, and yet mining has appeared in this book as a domestic affair dominated by big business and top-level politicians. It is certainly true that India's mineral commodities are now traded internationally in ways that were not possible before the late 1980s. These changes, along with more specific ones related to aluminium technology, made the bauxite projects of Eastern India seem feasible, at least at the planning stage. This book has emphasised continuity, rather than novelty, as a way of understanding the relationship of economic reform to electoral politics. From this point of view, the importance of state patronage has not been diminished with liberalisation, and this relates particularly to the crucial role of the state in controlling the transfer of vital resources such as land (Kitschelt and Wilkinson 2007; Kohli 2009; Sud 2009; Chandra 2015), which is regarded as 'the most important factor in inter-state competition for investment' (Levien 2012: 944).

The 'developmental alliance' (Kohli 2007) that sought to mine and refine bauxite in Andhra Pradesh certainly consisted of top-level state politicians and a big business group. Two features stood out amongst the decisions made by this group: first, the lack of public benefits in the initial agreement and in subsequent policy development; and second, the way that political interventions appeared to be directed against the implementation of environmental or social safeguards. The problem then is to explain such behaviour on the part of a democratically elected government that is supposed to work for the public benefit and is overwhelmingly dependent on the votes of poor rural people, some of whom are also tribal people.

The close collaboration between state and business was already apparent in the absence of any public debate over the memorandum of understanding (MoU). In that agreement, the private business partner committed to take care of virtually all technical and financial details, while the politicians could rationalise the inclusion of the state government as a vehicle to mediate in favour of the company on sensitive issues like the acquisition of land, the supply of ore that should have been reserved for the public sector under the terms of the Samatha judgment, and the obstruction of any democratic forums that were not directly under its control. The transfer of land itself required the state government to act as 'direct purchaser, property dealer, law interpreter, policymaker, and so forth' (Jenkins et al. 2014: 17).

It was hard to detect any significant debates or disagreements within the alliance. Uncertainties about royalty revenues for the state government or compensation for the loss of forest land have created controversies across India for decades, but did not generate significant problems for the JSW bauxite project. The almost complete lack of monetary benefits for the state government did not seem to trouble decision-makers, the company or even the project's opponents, all of whom chose to focus on other concerns. The preference to benefit private capital was not even accompanied by a clear strategy to achieve that outcome. This resembles the faltering national initiative to create 'special economic zones' across the country (Jenkins 1999; Jenkins et al. 2014).

Perhaps at no time in India's modern history were the potential gains from mineral industry investment greater than they were in the first decade of the present century, as international mineral prices reached all-time highs and the Indian domestic economy was amongst the fastest growing in the world. Despite widespread protests and the more recent downturn in international mineral prices, the industry remains a source of major profits for some investors, so further alliances between businessmen and politicians are likely to be formed around industries like alumina refining or steelmaking. The current collaboration is expected to continue so long as the politicians need to generate funds to ensure their own re-election and big companies are willing to provide the money in return for preferential treatment.

For politicians, any project is better than no project—however small the chances that it will actually be implemented—because of the possibility of collecting rents from projects that move ahead slowly or do not move at all. Indeed, this needs to be the case because large-scale industrial projects nearly always have a gestation period longer than five years, and elections every five years often throw politicians out of power. Frequent landlocks might even be preferred by some politicians who are then still needed 'as facilitators rather than as overseers of business' (Chandra 2015: 57). The state is not expected to undertake productive activities these days, but still has a role in the management of social protest. With different groups taking widely varying positions on whether and how projects should move ahead, protests are bound to continue. Since there is no apparent move to reduce the web of complicated, ambiguous and even contradictory legislation, just about any position on mineral extraction can find at least some amount of legal support to help intensify and further entrench the incidence of conflict.

One key question is whether India's present approach to industrialisation will remain acceptable to domestic industrialists when '[t]he credibility of the Indian state as a broker of compromises on a large scale is so damaged by its repeated failures … that compensation-based schemes find few takers and become unviable as deadlock-breaking solutions' (Jenkins 2011: 62). The deciding factor might be the capacity of at least some projects to make headway. In spite of frequent landlocks, a signed contract might represent the reservation of an ore deposit in the name of investors who believe they will be able to profit from it at some point in the future. If, on the other hand, there are too many cancelled projects and too much uncertainty, there could be a point in the future where a loss of patience with the messy politics of industrialisation will result in a push to reform the whole system. This is not likely to result in a radical transformation of the wider political economy, and might even imply 'a deepening of the stake of business in procedural democracy' (Chandra 2015: 56), given the length of time for which the present arrangements have been in place. It might, however, create the spaces where new alliances can start to form.

The large number of recent corruption cases in the mining sector might also indicate possibilities for improved accountability and governance.[1] Recent national legislation has even prescribed a minimum (26 per cent) public share of the profits to be derived from any mining project. While this would not have helped those people affected by bauxite mining in Andhra Pradesh, since the ore was to be sold at a self-determined price that would exclude the possibility of any meaningful revenues, it at least indicates a recognition of the existence of mine-affected communities that are not going to remain passive now that protests have started to gain more public notice.

There is a longstanding need to rework national policy to open up the mineral sector to public influence and align it to the changing roles of the state and the private sector (Lahiri-Dutt 2007, 2014). Numerous arrangements need to be worked out at local, regional and national levels to ensure that resources and decision-making powers are shared more equitably, and to allow some level of accountability to permeate the system. These are clearly significant challenges that come with the additional risk of further complicating an already very complex system of governance. Yet there are presently no obvious alternatives to increased public voice in resource extraction, and this must surely be preferable to the conflicts that too often lead to dispossession and environmental degradation, not to mention the plunder of resource wealth by the few individuals who can push their projects forward.

Systematically Distorted Communication

The landlock discussed in this book was the result of a number of informational problems that prevented meaningful deliberations when there was a proposal to use tribal land for the mining and refining of bauxite. The contestation, which came to be mainly about mining, involved a wide range of discursive and non-discursive struggles.

1 Newspaper coverage provides some details about the charges brought against a number of key officials in Andhra Pradesh in relation to other mining and industrial projects (Anon. 2011, 2012; Ramana 2011).

A considerable number of actors and organisations took part in these struggles, including industrialists, politicians, bureaucrats, judges, journalists, NGO representatives and political party workers. Material interests appeared to be a driving force for the first three groups of actors, and yet the multiplicity of groups involved in the contest, and the many separate public (and sometimes not so public) forums that were used to further their claims, also involved a set of discursively differentiated codes. These require the analysis of language and power in a setting like that of urban planning in Pakistan, where '[o]rder and disorder on every scale … are produced through the cease-less circulation of … maps, forms, letters, and reports' (Hull 2012: 4).

The approach taken here is not intended to deny the importance of power and resources in influencing outcomes. Instead, I have tried to use these as a foundation for the account of discursive contestations over the bauxite industry. The distribution of power shaped the disposition of resources—especially land—that were at stake in the project. But as the contestation moved further and further away from the proposed sites of implementation, factors other than the immediate livelihood needs of tribal people, or even the national economic development proclaimed as the primary goal of the project's promoters, came to be more important. The ability to access and make use of different forums were key to this contestation.

An analysis of how informational resources shaped the outcomes of the struggle represents a challenge to the idea of deliberation or deliberative justice as the best way to handle complex problems and move towards improved mutual understanding (Fraser 2009). It does this in two main ways. First, there was the strong reliance of all concerned on government information that was seen as being authoritative, despite a politically motivated process of data collection that used inadequate tools and methods. Second, the dispersed institutional setting across federal India, with its highly variable and challenging modes of access, ensured that only some in the opposition could hope to influence the outcomes and, when they did so, the result was a fragmentation of understandings.

The analysis in this book has drawn on Bohman's (2000) discussion of Habermas to suggest that the avoidance of deliberation, as opposed to engaging and winning debates, can be a useful strategy for influential groups such as those promoting the bauxite project in Andhra Pradesh. It was found that two factors encouraged the promoters to adopt this strategy. The first was the strength of the tribal land rights legislation and the knowledge that civil society objections to a potential amendment had spoiled earlier attempts to initiate bauxite mining in the state. It was well understood that oppositional groups and individuals would seek to challenge the plans and that an open contest would probably favour the project's opponents. The second factor was a seeming acceptance of rent-seeking behaviour for political gain as the price of the preferential treatment granted to the private investors. The bauxite alliance was therefore notably silent despite strong efforts by oppositional groups to elicit a response. Fundamental problems of communication, which I call 'Habermas's nightmare', arose when the dominant alliance of politicians and industrialists was unable to take advantage of its control over information production and key forums to ensure that its project would be implemented.

In the stalemate between the two sides, the outcomes were not simply dependent on the opposition's access to information. If they had been, then information could be viewed as a key resource in a political and economic power struggle. Instead, the opposition was found to have a relatively poor level of internal cooperation and sharing of information, but a great ability to organise protest meetings and to make use of the media and the courts to launch their challenges. These challenges restricted the operational freedom of the bauxite promoters and confronted the imperfect management of information within different government agencies. Uncertainty over the letter of the law in overlapping legal jurisdictions, at both state and federal levels, as well as in scheduled and non-scheduled areas, along with the limited capacity to obtain and process site-level information for use in planning documents, and the generally poor state of land records, were equally important in explaining the stalemate. At the same time, a setting characterised by complexity and uncertainty was seen as one that allowed for the manipulation of outcomes in favour of the bauxite promoters, thereby providing one answer to the question of why top decision-makers allowed the confusion to continue.

The opposition groups could have created alternative understandings, what Fraser (1989) would call alternative public forums, of what was being planned and who would be affected. But when many of the opponents, as well as supposedly independent experts, treated government plans and documents in very similar ways to the promoters, as resources to be used for political gain, what resulted was a fragmented understanding based on public information of deficient quality. To build functional alternative public spheres, it would not only be necessary to improve the distribution of information, but also to complement the poor quality of that which already existed in government plans with some truly independent knowledge production.

For now, the conclusion is that the many informational problems prevent any meaningful communication from taking place. This complete breakdown in communication seems to imply that contestations over mineral projects in tribal India are destined to move towards paralysing standoffs in which little productive work can be accomplished, and no advance is made in either the process of industrialisation or the advance of tribal social justice. Conversely, a few mineral projects with strong political support will be able to slowly push ahead, without mediation and despite the friction of local resistance, to the definite detriment of some of India's poorest and most vulnerable people.

Finding a way out of the current situation is clearly not a straightforward task. Increased transparency, mainly through freedom of information legislation, has been shown in this book to be at risk of creating further inequality, rather than reducing it, since procedural and other obstacles only allow those with superior resources to access the information. Even if greater transparency improves government behaviour, struggles will still have to take place to ensure that there is also justice.

New, alternative public forums could enable better communication and dialogue between the opposing discourses on mining and land use in Andhra Pradesh, as well as elsewhere across central India.

> While at an international level, the mining industry has at least acknowledged the importance of civil society organisations and stakeholders in their documents and policy papers, in Jharkhand, there is absolutely no space for people's representatives, civil society organisations, or NGOs to sit and dialogue with the government and mining industry today (George 2010: 185–6).

The international connection created since Vedanta Resources decided to list itself on the London Metal Exchange has not so far opened up new possibilities for communication abroad, despite the different institutional setting and the new actors that have come to be involved (Kumar 2014). There is also a risk that international discussions might not improve communication at a national level, since there are already too many forums across India, and although these often perform important functions, they can lead to a fragmentation of debate, with separate litigation or media strategies rather than collective and strategic interventions. While social concerns around mining projects are still relatively novel in India, and might become better articulated with the passage of time, it would seem that a reduction rather than an increase in the number of forums holds the promise of better outcomes. This is especially so if the remaining forums can be made more accessible to interested parties than is presently the case for any single forum.

The case presented here may not necessarily be typical of how land issues in Adivasi India are likely to play out, but a number of similar cases suggest that it is far from being unique (Oskarsson and Nielsen 2014). The most well-known of the resource projects facing landlocks are Vedanta's Niyamgiri bauxite mining and alumina refining complex, and the Posco steel plant and iron ore mine, both in the state of Odisha, and these have respectively lasted since 2003 and 2005.[2] The inability to reach any shared view of what should happen in these areas, despite the many years that have passed since they were first proposed, have led to grinding tests of endurance. It is remarkable that in both cases, despite a wealth of evaluation reports, fundamental local land use details cannot be accommodated in project planning circles.[3]

A 2014 decision against bauxite mining at Niyamgiri initially appeared as a final victory for a collection of 'heterogeneous actors and participants, with diverse interests and capacities, from around the world' (Kumar 2014: 196). And yet land struggles have, in a sense, been institutionalised, since Vedanta has already invested in a large refinery that is dependent on Niyamgiri ore, forcing the company to continue to seek support for mining the Niyamgiri hill. Not only do oppositional groups have virtually endless possibilities to launch different forms of appeal against new projects, the promoters can also object to decisions that go against them and find alternative routes, even in the face of seemingly clear denials. While bauxite ore only exists in a limited number of locations in India, the possibilities for appeals, modifications and workarounds create an endless circle of challenges and counter-challenges, with few options for more inclusive approaches to the politics of resource use.

2 Posco announced the suspension of its project in 2015 (Anon. 2015b). The movement against the project did not trust this announcement, however, nor was it able to secure a return of acquired land well into 2016 (Paikray 2016).

3 Examples would include the reliance of the Donghria Kondh on the area around Niyamgiri Hill for cultural and livelihood purposes, and use of the proposed Posco for betel leaf cultivation (Pingle et al. 2010; Amnesty International 2011). In both cases, old surveys stating that the land is forest are still accepted, without recognition of local uses, underpinning further controversy.

References

Ajay Kumar, P.S., n.d. 'Support 7 Days Dharna.' Campaign document produced by the AP Committee for Non-Scheduled Villages.

Amnesty International, 2010. 'Don't Mine Us Out of Existence: Bauxite Mine and Refinery Devastate Lives in India.' London: Amnesty International.

——, 2011. 'Generalisations, Omissions and Assumptions: The Failings of Vedanta's Environmental Impact Assessments for its Bauxite Mine and Alumina Refinery in India's State of Orissa.' London: Amnesty International.

Andhra Pradesh (Government of), 1991. 'Eighth Five Year Plan (1992–97) Andhra Pradesh—Volume II: Sectoral Programs 5: Industries and Minerals.' Hyderabad: Finance and Planning Department.

——, 2005a. 'Minutes of the Meeting held on 22nd April 2005 in the Chambers of Hon'ble Chief Minister on Issues Relating to Grant of Leases for Bauxite.' Hyderabad: Industries and Commerce Department.

——, 2005b. 'Memorandum of Understanding Between the Government of Andhra Pradesh and Jindal South West Ltd.' Signed 1 July.

——, 2005c. 'Minutes of the Meeting held on 02.07.2005 in the Chambers of the Hon'ble Minister for Revenue.' Hyderabad: Industries and Commerce Department.

——, 2005d. 'Resettlement and Rehabilitation Policy 2005: For Project Affected Families.' Hyderabad: Irrigation and CAD Department.

——, 2005e. 'Identification of Government Lands for Compensatory Afforestation.' Visakhapatnam: Visakhapatnam District Collector.

——, 2005f. Letter sent by the AP Government Irrigation and CAD Department to EIA Consultancy on the Alleged Supply of Information to People Opposing a Proposed Irrigation Dam. Hyderabad: Irrigation and CAD Department.

——, 2006a. 'Government Order Ms 119—Rehabilitation and Resettlement Policy of Government of Andhra Pradesh 2005—Amendment.' Hyderabad: Irrigation and CAD Department.

——, 2006b. 'Land Committee Report: Submitted to the Government of Andhra Pradesh.' Hyderabad: Andhra Pradesh Land Committee.

——, 2006c. Letter to Convene Gram Panchayat Meetings before End of December 2006. S. Kota: Mandal Development Organisation.

——, 2006d. 'Order in Writ Petition No. 1571 of 2006.' Hyderabad: High Court of Andhra Pradesh.

——, 2007a. 'Minutes of the 328th Meeting of the Board of Directors of the A.P. Mineral Development Corporation.' Hyderabad: Andhra Pradesh Mineral Development Corporation.

——, 2007b. 'Government Order Ms. No. 892.' S. Kota: Revenue Department.

——, 2007c. 'List of Households Displaced.' S. Kota: Revenue Department.

——, 2007d. 'Resettlement and Rehabilitation Package for JSW Refinery — Annexure II of Government Order Ms. No. 892.' S. Kota: Revenue Department.

——, 2007e. 'Memorandum of Understanding Between the Government of Andhra Pradesh and Jindal South West Ltd.' Signed 3 August.

——, 2007f. 'Memorandum of Understanding Between the Government of Andhra Pradesh and Jindal South West Ltd.' Signed 15 November.

——, 2007g. 'Request for Information on Environmental Impacts of Bauxite Mining under the Right to Information Act, 2005.' Hyderabad: Forest Department.

——, 2007h. 'Minutes of the Public Hearing held on 04/06/2007 in Connection with Establishment of Alumina Refinery and Co-Generation Power Plant by M/s JSW Aluminium.' Hyderabad: Pollution Control Board.

——, 2007i. 'Minutes of the Meeting for Review of Alumina Refinery Project of JSW Aluminium Limited held on 16th May, 2007 at 4.30 P.M. in the Chambers of Hon'ble Chief Minister, AP Secretariat, Hyderabad.' Hyderabad: Industries and Commerce Department.

——, 2007j. 'Minutes of the Meeting held by the Hon'ble Chief Minister on 5.5.2007 in his Chambers at the Secretariat with regard to the Establishment of Aluminium Company in Visakhapatnam District by the Government of Ras Al Kaimah.' Hyderabad: Industries and Commerce Department.

——, 2007k. 'Notes on Supply of Water from Thatipudi Reservoir to JSW Aluminium Limited in S. Kota Mandal of Vizianagaram District.' Visakhapatnam: Irrigation and CAD Department.

——, 2007l. 'Revised Masterplan for Visakhapatnam Metropolitan Region—2021.' Visakhapatnam: Visakhapatnam Urban Development Authority.

——, 2007m. Letter Sent from GVMC to JSW Aluminium for Supply of Water to the S. Kota Alumina Refinery. Visakhapatnam: Greater Visakhapatnam Municipal Corporation.

——, 2007n. 'This is Our Right: Pamphlet on the Implementation of the Forest Rights Act 2006.' Hyderabad: Integrated Tribal Development Agency.

——, 2008a. 'Minutes of the Meeting of High Powered Committee Held on 23 Jan 2008 for Fixing of Sale Price for Bauxite Ore to be Supplied by APMDC to End User Aluminium Companies in Andhra Pradesh.' Hyderabad: Industries and Commerce Department.

——, 2008b. '2007–2008 Kharif Agricultural Census of S. Kota Mandal.' S. Kota: Revenue Department.

——, 2008c. 'Government Order Ms. No. 178.' S. Kota: Revenue Department.

——, 2008d. 'Additional Documents Added to Government Order Ms. No. 892.' S. Kota: Revenue Department.

——, 2008e. 'Memo No. 10810/Assn 1(2)2008-1 Dated 13/3/2008.' S. Kota: Revenue Department.

——, 2008f. 'Land Acquisition Notice 512/2006 Dated 19/3/2008.' S. Kota: Revenue Department.

——, 2008g. 'Reply to Right to Information Request on Supply of Water to Aluminium Factories.' Visakhapatnam: Greater Visakhapatnam Municipal Corporation.

——, 2009a. 'Statement of Not Paid Particulars.' S. Kota: Revenue Department.

——, 2009b. 'List of Land Losers Being Paid Minimum Wages.' S. Kota: Revenue Department.

——, 2009c. 'List of Pending Cases.' Hyderabad: Andhra Pradesh Pollution Control Board.

Anon., 2006a. 'APMDC must Control Bauxite Mining: CM.' *Hindu Business Line*, 23 January.

——, 2006b. 'Bauxite Mining Helps in Tree Growth'. *The Hindu*, 5 July.

——, 2007a. 'GVMC Under Pressure to Give Water to Jindals.' *Hindu Business Line*, 10 July.

——, 2007b. 'GVMC Refuses Water to Jindal Alumina Refinery.' *Hindu Business Line*, 4 July.

——, 2007c. 'GVMC Softens Stand on Water Supply to Jindal.' *The Hindu*, 12 July.

——, 2007d. 'Vizag Mayor Promises Water to Jindal Plant.' *Hindu Business Line*, 12 July.

——, 2007e. 'TDP MLA Slams Konathala.' *The Hindu*, 3 June.

——, 2007f. 'Maoists Shoots ZP Vice-Chairman to Death in AP.' *New Indian Express*, 29 May.

——, 2007g. 'ZP Vice-Chairman's Killing: 2 Militants Held.' *The Hindu*, 11 June.

——, 2007h. 'Mobile Health Unit Launched in Agency.' *The Hindu*, 20 August.

——, 2007i. 'Back-Door Strategies.' *Eenadu* (date not recorded).

——, 2008a. 'Nalco Gets Mining Rights in AP.' *Hindu Business Line*, 22 February.

——, 2008b. 'Bauxite Mining May Wipe Out Ananthagiri Coffee.' *Financial Express*, 22 August.

——, 2008c. 'APMDC View on Gram Sabha Decried.' *The Hindu*, 22 June.

——, 2008d. 'Jindal to Take Water from GVMC.' *The Hindu*, 12 July.

——, 2008e. 'Diversion of Godavari Water Opposed.' *The Hindu*, 10 June.

——, 2008f. 'Maoists Afraid of Proposal.' *Deccan Chronicle*, 23 September.

——, 2008g. 'Mining Lease Issue Rocks A.P. Assembly.' *The Hindu*, 14 March.

——, 2008h. 'New Land Acquisitions in Boddavara Zindal's—Land Acquisition Strategy Full of Loopholes and Misappropriations.' *Eenadu*, 17 March.

——, 2008i. 'In the Name of Settlements … Lakhs of Rupees Hushed-Up.' *Eenadu* (date not recorded).

——, 2009a. 'Forest Beat Officer Sacked for Graft.' *The Hindu*, 8 April.

——, 2009b. 'Stage Set for Public Hearing on Bauxite Mining in Araku.' *Times of India*, 7 August.

——, 2009c. 'Court Notice on Water to Jindal.' *The Hindu*, 31 July.

——, 2009d. 'SP Condemns Maoist Statement.' *The Hindu*, 30 May.

——, 2009e. Bauxite Mining: Concern over Fate of Tribals.' *The Hindu*, 19 July.

——, 2009f. 'Mining Lease Issue Rocks Assembly.' *Indian Express*, 5 August.

——, 2010a. 'AP Congress Leaders against Ramesh's Re-Nomination to RS.' *The Hindu*, 11 May.

——, 2010b. 'Maoists Target Bauxite Mining Supporter.' *The Hindu*, 18 February.

——, 2010c. 'Andhra: Uproar over Bauxite Mines.' *Indian Express*, 13 March.

——, 2011. 'Mining Case: IAS Officer Srilakshmi Remanded to CBI Custody.' *Hindu Business Line*, 29 November.

——, 2012. 'B.P. Acharya Granted Bail.' *The Hindu*, 17 October.

——, 2013. 'There are Inter-Corporate Rivalries at Play: Sajjan Jindal, JSW Steel.' *Economic Times*, 2 September.

——, 2014. 'CAG Rips YSR Government's Bauxite Mining Lease.' *Times of India*, 7 September.

——, 2015a. 'TDP U-turn on Bauxite Mining Draws Opposition Ire.' *Times of India*, 7 November.

——, 2015b. 'Posco Pulls the Plug, Parties Take Potshots at Each Other.' *New Indian Express*, 17 July.

Arnold, D., 1984. 'Rebellious Hillmen: The Gudem-Rampa Rebellions (1829–1914).' In R. Guha (ed.), *Subaltern Studies I: Writings on South Asian History and Society*. New Delhi: Oxford University Press.

Arnold, D. and R. Guha, 1995. *Nature, Culture, Imperialism*. Oxford: Oxford University Press.

Atluri, M., 1984. 'Alluri Sitarama Raju and the Manyam Rebellion of 1922–1924.' *Social Scientist* 12: 3–33. doi.org/10.2307/3517081

Auty, R., 2002. *Sustaining Development in Mineral Economies: The Resource Curse Thesis.* London: Routledge.

Azeez, P.A., S. Bhupathy, S.N. Prasad, R. Chandra and T. Selva Kumar, 2008. 'Status of Blewitt's Owl in Araku Valley and Environmental Management Plan in View of the Proposed Bauxite Mines.' Coimbatore: Salim Ali Centre for Ornithology and Natural History.

Bainton, N.A., 2010. *Lihir Destiny: Cultural Responses to Mining in Melanesia.* Canberra: ANU E Press (Asia-Pacific Environment Monograph 5). doi.org/10.22459/LD.10.2010

Baken, R.J., 2003. *Plotting, Squatting, Public Purpose, and Politics.* Aldershot: Ashgate.

Balagopal, K., 1989. 'Pitting the Tribals against the Non-Tribal Poor.' *Economic and Political Weekly* 24: 1149–1154.

——, 2004. 'Andhra Pradesh: Beyond Media Images.' *Economic and Political Weekly* 39: 2425–2428.

——, 2006. 'The Maoist Movement in Andhra Pradesh.' *Economic and Political Weekly* 41: 3183–3187.

——, 2007a. 'Land Unrest in Andhra Pradesh—III: Illegal Acquisition in Tribal Areas.' *Economic and Political Weekly* 42: 4029–4034.

——, 2007b. 'Land Unrest in Andhra Pradesh—I: Ceiling Surpluses and Public Lands.' *Economic and Political Weekly* 42: 3829–3833.

——, 2008. Speech at the Southern Regional Strategy Meeting on Special Economic Zones, 13 September, Chennai.

Ballard, C. and G. Banks, 2003. 'Resource Wars: The Anthropology of Mining.' *Annual Review of Anthropology* 32: 287–313. doi.org/10.1146/annurev.anthro.32.061002.093116

Banerjee, S., 2006. 'Maoist Movement in India—Beyond Naxalbari.' *Economic and Political Weekly* 41: 3159–3163.

Barham, B., S.G. Bunker and D. O'Hearn, 1994. *States, Firms, and Raw Materials: The World Economy and Ecology of Aluminum.* Madison: University of Wisconsin Press.

Bates, C. and A. Shah (eds), 2014. *Savage Attack: Tribal Insurgency in India.* New Delhi: Social Science Press.

Baviskar, A., 1994. 'Fate of the Forest: Conservation and Tribal Rights.' *Economic and Political Weekly* 29: 2493–2501.

——, 1995. *In the Belly of the River: Tribal Conflicts over Development in the Narmada Valley*. New Delhi: Oxford University Press.

——, 2005. 'Adivasi Encounters with Hindu Nationalism in MP.' *Economic and Political Weekly* 40: 5105–5113.

——, 2007. 'Is Knowledge Power? The Right to Information Campaign in India.' Brighton: Institute of Development Studies.

——, 2008. 'Introduction.' In A. Baviskar (ed.), *Contested Grounds: Essays on Nature, Culture, and Power*. New Delhi: Oxford University Press.

Bebbington, A., 2011. *Social Conflict, Economic Development and Extractive Industry: Evidence from South America*. London: Routledge.

Bebbington, A., D.H. Bebbington, J. Bury, J. Lingan, J.P. Muñoz and M. Scurrah, 2008. 'Mining and Social Movements: Struggles Over Livelihood and Rural Territorial Development in the Andes.' *World Development* 36: 2888–2905. doi.org/10.1016/j.worlddev.2007.11.016

Bedi, H.P., 2013. 'Environmental Mis-Assessment, Development and Mining in Orissa, India.' *Development and Change* 44: 101–123. doi.org/10.1111/dech.12000

Behera, D.K., 2008. 'Inspection Report on M/S Vedanta Aluminium Limited.' Bhubaneshwar: Odisha State Pollution Control Board.

Bhaduri, A., 2007. 'Alternatives in Industrialisation.' *Economic and Political Weekly* 42: 1597–1600.

Bhagwati, J.N., 1993. *India in Transition: Freeing the Economy*. Oxford: Oxford University Press. doi.org/10.1093/acprof:oso/9780198288473.001.0001

Bhushan, C. and M. Zeya Hazra, 2008. *Rich Lands Poor People: Is 'Sustainable' Mining Possible?* New Delhi: Centre for Science and Environment.

Bohman, J., 2000. 'Distorted Communication: Formal Pragmatics as a Critical Theory.' In L.E. Hahn (ed.), *Perspectives on Habermas*. Chicago: Open Court Publishing.

BS Envi Tech, 2008. 'Draft Environmental Impact Assessment Report of Integrated Aluminium Complex by ANRAK Aluminium at Makavaripalem Mandal, Visakhapatnam District, Andhra Pradesh.' Hyderabad: Report to ANRAK Aluminium.

BTVPC (Bauxite Tavvakala Vytireka Porata Committee), 2008. 'Chalo S. Kota: A Call for Public Meeting by BTVPC, S. Kota Branch.' S. Kota: BTVPC.

Bunker, S.G., 1994. 'Flimsy Joint Ventures in Fragile Environments.' In B. Barham, S.G. Bunker and D. O'Hearn (eds), *States, Firms, and Raw Materials: The World Economy and Ecology of Aluminum*. Madison: University of Wisconsin Press.

Bunker, S.G. and P. Ciccantell, 1994. 'The Evolution of the World Aluminum Industry.' In B. Barham, S.G. Bunker and D. O'Hearn (eds), *States, Firms, and Raw Materials: The World Economy and Ecology of Aluminum*. Madison: University of Wisconsin Press.

Carmichael, D.F., 1869. *A Manual of the District of Vizagapatam in the Presidency of Madras*. Madras: W. Thomas.

CGNAP (Citizen Groups of Northern Andhra Pradesh), 2007. 'Water Declaration on Bauxite Mining.' Viewed 11 April 2017 at: www.samataindia.org.in/documents/water_delcaration.htm

Chandra, K., 2015. 'The New Indian State.' *Economic and Political Weekly* 50: 46–58.

Chatterji, A., 2004. 'The Biopolitics of Hindu Nationalism.' *Cultural Dynamics* 16: 319–372. doi.org/10.1177/0921374004047753

Chibber, V., 2003. *Locked in Place: State-Building and Late Industrialization in India*. Princeton: Princeton University Press.

CMPDI (Central Mine Planning and Design Institute), 2006. 'Interim Report on Hydrological Investigations Lanjigarh Bauxite Mines M/s Orissa Mining Corporation, Ranchi, India.' Ranchi: CMPDI.

Concerned Scholars, n.d. 'Bharat Aluminium Company: Gandhamardhan Hills and Peoples Agitation.' Unpublished paper.

Croton, J.T. and A.J. Reed, 2007. 'Hydrology and Bauxite Mining on the Darling Plateau.' *Restoration Ecology* 15: S40–S47. doi.org/10.1111/j.1526-100X.2007.00291.x

Damodaran, H., 2008. *India's New Capitalists: Caste, Business, and Industry in a Modern Nation*. Ranikhet: Permanent Black.

Dandekar, A. and C. Choudhury, 2010. 'PESA, Left-Wing Extremism and Governance: Concerns and Challenges in India's Tribal Districts.' Anand: Institute of Rural Management for Ministry of Panchayati Raj.

Dasgupta, B., 1973. 'Naxalite Armed Struggles and the Annihilation Campaign in Rural Areas.' *Economic and Political Weekly* 8: 173–188.

Dixon, C.T. and A. Watve, 2015. 'Lateritic Plateaus in the Northern Western Ghats, India: A Review of Bauxite Mining Restoration Practices.' *Journal of Ecological Society* 28: 25–44.

Dreze, J. and R. Khera, 2009. 'Lok Adalat or Joke Adalat?' *The Hindu*, 22 February.

D'Souza, D., 2002. *The Narmada Dammed: an Inquiry into the Politics of Development*. New Delhi: Penguin Books.

Dutta, R., 2009. 'Why Govindrajan Is Happy? The Collapse of Environmental Governance in India.' *Environmental Resource Centre Journal* 2: 4–9.

Edgar, A., 2006. *Habermas: The Key Concepts*. London: Routledge.

EIPPCB (European IPPC Bureau), 2001. 'Reference Document on Best Available Techniques in the Non Ferrous Metals Industries.' Sevilla: EIPPBC.

Epp, C.R., 1998. *The Rights Revolution: Lawyers, Activists, and Supreme Courts in Comparative Perspective*. Chicago: University of Chicago Press.

Escobar, A., 1995. *Encountering Development: The Making and Unmaking of the Third World*. Princeton: Princeton University Press.

Ferguson, J., 2006. *Global Shadows: Africa in the Neoliberal World Order*. Durham: Duke University Press. doi.org/10.1215/9780822387640

Fernandes, W., 2007. 'Singur and the Displacement Scenario.' *Economic and Political Weekly* 42: 203–206.

——, 2009. 'Displacement and Alienation from Common Property Resources.' In L. Mehta (ed.), *Displaced by Development: Confronting Marginalisation and Gender Injustice*. New Delhi: Sage. doi.org/10.4135/9788132100959.n5

Foil Vedanta, 2015. 'Global Days of Action against Vedanta's 2015 AGM.' Foil Vedanta blogpost, 26 June. Viewed 7 March 2017 at: www.foilvedanta.org/uncategorized/global-days-of-action-against-vedantas-2015-agm/

Francis, A.A., 1981. *Taxing the Transnationals in the Struggle over Bauxite*. The Hague: Institute of Social Studies.

Fraser, N., 1989. *Unruly Practices: Power, Discourse, and Gender in Contemporary Social Theory*. Minneapolis: University of Minnesota Press.

——, 1997. *Justice Interruptus: Critical Reflections on the 'Postsocialist' Condition*. New York: Routledge.

——, 2009. *Scales of Justice: Reimagining Political Space in a Globalizing World.* New York: Columbia University Press.

Galanter, M. and J.K. Krishnan, 2003. 'Bread for the Poor: Access to Justice and the Rights of the Needy in India.' *Hastings Law Journal* 55: 789–834.

Gang, I.N., K. Sen and M.-S. Yun, 2008. 'Poverty in Rural India: Caste and Tribe.' *Review of Income and Wealth* 54: 50–70. doi.org/10.1111/j.1475-4991.2007.00259.x

Ganjivarapu, S., 2007. 'Bauxite Mining: Threatened Eastern Ghats of India.' New Delhi: Society for the Study of Peace and Conflict.

Gaventa, J. and A. Cornwall, 2008. 'Power and Knowledge.' In P. Reason and H. Bradbury (eds), *The Sage Handbook of Action Research: Participative Inquiry and Practice.* London: Sage. doi.org/10.4135/9781848607934.n17

Gendron, R.S., M. Ingulstad and E. Storli, 2013. *Aluminum Ore: The Political Economy of the Global Bauxite Industry.* Vancouver: UBC Press.

George, A.S., 2010. 'The Paradox of Mining and Development.' In N. Sundar (ed.), *Legal Grounds: Natural Resources, Identity, and the Law in Jharkhand.* New Delhi: Oxford University Press.

Gilberthorpe, E. and G. Banks, 2012. 'Development on Whose Terms? CSR Discourse and Social Realities in Papua New Guinea's Extractive Industries Sector.' *Resources Policy* 37: 185–193. doi.org/10.1016/j.resourpol.2011.09.005

Gilberthorpe, E. and G.M. Hilson, 2012. 'Introduction.' In E. Gilberthorpe and G.M. Hilson (eds), *Natural Resource Extraction and Indigenous Livelihoods: Development Challenges in an Era of Globalization.* Farnham: Ashgate Publishing.

Global Experts, 2008. 'REIA & EMP Report of Expansion of Alumina Refinery from 1 MMTPA to 6 MMTPA Capacity of M/s Vedanta Aluminium Limited.' Bhubaneshwar (unpublished report).

Godoy, R., 1985. 'Mining: Anthropological Perspectives.' *Annual Review of Anthropology* 14(1): 199–217.

Goodland, R., 2007. *Utkal Bauxite & Alumina Project: Human Rights and Environmental Impacts.* Washington (DC): Business and Human Rights Resource Centre.

—— (ed.), 2009. *Suriname's Bakhuis Bauxite Mine: An Independent Review of SRK's Impact Assessment*. Paramaribo: Vereniging van Inheemse Dorpshoofden in Suriname.

Gopal, K.R., 1996. 'Tribals and Their Health Status.' New Delhi: APH Publishing.

Guha, R., 1996. 'Savaging the Civilised: Verrier Elwin and the Tribal Question in Late Colonial India.' *Economic and Political Weekly* 31: 2375–2389.

——, 1999. *Savaging the Civilized: Verrier Elwin, His Tribals, and India*. Chicago: University of Chicago Press.

——, 2007. 'Adivasis, Naxalites and Indian Democracy.' *Economic and Political Weekly* 42: 3305–3312.

Gustavsson, H., S. Vinthagen and P. Oskarsson, 2013. *Law, Resistance and Transformation: Dynamic Interaction of Law and Activism in the Narmada Struggle*. Lund: Lund University.

Hardgrave, R.L. and S.A. Kochanek, 2000. *India: Government and Politics in a Developing Nation*. Fort Worth: Harcourt College.

Herbert, T. and K. Lahiri-Dutt, 2004. 'Coal Sector Loans and Displacement of Indigenous Populations: Lessons from Jharkhand.' *Economic and Political Weekly* 39: 2403–2409.

Hilson, G., 2002. 'An Overview of Land Use Conflicts in Mining Communities.' *Land Use Policy* 19: 65–73. doi.org/10.1016/S0264-8377(01)00043-6

Hjejle, B., 1988. 'Social Stratification in a Rice-Irrigated Economy: South Vizagapatam, 1870–1905.' In C. Dewey (ed.), *The State and the Market: Studies in the Economic and Social History of the Third World*. London: Sangam Books.

HRF (Human Rights Forum), 2008a. 'Press Release on APMDC Not Recognising PESA for Bauxite Mining Areas.' Hyderabad: HRF.

——, 2008b. 'Press Release Ahead of the Public Hearing for AnRak Aluminium.' Hyderabad: HRF.

Hull, M.S., 2012. *Government of Paper: the Materiality of Bureaucracy in Urban Pakistan*. Berkeley: University of California Press. doi.org/10.1525/california/9780520272149.001.0001

ICFRE (Indian Council of Forestry Research and Education), n.d. 'Environmental Impact Assessment with Detailed Ecological and Socio-Economic Studies for Proposed Galikonda Bauxite Mines Vishakhapatnam.' Dehradun: ICFRE.

——, 2008. 'Draft Report on Environment Impact Assessment and Environment Management Plan for Jerrila Block I Bauxite Mines, Visakhapatnam District, Andhra Pradesh.' Dehradun: ICFRE.

IFAD (International Fund for Agricultural Development), 1991. 'Report and Recommendation on a Proposed Loan for the Andhra Pradesh Tribal Development Project.' Rome: IFAD.

India (Government of), 1995. 'Report of MPs and Experts to Make Recommendations on the Salient Features of the Law for Extending Provisions of the Constitution (73rd) Amendment Act, 1992 to Scheduled Areas.' Delhi: Ministry of Rural Development, Bhuria Committee.

——, 1997. Judgement in the Case of 'Samatha versus the State of Andhra Pradesh and Others'. New Delhi: Supreme Court of India.

——, 1998. 'Report on Mining in Forest Areas.' Dehradun: Forest Survey of India.

——, 2000a. Appeal in the Case of 'Samatha versus the State of Andhra Pradesh and Others'. New Delhi: Supreme Court of India.

——, 2000b. 'Note for Committee of Secretaries Regarding Amendment of the Fifth Schedule to the Constitution of India in the Light of the Samatha Judgement.' New Delhi: Ministry of Mines.

——, 2001a. 'Census of India 2001: A 11 State Primary Census Abstract for Individual Scheduled Tribe.' New Delhi: Office of the Registrar General.

——, 2001b. 'Census of India 2001—Data Highlights Andhra Pradesh: The Scheduled Tribes.' New Delhi: Office of the Registrar General.

——, 2001c. 'Draft Approach Paper to the Tenth Five Year Plan (2002–2007).' New Delhi: Planning Commission.

——, 2001d. 'President's Address to the Nation on the Eve of Republic Day.' New Delhi: Press Information Bureau. Viewed 7 March 2017 at: pibarchive.nic.in/archive/releases98/lyr2001/rjan2001/r25012001.html

——, 2001e. Judgement in the Case of 'Balco Employees Union versus Union of India and Others'. New Delhi: Supreme Court of India. Viewed 11 April 2017 at: indiankanoon.org/doc/1737583/

——, 2002a. 'Tenth Five Year Plan (2002–2007).' New Delhi: Government of India, Planning Commission.

——, 2002b. 'Report of the Steering Group on Foreign Direct Investment.' New Delhi: Planning Commission.

——, 2002c. 'Report on Reforming Investment Approval & Implementation—Part I: Investment Approval Procedures – Government and Public Sector Projects.' New Delhi: Ministry for Commerce and Industry, Department of Industrial Policy and Promotion.

——, 2002d. 'Report on Reforming Investment Approval & Implementation—Part II: Downstream Issues—Implementation and Operation.' New Delhi: Ministry for Commerce and Industry, Department of Industrial Policy and Promotion.

——, 2005a. 'Site Inspection Report of the Fact Finding Committee Regarding its Visit to Orissa from 18th–23rd December 2004.' New Delhi: Supreme Court of India, Central Empowered Committee.

——, 2005b. 'State of Forest Report 2005.' Dehradun: Forest Survey of India.

——, 2006a. 'National Mineral Policy: Report of the High Level Committee.' New Delhi: Planning Commission.

——, 2006b. 'Environmental Impact Assessment Notifications and Amendments.' New Delhi: Ministry of Environment and Forests.

——, 2007a. 'The Constitution of India as Modified up to the 1st December, 2007.' New Delhi: Ministry of Law and Justice.

——, 2007b. 'Supplementary Report in No. 1324 and No. 1474 Regarding the Alumina Refinery Plant Being Set Up by M/s Vedanta Alumina Ltd.' New Delhi: Supreme Court of India, Central Empowered Committee.

——, 2007c. 'Minutes of the 15th Meeting of the Expert Appraisal Committee (Mining) Held during November 12–14, 2007.' New Delhi: Ministry of Environment and Forests.

——, 2007d. 'Minutes of the 73rd Meeting of the Reconstituted Expert Appraisal Committee (Industry) Held 24–26 Oct 2007.' New Delhi: Ministry of Environment and Forests.

——, 2007e. 'Environmental Clearance for Alumina Refinery (1.4 MTPA) and Co-generation Plant (90 MW) at Srungavarapukota, Vizianagaram, A.P. by JSW Aluminium Ltd.' New Delhi: Ministry of Environment and Forests.

——, 2008a. Final Judgment in the Case of 'Forest Diversion for Niyamgiri Bauxite Mine, I.A. No. 2134 of 2007.' New Delhi: Supreme Court of India.

——, 2008b. 'Final Report on the Investigation for Bauxite in Galikonda Block, Visakhapatnam District, AP.' New Delhi: Geological Survey of India.

——, 2008c. 'Minutes of the 27th meeting of the Expert Appraisal Committee (Mining) held during November 4–5, 2008.' New Delhi: Ministry of Environment and Forests.

——, 2008d. 'National Mineral Policy 2008.' New Delhi: Ministry of Mines.

——, 2008e. 'Note on Bauxite Mining in Orissa: Report on Flora, Fauna, and Impact on Tribal Population.' New Delhi: Ministry of Environment and Forests.

——, 2008f. 'Report of Expert Group to Examine the Schemes of Statutory Clearances for Industrial and Infrastructure Projects in India.' New Delhi: Ministry of Finance, Department of Economic Affairs.

——, 2009a. 'Circular on Diversion of Forest Land while Ensuring Compliance with the Implementation of Tribal Forest Rights Act.' New Delhi: Ministry of Environment and Forests.

——, 2009b. 'Order in Appeal No. 10 of 2009 on the Environmental Approval of Jerrila Bauxite Mines.' New Delhi: Ministry of Environment, Forest and Climate Change, National Environment Appellate Authority.

——, 2009c. 'Girijan Sangham Claim in Appeal No. 10 of 2009.' New Delhi: Ministry of Environment, Forest and Climate Change, National Environment Appellate Authority.

——, 2009d. 'APMDC Response in Appeal No. 10 of 2009.' New Delhi: Ministry of Environment, Forest and Climate Change, National Environment Appellate Authority.

Iyer, R.R., 2007. 'Towards a Just Displacement and Rehabilitation Policy.' *Economic and Political Weekly* 42: 3103–3107.

Jenkins, R., 1999. *Democratic Politics and Economic Reform in India.* Cambridge: Cambridge University Press.

——, 2011. 'The Politics of India's Special Economic Zones.' In S. Ruparelia, S. Reddy, J. Harriss and S. Corbridge (eds), *Understanding India's New Political Economy: A Great Transformation?* New York: Routledge.

Jenkins, R., L. Kennedy and P. Mukhopadhyay, 2014. *Power, Policy, and Protest: the Politics of India's Special Economic Zones.* New Delhi: Oxford University Press. doi.org/10.1093/acprof:oso/9780198097341.001.0001

Johnson, C., 2003. 'Decentralisation in India: Poverty, Politics and Panchayati Raj.' London: Overseas Development Institute (Working Paper 199).

Johnson, C., P. Deshingkar, and D. Start, 2003. 'Grounding the State: Poverty, Inequality and the Politics of Governance in India's Panchayats.' London: Overseas Development Institute (Working Paper 226).

Joshi Saha, S., 2009. 'Fund Crunch Hits JSW Cement, Aluminium Expansion Plans.' *Financial Express*, 1 June.

JSW Aluminium, 2007a. 'Combined Sketch of Five Villages for Proposed Plant Site of JSW Aluminium at Kiltampalem, Chinakandepalli, Chidipalem, Mushidipalli and M Boddavara, S Kota Mandal, Vizianagaram, A.P.' Visakhapatnam: JSW Aluminium Ltd.

——, 2007b. 'Water Supply for Alumina Refinery.' Press release.

JSW Energy, 2008. 'Draft Red Herring Prospectus for Issue of Public Equity Shares.' Mumbai: JSW Energy.

Kalesh, B., 2009. 'JSW Scouting for Partner to Fund Cement Operations.' Live Mint blogpost, 22 July. Viewed 7 March 2017 at: www.livemint.com/2009/07/22234453/JSW-scouting-for-partner-to-fu.html

Kalshian, R., 2007. *Caterpillar and the Mahua Flower: Tremors in India's Mining Fields*. New Delhi: Panos South Asia.

Kapur Mehta, A. and A. Shah, 2003. 'Chronic Poverty in India: Incidence, Causes and Policies.' *World Development* 31: 491–511. doi.org/10.1016/S0305-750X(02)00212-7

Karmali, N., 2008. 'India's 40 Richest.' Forbes blogpost, 11 December. Viewed 7 March 2017 at: www.forbes.com/2008/11/12/richest-Indian-billionaires-biz-indiarichest08-cx_nk_1112india_land.html

Katzenstein, M., S. Kothari and U. Mehta, 2001. 'Social Movement Politics in India: Institutions, Interests, and Identities.' In A. Kohli (ed.), *The Success of India's Democracy*. Cambridge: Cambridge University Press.

KGP (Kiltampalem Gram Panchayat), 2006. 'Kiltampalem Panchayat Resolution Approving Land Acquisition for Jindal.' Unpublished document.

Kitschelt, H. and S. Wilkinson, 2007. *Patrons, Clients, and Policies: Patterns of Democratic Accountability and Political Competition*. Cambridge: Cambridge University Press. doi.org/10.1017/CBO9780511585869

Kochanek, S.A., 2007. 'Liberalisation and Business Lobbying in India.' In R. Mukherji (ed.), *India's Economic Transition: The Politics of Reforms*. New Delhi: Oxford University Press.

Kohli, A., 2001. 'Introduction.' In A. Kohli (ed.), *The Success of India's Democracy*. Cambridge: Cambridge University Press.

——, 2004. *State-Directed Development: Political Power and Industrialization in the Global Periphery*. Cambridge: Cambridge University Press. doi.org/10.1017/CBO9780511754371

——, 2007. 'State, Business, and Economic Growth in India.' *Studies in Comparative International Development* 42: 87–114. doi.org/10.1007/s12116-007-9001-9

——, 2009. *Democracy and Development in India: from Socialism to Pro-Business*. Oxford: Oxford University Press.

Kohli, K., 2006. 'Mine? What Mine? Ah, Yes, the Mine.' *India Together*, 8 December.

Krishnakumar, A., 2004. 'A Tribal Struggle.' *Frontline*, 24 September.

Krueger, A.O., 2002. *Economic Policy Reforms and the Indian Economy*. Chicago: University of Chicago Press. doi.org/10.7208/chicago/9780226454542.001.0001

Kumar, K., 2004. 'Dispossessed and Displaced: A Brief Paper on Tribal Issues in Orissa.' Unpublished paper.

——, 2014. 'The Sacred Mountain: Confronting Global Capital at Niyamgiri.' *Geoforum* 54: 196–206. doi.org/10.1016/j.geoforum.2013.11.008

Kumar, K., P.R. Choudhary, S. Sarangi, P. Mishra and S. Behera, 2005. 'A Socio-Economic and Legal Study of Scheduled Tribes' Land in Orissa.' Unpublished study commissioned by the World Bank.

Kumar, K. and J.M. Kerr, 2012. 'Democratic Assertions: The Making of India's Recognition of Forest Rights Act.' *Development and Change* 43: 751–771. doi.org/10.1111/j.1467-7660.2012.01777.x

Lahiri-Dutt, K., 2007. 'Coal Mining Industry at the Crossroads: Towards a Coal Policy for Liberalising India.' Canberra: The Australian National University (ASARC Working Paper).

—— (ed.), 2011. *Gendering the Field: Towards Sustainable Livelihoods for Mining Communities*. Canberra: ANU E Press (Asia-Pacific Environment Monograph 6). doi.org/10.22459/GF.03.2011

—— (ed.), 2014. *The Coal Nation: Histories, Ecologies and Politics of Coal in India*. London: Routledge.

——, 2016. 'The Diverse Worlds of Coal in India: Energising the Nation, Energising Livelihoods.' *Energy Policy* 99: 203-213. doi.org/10.1016/j.enpol.2016.05.045

Lahiri-Dutt, K., R. Krishnan and N. Ahmad, 2012. 'Land Acquisition and Dispossession: Private Coal Companies in Jharkhand.' *Economic and Political Weekly* 47: 39–45. doi.org/10.2139/ssrn.2015125

Laxmaiah, A., K.M. Rao, R.H. Kumar, N. Arlappa, K. Venkaiah and G.N.V. Brahmam, 2007. 'Diet and Nutritional Status of Tribal Population in ITDA Project Areas of Khammam District, Andhra Pradesh.' *Journal of Human Ecology* 21: 79–86. doi.org/10.1080/09709274.2007.11905954

Levien, M., 2011. 'Rationalising Dispossession: The Land Acquisition and Resettlement Bills.' *Economic and Political Weekly* 46: 66–71.

——, 2012. 'The Land Question: Special Economic Zones and the Political Economy of Dispossession in India.' *Journal of Peasant Studies* 39: 933–969. doi.org/10.1080/03066150.2012.656268

LSP (Lok Satta Party), 2009. 'Lok Satta Demands ACB Inquiry into Jindal Land Scam.' Lok Satta Party blogpost, 29 June. Viewed 7 March 2017 at: www.loksatta.org/cms/index.php?option=com_content&view=article&id=292&Itemid=60

Maharatna, A., 2005. *Demographic Perspectives on India's Tribes*. New Delhi: Oxford University Press.

Mearns, R., 1999. 'Access to Land in Rural India.' Washington (DC): World Bank (Policy Research Working Paper 2123).

MGP (Mushidipalli Gram Panchayat), 2006. 'Mushidipalli Panchayat Resolution Approving Land Acquisition for Jindal.' Unpublished document.

Mishra, A.B., 1987. 'Mining a Hill and Undermining a Society: The Case of Gandhamardan.' In A. Agarwal, D. D'Monte and U. Samarth (eds), *The Fight for Survival: People's Action for Environment*. New Delhi: Centre for Science and Environment.

Mishra, B., 2006. 'People's Movement at Kalinga Nagar: An Epitaph or an Epitome?' *Economic and Political Weekly* 41: 551–554.

Mitta, M., 2000. 'When the Law Displaces.' *Indian Express*, 21 September.

Mohanty, D., 2003. 'Orissa Nod to Plants in Tribal Areas.' *The Telegraph* (Calcutta), 30 December.

Moody, R., 2007. 'The Base Alchemist.' In R. Kalshian (ed.), *Caterpillar and the Mahua Flower: Tremors in India's Mining Fields*. New Delhi: Panos South Asia.

Naandi Foundation, 2008. 'Inclusive Value Chains: Araku Case Study.' Unpublished paper.

Narasimha Rao, G., 2008. 'Helicopter Survey in Bauxite Mining Area Triggers Fresh Controversy.' *The Hindu*, 5 March.

——, 2010. 'Maoists Kill Vizag ZP Vice-Chairman.' *The Hindu*, 11 May.

Nathan, D., 2009. 'Social Security, Compensation and Reconstruction of Livelihoods.' *Economic and Political Weekly* 44: 22–26.

Nature, 2006. 'Survey Carried Out as Part of the EU STEP Project in Ananthagiri Mandal, Visakhapatnam District.' Unpublished paper.

Nayak, C.R., 2008. 'Inspection Report on M/S Vedanta Aluminium Limited Lanjigarh, Dist.' Kalahandi: Orissa Pollution Control Board.

Newell, P. and J. Wheeler, 2006. *Rights, Resources and the Politics of Accountability*. London: Zed Books.

Norway (Government of), 2007. 'Recommendation to Disinvest in Vedanta Resources.' Oslo: Ministry of Finance, Council of Ethics.

O'Faircheallaigh, C., 1999. 'Making Social Impact Assessment Count: A Negotiation-Based Approach for Indigenous Peoples.' *Society and Natural Resources* 12: 63–80. doi.org/10.1080/089419299279894

——, 2006. 'Aborigines, Mining Companies and the State in Contemporary Australia: A New Political Economy or "Business as Usual"?' *Australian Journal of Political Science* 41: 1–22. doi.org/10.1080/10361140500507252

O'Faircheallaigh, C. and T. Corbett, 2005. 'Indigenous Participation in Environmental Management of Mining Projects: The Role of Negotiated Agreements.' *Environmental Politics* 14: 629–647. doi.org/10.1080/09644010500257912

Orissa (Government of), 1996. 'Recommendations for Environmentally Sound Growth of Aluminium Industry in Orissa.' Bhubaneswar: State Pollution Control Board.

——, 2011. 'Writ Petition No. 19605 of 2010.' Cuttack: High Court of Orissa.

Oskarsson, P., 2012. 'AnRak Aluminium: Another Vedanta in the Making.' *Economic and Political Weekly* 47: 29–33.

——, 2013a. 'Dispossession by Confusion from Mineral-Rich Lands in Central India.' *South Asia* 35: 199–212. doi.org/10.1080/00856401.2012.739597

——, 2013b. *Visualising Resources on Gandhamardhan Hill: Mapping Revenue and Forest Land in Bargarh District of Western Odisha.* Hyderabad: Centre for Economic and Social Studies.

——, 2015. 'Governing India's Bauxite Mineral Expansion: Caught between Facilitating Investment and Mediating Social Concerns.' *Extractive Industries and Society* 2/3: 426–433. doi.org/10.1016/j.exis.2015.05.007

——, 2017. 'Diverging Discourses on Bauxite Mining in Eastern India: Life-Supporting Hills for Adivasis or National Treasure Chests on Barren Lands?' *Society & Natural Resources* 30: 994–1008. doi.org/10.1080/08941920.2017.1295496

Oskarsson, P. and K.B. Nielsen, 2014. 'Development Deadlock: Aborted Industrialization and Blocked Land Restitution in West Bengal and Andhra Pradesh, India.' *Development Studies Research* 1: 267–278. doi.org/10.1080/21665095.2014.967412

Padel, F., 2009. *Sacrificing People.* New Delhi: Orient BlackSwan.

Padel, F. and S. Das, 2007. 'Agya, What Do You Mean by Development?' In R. Kalshian (ed.), *Caterpillar and the Mahua Flower: Tremors in India's Mining Fields.* New Delhi: Panos South Asia.

——, 2010. *Out of This Earth: East India Adivasis and the Aluminium Cartel.* New Delhi: Orient BlackSwan.

Padhi, R. and N. Adve, 2006. 'Endemic to Development: Police Killings in Kalinga Nagar.' *Economic and Political Weekly* 41: 186–187.

Paikray, P., 2016. 'PPSS Update—18th April 2016.' *POSCO Pratirodh Sangram Samiti Newsletter*, 18 April.

Pati, B., 2011. *Adivasis in Colonial India: Survival, Resistance and Negotiation.* New Delhi: Orient BlackSwan.

Patnaik, S., 2007. 'GVMC Decision Puts Jindal in Fix.' *The Hindu*, 7 July.

——, 2008. 'Water for Refinery Raises Heat.' *The Hindu*, 25 July.

——, 2009. 'Bauxite Mining: Legal Tangle Upsets APMDC's Plans'. *The Hindu*, 21 February.

——, 2014. 'Fear of Fresh Bid for Bauxite Mining Haunts Tribal People.' *The Hindu*, 21 July.

Patra, S.H. and A. Murthy, n.d. 'Fact Finding Report of Nalco.' Bhubaneshwar: Vasundhara (unpublished report).

Pattanaik, C., S.N. Prasad and C.S. Reddy, 2009. 'Need for Conservation of Biodiversity in Araku Valley, Andhra Pradesh.' *Current Science* 96: 11–12.

Pingle, U. and C. von Führer-Haimendorf, 1998. *Tribal Cohesion in the Godavari Valley*. Hyderabad: Booklinks.

Pingle, U., D. Pandey and V. Suresh, 2010. 'Majority Report of the Committee Constituted to Investigate into the Proposal Submitted by POSCO India Pty Limited for Establishment of an Integrated Steel Plant and Captive Port in Jagatsinghpur District.' New Delhi: Ministry of Environment and Forests.

Prasad, A., 2003. *Against Ecological Romanticism: Verrier Elwin and the Making of an Anti-modern Tribal Identity*. New Delhi: Three Essays Collective.

Prasad, R.J., 2000. 'Eyeing Tribal Land.' *The Hindu*, 7 November.

PUDP (People's Union for Democratic Rights), 2005. 'Halting the Mining Juggernaut: People's Struggles against Alumina Projects in Orissa.' Unpublished paper.

Purushothaman, S., 2005. 'Land-Use Strategies for Tribals: A Socio-Economic Analysis.' *Economic and Political Weekly* 40: 5611–5619.

Rajpramukh, K.E. and P.D.S. Palkumar, 2005. 'Livelihood Challenges and Strategies: The Valmikis of Eastern Ghats.' *Anthropologist* 7: 153–160. doi.org/10.1080/09720073.2005.11890896

Ramamurthy, S., 1995. *Impacts of Bauxite Mining and Aluminium Industry in India*. New Delhi: Academy for Mountain Environics.

Ramana, K.V., 2011. 'AP's Former Top Mining Official Held.' *Daily News & Analysis* (Hyderabad), 14 November.

Ramanathan, U., 2010. 'Site Inspection Report for Diversion of Forest Land.' New Delhi: Ministry of Environment and Forests.

Rama Raju, S.V., n.d. 'Loopholes… Misinterpretations…' *Eenadu* (date not recorded).

Rama Raju, V., 2009. 'JSW Aluminium Ties up Funds for Rs 4,000-Cr Vizag Plant.' *Business Standard*, 19 January.

Ramesh, P., 2017. 'Rural Industry, the Forest Rights Act, and the Performance(s) of Proof.' In K.B. Nielsen and P. Oskarsson (eds), *Industrialising Rural India: Land, Policy, Resistance*. London: Routledge.

Randeria, S. and C. Grunder, 2011. 'The (Un)Making of Policy in the Shadow of the World Bank: Infrastructure Development, Urban Resettlement and the Cunning State in India.' In C. Shore, S. Wright and D. Però (eds), *Policy Worlds: Anthropology and the Analysis of Contemporary Power*. New York: Berghahn Books.

Rao, A.S., 2010. 'Andhra Pradesh Ministers on the Hit-List of Maoists.' *India Today* (Hyderabad), 14 May.

Rao, M.G. and P.K. Ramam, 1979. *The East Coast Bauxite Deposits of India*. Calcutta: Geological Survey of India.

Rao, N., 2003. 'Vision 2010: Chasing Mirages.' *Economic and Political Weekly* 38: 1755–1758.

Rao, S.L., P. Deshingkar and J. Farrington, 2006. 'Tribal Land Alienation in Andhra Pradesh: Processes, Impacts and Policy Concerns.' *Economic and Political Weekly* 41: 5401–5407.

Rao, V.N., B. Rama Krishna and K. Viswanath, 2000. 'Environmental Pollution by Red Mud of Damanjodi, Orissa.' In *Environment and Waste Management: Proceedings of National Seminar on Environmental Geology with Special Reference to Waste Management*. Visakhapatnam: Andhra University, Department of Geology.

Ras al-Khaimah (Government of), 2006. 'Sheikh Saud Inaugurates AED 400 m Pioneer Cement Industries Plant in RAK, 12 November.' Viewed 8 July 2008 at: www.ameinfo.com/101436.html (site discontinued).

Reddy, A.M., 1971. The Bagatha and the Related Tribes: A Study of Inter-Tribal and Intra-Tribal Pattern of Life in the Visakhapatnam Agency. Visakhapatnam: Andhra University (PhD thesis).

Reddy, M.G., K. Anil Kumar, P.T. Rao and O. Springate-Baginski, 2010. 'The Making of Andhra's Forest Underclass: An Historical Institutional Analysis of Forest Rights Deprivations.' Manchester: University of Manchester, Institutions and Pro-Poor Growth Program (Discussion Paper 42).

Reddy, M.G., K. Jayalakshmi and A.-M. Goetz, 2006. 'Politics of Pro-Poor Reform in the Health Sector: Primary Healthcare in Tribal Areas of Visakhapatnam.' *Economic and Political Weekly* 41: 419–426.

Reddy, M.G. and P. Mishra, 2010. 'Final Report on Livelihoods Change from AP Bauxite Projects.' Hyderabad: Centre for Economic and Social Studies (project report).

Reddy, N.S., 1977. 'Crisis of Confidence among the Tribal People and the Naxalite Movement in Srikakulam District.' *Human Organization* 36: 142–149. doi.org/10.17730/humo.36.2.ek4716323486417v

——, 1988. 'Depriving Tribals of Land: Andhra Move to Amend Land Transfer Laws.' *Economic and Political Weekly* 23: 1458–1461.

Reddy, S., 2006. *Kashipur: An Enquiry into Mining and Human Rights Violations in Kashipur*. Mumbai: Indian People's Tribunal on Environment and Human Rights.

Reddy, T.S., 2007. Speech at the Mining Engineer Association's Convention, 7 April, Hyderabad.

Reddy, V.R., M.G. Reddy, V. Saravanan, M. Bandi and O. Springate-Baginski, 2004. 'Participatory Forest Management in Andhra Pradesh: A Review.' Hyderabad: Centre for Economic and Social Studies (Working Paper 62).

Ross, M.L., 1999. 'The Political Economy of the Resource Curse.' *World Politics* 51: 297–322. doi.org/10.1017/S0043887100008200

Roy, A., 2009. 'The Heart of India is Under Attack.' *The Guardian* (London), 30 October.

——, 2010. 'Foreword.' In F. Padel and S. Das (eds), *Out of This Earth: East India Adivasis and the Aluminium Cartel.* New Delhi: Orient BlackSwan.

Roy Burman, B.K., 2003. 'Indigenous and Tribal Peoples in World System Perspective.' *Studies of Tribes and Tribals* 1: 7–27. doi.org/10.1080/0972639X.2003.11886480

Rudolph, L.I. and S.H. Rudolph, 2001a. 'Iconisation of Chandrababu: Sharing Sovereignty in India's Federal Market Economy.' *Economic and Political Weekly* 36: 1541–1552.

——, 2001b. 'Redoing the Constitutional Design: From an Interventionist to a Regulatory State.' In A. Kohli (ed.), *The Success of India's Democracy*. Cambridge: Cambridge University Press.

Sakti, n.d. 'Environment of Eastern Ghats in Relation to Bauxite and other Mineral Resources.' Anonymous post to Sakti website (www.sakti.in).

Sampat, P., 2008. 'Special Economic Zones in India.' *Economic and Political Weekly* 43: 25–29.

Sarin, M., 2009. 'Off the Green Track.' *The Tribune*, 2 August.

Sastry, V., 2006. 'Study of IKP's Work on Tribal Land Issues: Report Submitted to Rural Development Department.' Hyderabad: Government of Andhra Pradesh, Rural Development Department.

Saxena, N.C., 1997. *The Saga of Participatory Forest Management in India*. Jakarta: Center for International Forestry Research.

——, 2005. 'Draft National Policy for Tribals: Suggestions for Improvement.' Unpublished paper.

Saxena, N.C., S. Parasuraman, P. Kant and A. Baviskar, 2010. 'Report of the Four Member Committee for Investigation into the Proposal Submitted by the Orissa Mining Company for Bauxite Mining in Niyamgiri.' New Delhi: Ministry of Environment and Forests.

Scott, J.C., 1985. *Weapons of the Weak: Everyday Forms of Peasant Resistance*. New Haven: Yale University Press.

Seethalakshmi, S., 2009. *Special Economic Zones in Andhra Pradesh: Issues, Concerns and Ways Ahead*. Hyderabad: Society for National Integration through Rural Development and ActionAid.

Shah, A., 2007. 'The Dark Side of Indigeneity? Indigenous People, Rights and Development in India.' *History Compass* 5: 1806–1832.

Shiva, V., 1988. *Staying Alive: Women, Ecology, and Development*. London: Zed Books.

Simonson, P., 2001. 'Social Noise and Segmented Rhythms: News, Entertainment, and Celebrity in the Crusade for Animal Rights.' *Communication Review* 4: 399–420. doi.org/10.1080/10714420109359476

Singh, C., 1986. *Common Property and Common Poverty: India's Forests, Forest Dwellers, and the Law*. Delhi: Oxford University Press.

Sivaramakrishna, P., n.d. 'Lead Paper Made for Hyderabad Public Hearing of the People's Commission on Environment and Development.' Unpublished paper.

——, 2006. Letter to the Principal Secretary to Government of Andhra Pradesh, 27 December.

——, 2007. Letter to Ministry of Environment and Forests on Proposals to Mine Bauxite in Andhra Pradesh, 14 June.

Springate-Baginski, O. and P.M. Blaikie, 2007. *Forests, People and Power: The Political Ecology of Reform in South Asia*. London: Earthscan.

Sreenivas, J., 2009. 'Andhra Mining Plan New Naxal Flashpoint.' *Indian Express*, 16 June.

Srinivasan, K., V. Vyasulu and S. Rajagopalan, 1981. 'The Orissa Aluminium Complex: Points toward a Debate.' *Economic and Political Weekly* 16: 2005–2014.

Srinivasulu, K., 2002. 'Caste, Class and Social Articulation in Andhra Pradesh: Mapping Differential Regional Trajectories.' London: Overseas Development Institute (Working Paper 179).

——, 2009. 'Y.S. Rajasekhara Reddy: A Political Appraisal.' *Economic and Political Weekly* 44: 8–10.

——, 2010. 'Land Acquisition and Popular Resistance: Politics of Special Economic Zones in Andhra Pradesh.' Paper posted to India SEZ Politics website.

Subrahmanyam, K.V., 1982. 'The Orissa Aluminium Complex: Points toward a Debate.' *Economic and Political Weekly* 17: 168–172.

Sud, N., 2009. 'The Indian State in a Liberalizing Landscape.' *Development and Change* 40: 645–65. doi.org/10.1111/j.1467-7660.2009.01566.x

Sundar, N., 2006. 'Bastar, Maoism and Salwa Judum.' *Economic and Political Weekly* 41: 3187–3192.

Suri, K.C., 2004. 'Andhra Pradesh: Fall of the CEO in Arena of Democracy.' *Economic and Political Weekly* 39: 5493–5497.

——, 2005. 'The Dilemma of Democracy: Economic Reforms and Electoral Politics in Andhra Pradesh.' In J. Mooij (ed.), *The Politics of Economic Reforms in India*. New Delhi: Sage.

Thomas, J.J. and G. Parayil, 2008. 'Bridging the Social and Digital Divides in Andhra Pradesh and Kerala: A Capabilities Approach.' *Development and Change* 39: 409–435. doi.org/10.1111/j.1467-7660.2008.00486.x

Tingay, A., 2010. 'Comments on the Environmental Impact Assessments for Proposed Lanjigarh Bauxite Mine, Alumina Refinery and the Refinery Expansion.' Unpublished paper.

UNCTAD (United Nations Conference on Trade and Development), 2007. 'World Investment Report 2007.' New York: UNCTAD.

Upadhya, C.B., 1988. 'The Farmer-Capitalists of Coastal Andhra Pradesh.' *Economic and Political Weekly* 23: 1433–1442.

Vagholikar, N. and K.A. Moghe, 2003. *Undermining India: Impacts of Mining on Ecologically Sensitive Areas*. Pune: Kalpavriksh.

Venkateshwarlu, K., 2007. 'OMC Row Back in Focus.' *The Hindu*, 3 September.

Vijay Murty, B. and B. Saran, 2016. 'Jharkhand CM Determined to Changes in Land Laws.' *Hindustan Times*, 3 November.

Vimta Labs, 2006. 'Rapid Environmental Impact Assessment for the Proposed Capacity Expansion of Utkal Alumina Refinery from 1.0 Mtpa to 3.0 Mtpa at Doragurha, Rayagada Dist.' Hyderabad: Vimta Labs (unpublished report to Utkal Alumina).

——, 2007. 'Rapid Environmental Impact Assessment for the Proposed 1.4 Mtpa Alumina Refinery and Co-Generation Plant at Srungavarapu Kota, Vizianagaram District.' Hyderabad: Vimta Labs (unpublished report to Utkal Alumina).

Vyasulu, V., 1981. 'Alternate Development Strategies for Koraput.' *IFDA Dossier* 26: 29–40.

Wade, R., 1985. 'The Market for Public Office: Why the Indian State is Not Better at Development.' *World Development* 13: 467–497. doi.org/10.1016/0305-750X(85)90052-X

WII (Wildlife Institute of India), 2006a. 'Studies on Impact of Proposed Lanjigarh Bauxite Mining on Biodiversity Including Wildlife and Its Habitat.' Dehradun: WII.

——, 2006b. 'Supplementary Report on Impact of proposed Lanjigarh Bauxite Mining on Biodiversity Including Wildlife and its Habitat.' Dehradun: WII.

World Bank, 2006. 'The Outlook for Metals Markets Prepared for G20 Deputies Meeting Sydney 2006.' Washington (DC): World Bank (background paper).

Xaxa, V., 1999. 'Tribes as Indigenous People of India.' *Economic and Political Weekly* 34: 3589–3595.

Yadav, A., 2016. 'In Jharkhand, Protests Break Out over Changes to Land Tenancy Law in Adivasi Areas.' Post to Scroll.in blog, 27 November. Viewed 29 November 2016 at: scroll.in/article/822586/in-jharkhand-protests-break-out-over-changes-to-land-tenancy-law-in-adivasi-areas

Yadav, K.P.S., 2003. 'Orissa Okays Mining in Tribal Territory.' Down to Earth website, 15 August. Viewed 8 March 2017 at: www.downtoearth.org.in/news/orissa-okays-mining-in-tribal-territory-13306

www.ingramcontent.com/pod-product-compliance
Lightning Source LLC
Chambersburg PA
CBHW050811270326
41926CB00052B/4636
* 9 7 8 1 7 6 0 4 6 2 5 0 5 *